THE NEW GUIDE *to*
BEER

THE NEW GUIDE *to*
BEER

BRIAN GLOVER

This edition first published in 1998 by Hermes House

© Anness Publishing Limited 1998

Hermes House
books are published by
Anness Publishing Limited
Hermes House 88–89 Blackfriars Road London SE1 8HA
and in the USA by Anness Publishing Inc.,
27 West 20th Street New York NY10011

This edition distributed in Canada by Raincoast Books
8680 Cambie Street, Vancouver, British Columbia V6P 6MY

ISBN 1 84038 069 1

A CIP catalogue record for this book is available from the British Library

Publisher: Joanna Lorenz
Project Editor: Jo Wells
Researchers: Alison Heatherington, Daniel King
Designer: Siân Keogh, Axis Design
Jacket Designer: Lisa Tai
Photographer: David Jordan Photography

Previously published as part of a larger compendium, *The World Encyclopedia of Beer*.

Printed and bound in Singapore

1 3 5 7 9 10 8 6 4 2

Acknowledgements
The publishers would like to thank the following for additional images reproduced in this book: Axiom Photographic Agency: pp143br;
The Beer Cellar and Co. Ltd.: pp68b; Bruce Coleman Picture Library: pp98tr; Edifice: pp144b, 155t; ET Archive: pp117b; Greg Evans Photo Library: pp108, 189b;
John Freeman: pp 37b; Guinness Archives: pp14tr, 15tr; Jayawardene Travel Photography Library: pp104t, 135, 154b; Peter Newark's Historical Pictures: pp15tl,
15tc, 19t, 20bl, 21br, 89tr; Peter Newark's Western Americana: pp175b, 181br; Trip Photographic Library: pp179br (photo R. Powers), 106, 107, 109t
(photos T. Noorits), 109b (photo I. Burgandinov), 139 (photo D. Saunders), 187b (photo R. Belbin); Zefa Pictures: pp89tl, 89b.
The publishers would also like to thank Brian Glover for images from his archive.

CONTENTS

A WORLD TOUR

A globe-trotting journey around the world of beer, giving a glimpse into the thousands of beers brewed worldwide today. The world of beer is a complex one, so for ease we have chosen the main brews of note in each country or region. Large international brewers and brands can be found in their country of origin and in each country the main emphasis is on the native beers and brewers.

HISTORY

Beer has always been the drink of the people. Malt and hops may not have inspired as many precious pens as the noble grape, but they have always provided good company. Beer is much more sociable. It is the best long drink in the world.

THERE ARE NO BARRIERS around a shared jug. "Beer cheers and heartens. It is the accompaniment of simple friendliness," said a churchman during the dark days of the Second World War. "In times such as these, people need some liquid sunshine." Beer is a most ancient drink that has had a chequered and varied history. It has been used by preachers as a religious symbol, by doctors as a medicinal treatment and by workers as a means of relaxation after a hard day's toil. Throughout the ages, in different countries beer has been both promoted as a health drink and reviled as the draught of the devil.

The brewing industry has changed fundamentally since the early medieval ale wives brewed from their kitchens, and it has been affected profoundly by the advances in technology sparked by the Industrial Revolution of the 19th century and continuing innovation of the 20th century. It has developed into one of the largest and most modern multinational industries. Beer is shipped all around the globe and large companies produce their brews thousands of miles from home. But there is still room for the small-scale producer in today's richly varied marketplace.

The huge range of beers that is drunk all over the world is dazzling, as is the variety of customs associated with it. A glass of beer does not just mean a sparkling golden lager, familiar in every land. It could be a stout or strong ale, a white beer, a wheat beer, a porter or a double bock. All are waiting to be enjoyed. This book will show you some of the glasses to raise on your journey around the global bar.

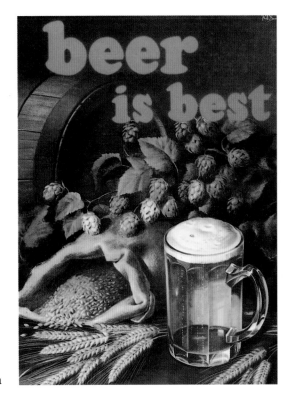

Above: "Beer is Best". An advertisement from 1933 emphasizes beer's nourishing qualities.

Opposite: "A Warming Brew", from the painting by Edwin Thomas Roberts, 1840-1917.

JOSEF SIGL

BRAUEREI·UND REALITÄTENBESITZER

OBERTRUM
BEI SALZBURG.
GEGRÜNDET 1601.

Left: In the 19th century large breweries were appearing all around Europe. This print shows the original Salzburg premises of Josef Sigl, an Austrian brewery that is still going strong.

IRELAND

When people think of Irish beer, they picture a dark glass of stout. Ireland is the only country in the world where this creamy brew is the most popular drink, consumed in great quantities in the famous Irish pubs.

THE IRISH HAVE PROBABLY BEEN BREWING since the Bronze Age. Although spirits have always been popular, beer is very much a traditional tipple and brewing is a major industry, with the majority of the malting barley crop going directly into whisky and beer production. One particular type of beer – stout – still accounts for around half of all beer sold in Ireland, the vast bulk of it Guinness. The only serious competition comes from Cork where Beamish and Murphy's, both now owned by foreign companies, brew rivals. But even in Cork, Guinness control half the market.

Dry, bitter stout is the quintessential Irish drink and some obliging barmen will even sketch a shamrock leaf in the foam, to prove it. But Irish stout is actually based on a dark English beer, porter, imported into Ireland in the 18th century.

Irish brewers copied the increasingly popular style, then in the early 19th century Guinness introduced its own, bigger-bodied, drier version – Extra Stout Porter – which eventually became known simply as stout.

In Ireland drinking is a highly sociable tradition. The nation is full of bars and pubs, famous the world over for their good music and convivial atmosphere. It is here that beer is generally consumed, rather than at home, and as a result most beer (more than 80%) is still served on draught. Up until the 1950s, stout was served through a two-cask system. One wooden cask contained fresh, still-fermenting stout, while another contained more mature stout. The glass was filled with the fresh brew, and then, when the foam had settled, was topped up with the older, flatter stout. This system was replaced in the 1960s by pressurized containers which used nitrogen to give a smoother, creamier texture. The beer was served from one keg and was filtered and pasteurized. At the same time weaker porter was phased out and the strength of stout was lowered from around 5% alcohol by volume to 4%. Today, there is an increasing tendency to chill it, thereby reducing its flavour and aroma.

Above: Drinking in Ireland generally means a pint of stout in the pub. But brewers have tried to bottle the experience to be enjoyed at home.

THE BEERS

Beamish Red Ale

This recent addition to the Beamish range is a smooth, traditional Irish-style red ale (4.5%). It has a rich, red colour, created by the black and crystal malts that are used in the brew. It has a full, sweet flavour.

Beamish Stout

The chocolatey Beamish Stout (4.2%) is the only stout brewed nowhere but Ireland. In fact it is not even brewed outside the town of Cork. Its distinctive flavour is partly due to the use of malted wheat, as well as barley, in the mash. Beamish is exported to Britain, Europe and North America.

Black Biddy Stout

A rare, cask-conditioned stout (4.4%) brewed at the Biddy Early pub, County Clare.

Caffrey's Irish Ale

This strong, creamy, traditional, Irish ale (4.8%) is brewed at the Ulster brewery in County Antrim. It is named after Thomas R. Caffrey, who founded the brewery in 1891. Caffrey's pours like an old-fashioned stout and takes about three minutes to settle from a creamy liquid to a rich auburn colour, topped with a creamy head. The beer is served chilled like a lager, but has the flavour of an ale. It was launched in the UK on St Patrick's Day 1994.

Great Northern Porter

This rare cask Irish porter (4%) is a black, traditional seasonal brew with a rich, sweetish, burnt flavour, from the Hilden brewery.

Guinness Draught

Draught Guinness (4.1%) is a smooth and creamy stout (partly due to the nitrogen- dispensing system) with a refreshing, roasted flavour and a rich black hue. It is filtered and pasteurized. In 1989, canned "draught" Guinness was launched, after five years' research, so that dedicated Guinness drinkers could enjoy the smooth brew in the comfort of their homes.

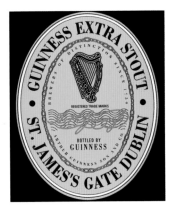

Guinness Extra Stout

This quality bottled stout (4.3%) uses unmalted, roasted barley and is heavily hopped to give a ruby-black colour and a complex, bitter flavour. It is still unpasteurized in Ireland. One of the world's classic beers.

Guinness Foreign Extra Stout

A strong export stout with a richly astringent taste (7.5%), it is a partly blended brew, using specially matured stout.

Guinness Special Export

This delicious, strong, mellow export stout (8%) is produced exclusively for the Belgian market.

Harp Export

This is a stronger (4.5%) version of Harp Lager and is produced at Guinness's Great Northern Brewery in Dundalk.

Harp Lager

This pioneering golden lager (3.6%) was developed by Guinness in 1959, to mark the bicentenary of the firm. Harp was launched in 1960 and was named after the company's famous Irish harp logo. It is brewed at the Great Northern Brewery in Dundalk.

The Crack

Irish pubs are famous the world over for their great beer and convivial atmosphere. The pub, as much as the church, is the traditional meeting place for the local community and is a place for good talk, good music and good drink. "The Crack" as it is known is one of the country's best known exports as "Irish pubs" spring up as far afield as Milan and Sydney.

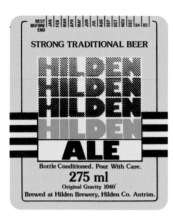

Hilden Ale

This hoppy, cask bitter (4%), produced by the Hilden Brewery, is a hoppy, light-amber brew, which is mainly exported to Britain.

Hilden Special Reserve

A dark, amber mild (4.6%), brewed using dark malts, by the Hilden brewery.

Hoffmans Lager

This lager (3.3%) is produced in Waterford for south-east Ireland.

Irish Festival Ale

This amber-coloured, fruity bitter (5%) was originally brewed for important calendar events and beer festivals, but it is now a regular offering from the Hilden brewery.

Kaliber

This is a non-alcoholic lager brewed by Guinness.

Kilkenny Irish Beer

This red ale (4.3%) is a creamy, premium ale, initially produced for export in 1987 by Smithwick's. It was launched in Ireland in 1995. A stronger version (5%) is exported to the United States.

Macardles Ale

This Irish ale (4%) is produced at the small traditional Macardle Moore brewery in Dundalk.

Murphy's Irish Stout

This is a relatively light, smooth stout (4%). It should be served cooled to lager temperature, with a head about 1½ cm (½ in) deep.

Murphy's Red Beer

This pressurized red ale (5%) was launched by Murphy's in 1995. Its distinctive red hue is entirely natural.

Oyster Stout

This classic Irish beer (4.8%) includes real oysters in the boil. It is produced by the Porter House brewpub in Dublin. In its first year this stout won two awards.

Phoenix

This traditional Irish ale (4%) is produced at Macardle Moore of Dundalk.

Plain Porter

This classic, light stout (4.3%) has a dry, roast flavour and an uncompromizing black colour. Yet another quality brew from the Porter House brewing company, Parliament Street, Dublin.

Porter House Red

A traditional Irish red ale (4.4%) with a hoppy, caramel flavour. Produced by the Porter House brewery.

Smithwick's Barley Wine

Despite its name, this barley wine (5.5%) is actually brewed at Macardle's brewery in Dundalk.

Smithwick's Export

This auburn Irish ale (5%) is brewed in Ireland for the Canadian market.

Whitewater Mountain Ale

This cask-conditioned Irish ale (4.2%) is produced by the Whitewater brewery, a new brewery founded in 1996 in Kilkeel, County Down.

Wrasslers XXXX Stout

This fine stout (5%) is made to a recipe using four different types of malt, originally brewed by Deasy's of West Cork in the 1900s. The Hilden brewing company bills it as "a stout like your grandfather used to drink".

THE BREWERS

Beamish and Crawford

The Cork-based brewers first produced porter in 1792 and early in the 19th century they were the largest brewers in the land, bigger than Guinness. However, by the mid-20th century the brewery was run down and since 1962 it has been owned by a succession of foreign breweries. A modern brewhouse now stands alongside the half-timbered city centre offices. As well as Beamish Stout, it also produces a Beamish Red Ale.

Guinness

This international giant is, perhaps, one of the most renowned brewers in the world. The name has become almost synonymous with Irish stout (see next page).

Hilden Brewery

This small brewery located alongside a Georgian country house in Lisburn, County Antrim, was set up in 1981. It is the oldest surviving independent brewery in Northern Ireland.

Lett's

The Ghost Brewer of Ireland, Lett's, ceased brewing at Enniscorthy in County Wexford in 1956, but an enterprising member of the family – George Killian Lett – licensed two major foreign brewers to produce their Ruby Ale. Pelforth of France produce George Killian's Bière Rousse, while Coors of the United States brew a lighter Killian's Irish Red. English brewers Greene King have since also rolled out Wexford Irish Cream Ale brewed to a Letts recipe.

Murphy's

Murphy's was established in 1856 by the Murphy brothers, on the Lady's Well site in Cork. Following a disastrous trading agreement with English brewers Watney's in the 1960s to sell keg Red Barrel in Ireland, the Lady's Well brewery had to be rescued by the Irish Government and a consortium of publicans before being bought by Dutch giants Heineken in 1983. Today Murphy's Stout (4%) is exported to more than 50 countries.

Above: A village pub advertises its wares – beer, food and music – in Killarney, County Kerry.

Porter House

A brewpub brewing classic Irish beers. Porter House opened in 1996 in the heart of Dublin in Parliament Street. Its brews include Porter House Plain Porter (4.3%), Porter House Red (4.4%), 4X Stout (5%) and an Oyster Stout (4.8%).

Smithwick's

Ireland's oldest brewery, built around the impressive ruins of Kilkenny's St Francis Abbey, dates from 1710. It is now owned by Guinness. The soft, red Smithwick's (3.5%) is Ireland's best-selling draught ale. It also produces Kilkenny Irish Beer (4.3%), mainly for export.

THE GUINNESS STORY

Arthur Guinness began brewing in Dublin in 1759.

For many, Guinness is the first, last and only word on Irish beer. Initially Arthur Guinness produced ale, but seeing the success of imported porter from England, he completely switched to brewing the dark drop by 1799. He reversed the beer trade, sending exports to England. By 1815, Guinness was so well known that wounded officers at the Battle of Waterloo were calling for the beer by name.

In the 1820s, the second Arthur Guinness (1768–1855) perfected an extra stout porter which eventually became known simply as stout. He made Guinness the largest brewer in Ireland. His son Benjamin (1798–1868) turned St James's Gate into the largest brewery in the world. Its stout sold around the globe.

A franchise was granted to McMullen of New York in 1858; Speakman Brothers of Melbourne started distribution in Australia in 1869. The familiar buff label with its harp trademark first appeared in 1862, and in 1878 a completely new brewhouse was built under Edward Guinness (1847–1927).

By 1910, the ever-expanding plant was producing two million hogsheads (54-gallon/245-litre casks) of stout a year. A quarter of a million wooden barrels were stacked in mountains on the 64-acre (26-hectare) site.

In 1936 a second brewery was opened at Park Royal in London to meet demand in England. Since 1962, Guinness has built breweries around the world: in Nigeria, Malaysia, Cameroon, Ghana and Jamaica. In addition, the stout is brewed under licence from North America to Australia.

In the 1950s, Guinness re-entered the ale trade through Irish Ale Breweries, with a beer called Phoenix from Waterford. The firm celebrated its bicentenary in 1959 by planning its own Harp lager. The black stuff, however, remains at the heart of the business.

Guinness stout varies in strength and character, depending on the market that it is being sold in. Stronger stouts are brewed for export, partly blended using specially matured stout. St James's Gate also exports concentrated versions of mature stout to blend into Guinness brewed abroad to provide the characteristic flavour and

Above: By the 19th century the St James's Gate brewery had become a city within a city, complete with its own power station and internal railway system, and employing an army of men.

colour. Sweeter and stronger Guinness is especially popular in Africa and the Caribbean.

Besides its Dublin brewery, Guinness in Ireland also owns ale and lager breweries at Kilkenny, Dundalk and Waterford.

Since it merged with United Distillers in 1986 and Grand Metropolitan in 1997 it has become one of the world's top drinks companies.

Below: Altogether, Guinness is brewed in 50 countries and is on sale in a further 100.

NUTRITIOUS AND DELICIOUS

Dublin's famous stout brewer Guinness was one of the first brewers to achieve international recognition. It had little choice, since it had already saturated its home market. By 1959, when the Irish brewer celebrated its bicentenary, 60% of production at its huge Dublin plant was for export.

Despite its huge success Guinness never ceased its search for new sales, and as a result its distinctive advertising campaigns have become well known the world over.

Above: The Guinness toucan.

Above: A drink to come home to.

Above: A cartoon by H. Bateman and J. Gilroy.

Above: Guinness has used several effective slogans but this one probably made the most lasting impact.

WALES

As you step from the train in the Welsh capital of Cardiff, you cannot miss the heady aroma of malt and hops drifting across the platform from Hancock's brewery behind the station and Brains old brewery in the city centre.

THE WELSH have a long brewing tradition. However, a chilling draught of takeovers and closures swept through the industry in the 1960s. Today, two English companies, Bass and Whitbread, dominate South Wales, alongside the family brewery, Brains of Cardiff. Further west, in Llanelli, another two breweries – Felinfoel and Crown Buckley – still operate, though in 1997 Brains took over Crown Buckley.

The Welsh beer trade was built in the 19th century on the raging thirst of miners and steelworkers who worked in the heavy industries of the valleys. At the same time, however, there was a strong temperance movement led by the powerful Methodist chapels of the area. Demon drink was top of the sin list during the religious revivals of the 19th century. At a temperance meeting in Tredegar in 1859, 7,000 signed the teetotal pledge. That summer the receipts of the local Rhymney brewery plunged by £500 a month.

The twin influences of heavy industry and temperance ensured that the typical Welsh ale was a low-gravity brew, relative to English beers. It was brewed for drinking in quantity. The two leading brands today, Allbright from Welsh Brewers (Bass) and Welsh Bitter from Whitbread, reflect this weak tradition: both are light-processed beers. However, some tastier traditional brews still survive, notably Brains Dark and Worthington Dark.

Above right: Roberts of Aberystwyth is one of the many breweries which have vanished.

Above: The Brains brewery of Cardiff has long kept the flag of cask-conditioned ales flying. It has only recently released its premium brew S-A in bottles.

When Welsh brewing recovered somewhat in the early 1980s, 20 new breweries frothed up to meet the demand for traditional cask ale. Most, however, found it difficult to establish a reliable trade and went rapidly to the brewhouse wall. The only survivors from this period are the Bullmastiff brewery in Cardiff and Plassey near Wrexham.

In the mid-1990s, a second wave of new ventures appeared, led by Dyffryn Clwyd of Denbigh, Cambrian of Dolgellau and Tomos Watkin of Llandeilo.

THE BEERS

Allbright

This is the most popular beer in Wales. It is a standard, pale-amber keg bitter (3.2%), produced by Bass-owned Welsh Brewers in Cardiff.

Archdruid

This flavoursome ale (3.9%) is one of a range of beers from the small Dyffryn Clwyd brewery, located in the old, stone butter market in the centre of Denbigh.

Brains Bitter

This hoppy, golden-amber cask bitter (3.7%), is Brains' best-selling brew.

Brains Dark

This lightly hopped, dark mild (3.5%) is traditionally served with a creamy head. Brains Dark is a smooth brew that is less sweet than most beers of the dark mild type, a stronger (4%) processed version is sold as Dark Smooth.

Brenin

Crown Buckley's low-gravity keg bitter (3.4%) takes its name from the Welsh word for "king".

Brindle

A strong, tasty ale (5%), produced by the small Bullmastiff brewery.

Buckley's Best Bitter

This well-balanced bitter (3.7%) has a pleasing, hoppy character. It has been famous for generations in west Wales and is still Crown Buckley's best-selling brew. Buckley's Best Bitter is available in cask, keg and cans.

Bullmastiff Best Bitter

A malty, fruity beer (4%) brewed by Bullmastiff of Cardiff.

Cambrian Original

Hoppy, session bitter from the Cambrian brewery of Dolgellau. They also brew a malty Best Bitter (4.2%) and full-bodied Premium (4.8%).

CPA

Crown Pale Ale is the light-amber, refreshing bitter (3.4%) that was once known as "the champagne of the valleys", when it slaked the thirsts of the miners. It is brewed by Crown Buckley.

Cwrw Castell

The name of this beer (4.2%) means "Castle Bitter" in Welsh. It is produced by Dyffryn Clwyd.

Cwrw Tudno

This is Plassey's malty premium bitter (5%). "Tudno" is the patron saint of the seaside resort of Llandudno.

Dr Johnson's Draught

This traditional draught beer (3.6%) is one of the range from Dyffryn Clwyd.

Double Dragon

Felinfoel's famous full-bodied premium bitter (4.2%) won the Challenge cup for cask beer at the Brewers' Exhibition in London in 1976. A stronger version of the dark-amber, moderately malty, delicately hopped brew is bottled for export, mainly to the US.

Dragon's Breath

This is Plassey's fiery, spicy-flavoured, dark-amber winter warmer (6%).

Ebony Dark

This distinctive, rare cask ale (3.8%) comes from Bullmastiff in Cardiff.

Felinfoel Bitter

An amber, lightly hopped session bitter (3.2%) brewed using pale pipkin malt in the mash by the Felinfoel brewery.

Felinfoel Dark

This deep, dark beer (3.2%) is brewed using extra caramel to produce a slightly sweeter brew than the standard.

Gold Brew

This amber-coloured, tasty, cask ale (3.8%) is produced by the Bullmastiff brewery in Cardiff.

Hancock's HB

Hancock's HB is a malty, cask bitter (3.6%) from the Bass-owned Hancock's brewery in Cardiff.

Jolly Jack Tar Porter

This is Dyffryn Clwyd's dark, dry traditional porter (4.5%).

Main Street Bitter

This is the Pembroke brewery's fine, cask-conditioned bitter (4.1%).

Off the Rails

This strong beer (5.1%) is produced at the Pembroke brewery, for the free trade. It is available at the Station Inn at Pembroke Docks.

Old Nobbie Stout

A dark beer from the Pembroke brewery (4.8%). It is available for the free trade and at the Station Inn.

Pedwar Bawd

This strong ale (4.8%) comes from Dyffryn Clwyd of Denbigh. The name means "four thumbs". In 1994, it won the CAMRA accolade of "Welsh Beer of the Year".

Plassey Bitter

A straw-coloured beer (4%) with a fruity flavour from Plassey brewery.

Reverend James

Buckley's full-bodied, warming, spicy, fruity premium ale (4.5%) is named in honour of the Reverend James Buckley. A Methodist minister, Buckley combined saving souls with satisfying thirsts when he inherited the brewery in Llanelli from his father-in-law in the 1820s.

BRAGOT

Centuries ago, Welsh ale was a highly prized commodity throughout Britain. For example, when King Ine of Wessex in southern England drew up a law concerned with payments in kind received in return for land, some time between 690 and 693 AD, he decreed that for every ten hides of land, the food rent paid should include 12 ambers (an ancient liquid measurement) of Welsh ale.

Records of the Saxon period divide ale into three types – clear, mild and Welsh. Welsh ale, which was known as Bragawd or Bragot, was more highly valued than either clear or mild ale. It was recognized as a separate style, and did not necessarily have to be brewed in Wales. The savoury brew, which was flavoured with expensive spices and honey, was driven west by the invading Saxons, but then welcomed back into England by the new masters who greatly appreciated its heady flavour. In ancient Britain, Welsh ale was second only to mead, that other honey brew.

S-A

Brains' best-known beer is a dark-amber, malty, fruity premium bitter (4.2%) that is affectionately known as "Skull Attack" by Welsh drinkers. However, its name actually comes from the initials of the brewery's founder, Samuel Arthur Brain. S-A is exported to the United States under the name Traditional Welsh Ale.

SBB

Special Best Bitter (3.7%) is brewed by Crown Buckley in Llanelli. This rounded, mature, cask-conditioned bitter is particularly popular with beer drinkers in the Cynon valley.

Son of a Bitch

This full-bodied and dangerously drinkable ale is the strongest, regularly brewed, cask beer in Wales (6%). It comes from Bullmastiff of Cardiff.

Watkin BB

A malty bitter (4%) from Tomos Watkin of Llandeilo.

Watkin OSB

A slightly stronger old style bitter (4.5%) from Watkin.

Welsh Bitter

Whitbread's well-known weak keg bitter (3.2%) from its vast plant at Magor.

Worthington Dark

Welsh Brewers' dark-ruby, creamy mild (3%), named after the famous Burton brewers. It is popular in the Swansea area.

Worthington Draught

A smooth, creamy bitter (3.6%) from Welsh Brewers with subtle bitterness and pear-and-peach aroma.

THE BREWERS

Brains

This traditional family brewery has been operating in Cardiff since 1882. The brewery is famous for its slogan "It's Brains you want". It produces three cask ales for its 189 pubs.

Bullmastiff

Bob Jenkins founded this colourful brewery in 1987, and named it in honour of his pet dogs. Now located in Cardiff, this small brewery produces distinctive but hard-to-find cask beers, including Gold Brew and Ebony Dark, Best Bitter, Brindle and the infamous Son of a Bitch.

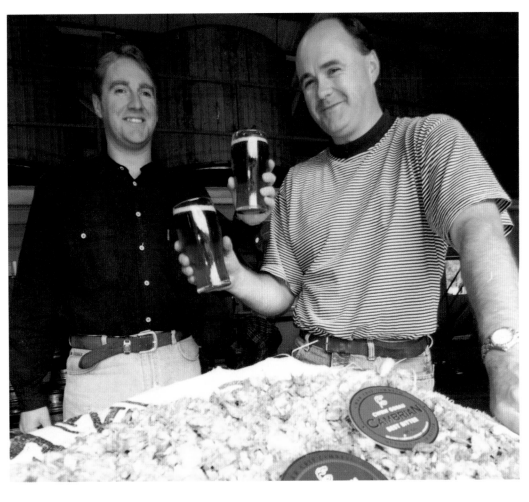

Cambrian

Brothers Kevin and Keith Williams set up the only brewery in north-west Wales in 1996, to serve the mountainous Snowdonia National Park. Based in Dolgellau, the small brewery

Above: The Williams brothers toast the success of their fledgling Cambrian brewery.

produces Cambrian Original, Best Bitter, Premium and Mountain Ale, as well as various seasonal brews.

Crown Buckley

Buckley's brewery in Llanelli claims to be the oldest in Wales, dating back to 1767. Crown brewery, which was previously D.T. Jenkins of Pontyclun, has been rolling out barrels as Crown since 1919. D.T. Jenkins became Crown when the local clubs banded together to buy their own brewery in an attempt to overcome shortages of beer caused by rationing. In 1989 Crown and Buckley merged, and the

brewing was then concentrated at the former Buckley site in Llanelli. The old Crown site is used for bottling and kegging. In 1997 the company was taken over by Brains of Cardiff and is now known as Brain Crown Buckley.

Above: Vans load up with barrels of Brains for the pubs (c. 1930).

Dyffryn Clwyd

A small brewery located in the old, stone butter market in the centre of Denbigh.

Felinfoel

This village brewery, situated just outside Llanelli, is one of only two surviving breweries in west Wales. In 1935, it became the first brewery to can beer in Europe, in an effort to help the local tinplate industry during the Depression. Felinfoel is best known for its robust and patriotically named Double Dragon ale (a red dragon is the symbol of Wales). It also brews a fine bitter and a tasty dark (both 3.2%) for its 85 pubs.

Hancock's

William Hancock took over North and Low's Bute Dock brewery in Cardiff in 1883. From there the company expanded by taking over several other breweries around South Wales, until eventually it could easily claim to be the largest brewer in Wales. When this regional force was taken over by the English giant Bass in 1968, Welsh Brewers was born through a merger of Hancock's with Webb's of Aberbeg and Fernvale of the Rhondda. Today only Hancock's Brewery in Cardiff remains.

Pembroke

David Lightley set up this small brewery in 1994, in converted stables behind his 18th-century guest house. Pembroke mainly supplies his pub, the Station Inn, on the railway platform at Pembroke Docks. Beers produced include a rare cask-conditioned lager (4.1%).

Plassey

This small brewery was set up in a caravan site at Eyton in 1985. Plassey produces a hoppy Plassey bitter (4%), a dry stout (4.6%) and two stronger ales for the three bars on the caravan site, as well as for the local free trade.

Watkin

Tomos Watkin and Sons is named after a former Llandovery brewery. It was established in 1995 in Llandeilo in south-west Wales by Simon Buckley, a member of the famous Buckley brewing family. The plant produces two cask

beers: Watkin's Brewery Bitter and Watkin's Old Style Bitter. Watkin has ambitious plans to expand to larger premises and to build up a pub estate.

Welsh Brewers

Bass's South Wales subsidiary is based in Cardiff.

Whitbread

This famous company is England's third largest brewing group. It has a weighty presence in Wales through its huge plant at Magor. As well as the best-

Below: Tin plating was a traditional industry of West Wales. Its decline prompted Felinfoel to adopt beer in cans more readily than most in a bid to boost the tin industry and the pockets of its local drinkers.

selling Welsh Bitter, it also brews many foreign beers at the plant for the Welsh market.

HOME-BREW PUBS

Wales has four pubs that brew their own beers:

• The Joiners Arms, Bishopston. The Swansea Brewing Co. was set up behind this pub in 1996. The main beer is Bishopswood Bitter.

• The Nag's Head, Abercych, near Newcastle Emlyn, is a restored old smithy producing Old Emrys (4.1%).

• The Red Lion, Llanidloes, Powys, brews Blind Cobbler's Thumb (4.2%), Witches' Brew (7.5%) and, at Christmas, the powerful barley wine Blind Cobbler's Last (10.5%).

• The Tynllidiart Arms, Capel Bangor, near Aberystwyth, is a cottage brewpub that produces Rheidol Reserve (4.5%).

WREXHAM LAGER

Wrexham was once the centre of beer making in Wales, as its springs provided ideal water for brewing. The town boasted 19 breweries, and its beers were famous across Britain. The last of the Wrexham ale breweries, Border, closed in 1984 – but one unique concern remains.

German and Czech immigrants established the Wrexham Lager Beer Company in 1882. When it first began brewing, it claimed to be the first lager brewery in Britain. Much of its early production was shipped abroad, particularly by the army.

Burton brewer Ind Coope took over Wrexham in 1949, and it switched to producing foreign lagers under licence. It was the first brewery in Britain to brew American Budweiser. It still brews a light Wrexham lager for the local trade and occasional export.

Below and above: The Wrexham brewery struggled to convert Britain's ale drinkers with its lager beer.

21

ENGLAND

In the first half of the 20th century, the main beer in England was mild, the worker's drink. Since the Second World War mild has been replaced by another top-fermenting ale, the stronger, more heavily hopped bitter.

D ESPITE THE FACT that the golden tide of lager has washed over the shores of England, in the shape of imitations of the Pilsner style from overseas, ales are still very popular and account for around half the market. No country in the world drinks more. Ale, which varies in colour from pale gold through to dark ruby, is a social drink, usually of modest strength, from 3.5 to 4.5% alcohol by volume. It is brewed for drinking in quantity (usually in pints or halves) in company.

To find the native beers of England, walk into an English pub (public house) where the bulk of beer is still enjoyed on draught, served over the bar usually from a tall handpump, rather than being bought in a bottle or a can in a shop or supermarket and drunk at home. Traditional English beer is cask-conditioned – it is a living beer which continues to ferment and mature in the cask in the pub cellar after leaving the brewery. This allows the beer's flavour to develop fully.

English beer has a reputation for being "warm", but though it should not be heavily chilled, like lagers, it should always be served cellar cool.

In the 1960s the major breweries in England tried to replace cask beer with easier-to-handle keg beer, which was filtered and pasteurized at the brewery (to make it easier to store), then served chilled and carbonated at the bar. But the beer drinkers of England rose in revolt. Many objected to losing their traditional local tastes. They wanted cask beer's fuller flavour. A campaign was launched in the early 1970s called CAMRA – the Campaign for Real Ale. It sparked a major revival of cask beer. As a result around 55 traditional local and regional breweries have survived, and some of the national companies have relaunched their own cask beers. CAMRA began a brewing revolution, and following that hundreds of new breweries have been set up since the 1970s, some reviving old styles of ale such as porter.

Above: English beer is brewed to be drunk in quantity. Stronger ales such as Fuller's 1845 are for special occasions.

THE BEERS

Abbot Ale

This robust, bright-amber, fruity premium bitter (5%) from Greene King is named after the last abbot of Bury St Edmunds in East Anglia – the brewer's home town.

Adnams Bitter

Adnams bitter is a dark-gold classic of its type (3.7%), with a hoppy, orangey flavour. Adnams also brews a smooth, malty, dark mild (3.2%), Regatta Ale (4.3%), a light summer ale, and its Extra, a pleasant best bitter with a dry, hoppy flavour, was voted Champion Beer of Britain in 1993.

AK

This long-established and popular ale (3.7%), produced by McMullens of Hertford, is a refreshingly light bitter.

Amazon Bitter

Additive-free beer (4%) from the Masons Arms brewpub, Cartmel Fell, Cumbria.

Ansells Mild

A liquorice-tasting, dark mild (3.4%) brewed by Ind Coope at Burton-on-Trent.

A Pint-a Bitter

A tasty, cask-conditioned bitter (3.5%) from the Hogs Back brewery in Surrey. Also known as APB.

Archers Best

A malty, fruity bitter from Archers of Swindon.

Arthur Pendragon

A full-bodied, fruity, premium ale (4.8%) from the Hampshire brewery in Andover, Hampshire.

Arundel Best Bitter

This gold-coloured, additive-free bitter (4%) is produced by Arundel of Sussex.

Badger

The popular name for a range of beers by the historic Hall and Woodhouse brewery in Blandford Forum, Dorset.

Ballard's Best

Copper-coloured malty ale from the Sussex country brewery, Ballard's of Nyewood.

Banks's Ale

A reddish-amber mild (3.5%), made with Maris Otter malt, Fuggles and Golding hops and caramel.

Banks's Bitter

A bittersweet, crisp bitter (3.8%) from Banks's brewery in Wolverhampton.

Banner Bitter

A flavoursome, light-brown bitter (4%) from the Butterknowle brewery in Bishop Auckland.

Barn Owl Bitter

A darkish-brown, fruity, rich bitter (4.5%) from the Cotleigh brewery, Somerset.

Batham's Best

Sweetish, golden bitter (4.3%) from the famous Black Country brewery, Batham's, of Brierley Hill.

Battleaxe

A smooth, slightly sweet cask beer (4.2%) from the Rudgate brewery, near York.

Beacon Bitter

A refreshing bitter (3.8%) brewed by Everard in Narborough, near Leicester.

Beast

A potent winter brew (6.6%) from the Exmoor brewery in Wiveliscombe, Somerset.

Beaumanor Bitter

This light-brown, strong-tasting bitter (3.7%) is brewed by the Hoskins brewery in Leicester.

Beechwood

A full-bodied draught beer (4.3%) with a nutty character from the Chiltern brewery.

Benchmark

A pleasantly bitter, malty ale (3.5%) produced by Bunces brewery, Wiltshire.

Bishops Ale

A potent, full-flavoured, warming barley wine (8%) from Ridleys brewery near Chelmsford.

Bishops Finger

A ruby-red ale (5.4%) with a fruity flavour and a malty aftertaste from the Shepherd Neame brewery in Kent.

Blunderbus

An intense porter (5.5%) from the Coach House brewery in Warrington.

Bosun Bitter

This smooth, amber, cask beer (4.6%) has a strong malt flavour. Brewed by the Poole brewery, Dorset.

Bosun's Bitter

A refreshing, amber cask bitter (3.1%) with a bitter, hops taste from the St Austell brewery, Cornwall.

Black Diamond

A dark-ruby-coloured, rich, malty bitter (4.8%) from the Butterknowle brewery in Bishop Auckland.

Black Jack Porter

A rich, black, winter beer (4.6%) with a fruity, sweetish flavour, from Archers in Swindon, Wiltshire.

Black Magic

Bitter stout (4.5%) from Oakhill brewery of Somerset.

Black Rock

A strong ale (5.5%) from the Brewery-on-Sea, Lancing, Sussex.

Boddingtons

A straw-coloured brew (3.8%) from this famous Manchester brewery. It was once worshipped for its parch-dry bitterness, but it now has a smoother flavour.

Brakspear Bitter

A well-hopped, aromatic light bitter (3.4%) produced by this Oxfordshire brewery.

Brakspear Special

A golden-brown, malty, dry bitter (4.3%).

Brand Oak Bitter

This well-balanced cask beer (4%) has a dry finish and a citrus, sweet flavour. It is brewed by the Wickwar brewery in Gloucestershire.

Branoc

An amber bitter (3.8%) brewed by Branscombe Vale in Devon using the local spring water.

Bishop's Tipple, The

A strong, rich, deep-amber barley wine (6.5%) with a sweet and smokey, complex flavour brewed within view of the city's towering cathedral spire by Gibbs Mew of Salisbury.

Black Adder

This dark stout (5.3%) with a roast-malt character, from the Mauldon brewery, was voted Champion Beer of Britain in 1991.

Black Cat Mild

A dark, full-tasting cask bitter (3.2%) from the Moorhouse brewery, Lancashire.

Black Sheep Best

A hoppy bitter (3.8%) fermented in traditional Yorkshire stone squares at the Black Sheep brewery, Masham, North Yorkshire.

Black Sheep Special

A full, amber ale (4.4%) brewed in traditional stone squares. It is sold bottled as Black Sheep Ale.

Bombardier

A mild, smoky, malty cask beer (4.3%) from the Charles Wells brewery in Bedford.

Boro Best

A full-bodied cask beer (4%) from the North Yorkshire brewery in Middlesborough.

Brew XI

A sweetish, malty cask bitter (3.8%) from the Mitchells & Butlers brewery in Birmingham.

Brew 97

A full-bodied, malty cask beer (5%) with a good hops taste, from the Moles brewery, Wiltshire.

Brewer's Droop
A strong ale (5%) available on draught and in bottles from the Marston Moor brewery, North Yorkshire.

Brewer's Pride
An amber, light, refreshing, fruity cask bitter (4.2%) from the Marston Moor brewery, North Yorkshire.

Bridge Bitter
A fruity, hoppy bitter (4.2%), brewed by Burton Bridge in Burton-on-Trent.

Bristol Stout
A tasty, seasonal stout (4.7%) from the Smiles brewery, Bristol. It has a red-brown hue and a pleasant roast malt taste.

Broadside Ale
Adnams' strong garnet-coloured, bitter, hoppy ale (4.7%) was brewed to mark the 300th anniversary of the battle of Sole Bay in 1672. The ale in its bottle version (6.3%) packs more cannon fire than the draught beer.

Buccaneer
A light, pale gold bitter with a sweet malty taste (5.2%) brewed by Burtonwood.

Bullion
Fruity dark ale (4.7%) from the Old Mill brewery, Snaith, Yorkshire.

Bulldog Pale Ale
A strong, yellow-coloured, hoppy, bottled pale ale (6.3%), produced by Courage in Bristol.

Bunce's Best Bitter
This aromatic, fresh and fruity bitter (4.1%) is brewed in a watermill in Netheravon, Wiltshire.

Burton Porter
This tawny-brown, dry porter (4.5%) has a light, malty taste. It is also available as a bottle-conditioned beer. Brewed by the Burton Bridge brewery in Burton-on-Trent.

Burtonwood Bitter
A smooth, smoky-tasting bitter (3.7%), brewed near Warrington at the Burtonwood brewery.

Butcombe Bitter
A dry, hoppy bitter (4%) brewed near Bristol in the Mendip Hills.

Buzz
A cask beer primed with honey (4.5%) produced by the Brewery-on-Sea, Lancing, Sussex.

Cains Bitter
A dry, spicy, amber bitter (4%) from this popular Merseyside brewery in Liverpool.

Cambridge Bitter
A traditionally brewed, amber, hoppy bitter (3.8%) from the Elgood brewery in the Fens at Wisbech.

Camerons Bitter
An orange-coloured, light, malty bitter (3.6%) from the Hartlepool brewer, which is very popular with the local workers.

Carling Black Label
This smooth, sweet lager (4.1%) is Britain's best-selling beer. It was introduced to England from Canada in 1953 and was adopted by Bass as its leading lager brand.

Castle Eden Ale
An amber-coloured, sweet, malty ale (3.8%) from the Durham-based brewery owned by Whitbread.

Castle Special Pale Ale
One of a range of bottled beers (5%) from the McMullen brewery in Hertford.

Challenger
A premium bitter (4.1%), which despite carrying the name of a hop, has a fruity, malty flavour. It is brewed by the Ash Vine brewery, Trudoxhill, Somerset.

Chiltern Ale
A tangy, light draught beer (3.7%) from the Chiltern brewery of Terrick.

Chiswick Bitter
This refreshing bitter (3.5%) with a subtle, floral, smoky flavour, from Fullers of London, is much acclaimed.

Coachman's Best
A medium-coloured full-bodied bitter (3.7%) with a hoppy, fruity flavour, from the Coach House brewery in Warrington.

Cocker Hoop
A golden, refreshing bitter (4.8%) with a hoppy, fruity flavour, from the independent Jennings brewery in the Lake District.

College Ale
A strong seasonal, winter cask ale (7.4%) from the Morrells brewery, Oxford.

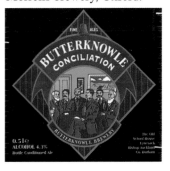

Conciliation
This dark, tawny-brown bitter (4.3%) has a good, hoppy taste. It is the flagship brew of the Butterknowle brewery in Bishop Auckland, County Durham.

Coopers WPA
A popular, refreshing, yellow-gold cask beer (3.5%) with a hoppy, citrus tang, which comes from the Wickwar brewery in Gloucestershire.

Country Best Bitter

A full and fruity, clean-tasting bitter (4.3%) from the McMullen brewery in Hertford.

Country Stile

A mid-brown draught beer (4.1%), produced by Daleside brewery in Harrogate, Yorkshire.

Courage Best

A traditional golden-brown, malty, dry cask bitter (4%) brewed in Bristol by Courage.

Craftsman

A hoppy, gold, premium ale (4.2%) from Thwaites brewery in Blackburn, Lancashire.

Cromwell Bitter

A gold, fruity cask bitter (3.6%) from the Marston Moor brewery, North Yorkshire.

Cumberland Ale

A gold-coloured bitter (4%) with a delicate flavour, from the Jennings brewery in Cockermouth in the Lake District.

Daredevil Winter Warmer

A smooth, fruity brew (7.1%) with a strong, mature flavour, produced by Everards in Narborough, near Leicester.

Deacon

A pale-gold, orangey, dry bitter (5%) from the Gibbs Mews brewery in Salisbury, Wiltshire.

Deep Shaft Stout

This black stout (6.2%) produced by the Freeminer brewery, Gloucestershire, has a roast-malt flavour.

Devon Gold

A straw-coloured, fruity, summer brew (4.1%) from Blackawton in South Devon.

Director's

A traditional dark, rich, cask bitter (4.8%) brewed in Bristol by Courage.

Dolphin Best

This dry, amber, cask bitter (3.8%) is brewed by the Poole brewery, Dorset.

Dorset Best

Also known as Badger Best Bitter (4.1%). This Hall and Woodhouse cask ale has a bitter hop and fruit flavour.

Double Chance

A malty bitter (3.8%) from the Malton brewery of North Yorkshire.

Double Diamond

Ind Coope's famous dark-amber bottled pale ale from Burton-on-Trent, which after a period of promotion as a weak keg beer, has seen its reputation restored as a bottled ale (4%), particularly in the stronger export version (5.2%). Also occasionally available as a cask beer.

Double Maxim

A classic, strong, amber-coloured brown ale (4.7%) with a smooth, fruity taste from the giant Vaux brewery.

Double Stout

An old-fashioned stout (4.8%), revived in 1996 after 79 years by the Hook Norton brewery in Banbury.

Dragonslayer

A yellowish real ale (4.5%) with a dry malt and hops flavour, from B&T, Bedfordshire.

Draught Bass

A superb bitter (4.4%) with a malty flavour and light hop bitterness. This is the biggest-selling premium ale in the country.

Draught Burton Ale

A full-bodied ale (4.8%) from the Carlsberg-Tetley brewery in Burton-on-Trent.

Drawwell Bitter

A cask beer (3.9%) from the Hanby brewery in Shropshire.

Eagle IPA

A sweet, malty, amber-coloured cask beer (3.6%) from the Charles Wells brewery in Bedford.

Eden Bitter

A smooth, sweet bitter (3.6%) from the Castle Eden brewery in County Durham.

Edmund II Ironside

A tasty, cask-conditioned bitter (4.2%) from the Hampshire brewery in Andover.

Elizabethan

A golden, barley wine (8.1%) originally brewed to mark the Queen's coronation in 1953 by Harveys brewery.

Enville Ale

One of a range of honey beers produced by the Enville Farm brewery in Staffordshire. The pale-gold ale (4.5%) is primed with honey after a rapid initial fermentation and then lagered. The brewery uses its own honey and barley.

Enville White

A golden wheat beer (4%) with a clean, sweet flavour from Enville Farm brewery.

ESB

The revered Extra Special Bitter (5.5%) from Fuller's of London is much stronger than most bitters. It has great character with a complex malt, fruit and hops flavour and has won the Champion Beer of Britain title an unprecedented three times.

ESX Best

A fruity cask bitter (4.3%) produced by Ridleys brewery, near Chelmsford, Essex.

Everard Mild

A dark mild (3.3%) which forms an unusually large head when it is poured. It is brewed in Narborough, near Leicester by Everard.

Exmoor Ale
This pale-brown, malty bitter (3.8%), from the Exmoor brewery in Wiveliscombe, Somerset, won the best bitter award at the Great British Beer Festival in 1980.

Exmoor Gold
An amber bitter (4.5%) from the Exmoor brewery.

Fargo
A rich, amber-coloured cask ale (5%) with a soft hop and roast-malt taste, from the Wells brewery in Bedford.

Farmer's Glory
A dark, fruity premium bitter (4.5%) from Wadworth's of Devizes, Wiltshire.

Fed Special
This bright, pale-amber, filtered bitter (4%) is brewed for the working men's clubs by the Federation Brewery in the north-east of England.

Festive
A fruity premium ale (5%) from the King & Barnes brewery, Horsham, Sussex.

Flowers IPA
A coppery-coloured, creamy pale ale (3.6%) produced by Whitbread in Cheltenham.

Flowers Original
A tasty bitter (4.5%) with a good malt and hop balance, produced by Whitbread in Cheltenham, Gloucestershire.

Flying Herbert
This red, refreshing, malty cask bitter is from the North Yorkshire brewery.

Formidable Ale
Strong golden-coloured ale (5%) with a full taste from Cains brewery, Liverpool.

Fortyniner
A well-balanced, fruity bitter (4.8%) from the Ringwood brewery, Hampshire.

Founders
A pale-brown bitter (4.5%) with a slight citrus and sweet-malt taste, from the Ushers brewery in Wiltshire.

Franklin's Bitter
A distinctive floral, aromatic, hoppy bitter (3.8%) brewed in Harrogate, Yorkshire.

Freedom Pilsener
This fresh, slightly fruity Pilsner (5.4%) is brewed by the Freedom brewery in Fulham, London.

Freeminer Bitter
A pale, hoppy bitter (4%) from the Forest of Dean, Gloucestershire.

Fuggles Imperial
A pale, strong, premium bitter (5.5%) from Whitbread's Castle Eden brewery, County Durham.

Gargoyle
A tasty cask bitter (5%) from the Lichfield brewery in the Midlands.

GB Mild
A smooth, malty, fruity brew (3.5%) brewed by the Lees family brewery in north Manchester.

Georges Bitter Ale
A light, refreshing bitter (3.3%) from the Courage brewery which was formerly Georges, in Bristol.

Gingersnap
A dark, orangey-coloured wheat beer (4.7%), brewed with fresh root ginger from the Salopian brewery, Shrewsbury.

Ginger Tom
A ginger-flavoured ale (5.2%) from the Hoskins & Oldfield brewery, Leicester.

Gladstone
A refreshing, smooth bitter (4.3%) from the McMullen brewery, Hertford.

Golden Best
A fine mild (3.5%) from the Timothy Taylor brewery, Keighley, Yorkshire.

Golden Bitter
A fruity bitter (4.7%) from Archers in Swindon.

Golden Brew
A golden, aromatic, bitter (3.8%) from the Smiles brewery, Bristol.

Gold Label
England's best-known bottled barley wine. This spicy, warming brew (10.9%) is produced by Whitbread.

Gothic Ale
A dark ale (5.2%) from the Enville Farm brewery, Staffordshire.

Governor
An amber bitter (4.4%) from the Hull brewery.

Graduate
A roasted-malt-flavoured premium bitter (5.2%) from the Morrells brewery, Oxford.

Granary Bitter
An amber-coloured brew with a bitter, fruity character (3.8%), from the Reepham brewery near Norwich.

GSB
A dry, fruity bitter (5.2%) from the Elgood brewery near Wisbech.

Gunpowder
A liquorice-black mild (3.8%) from the Coach House brewery, Warrington.

Hammerhead
A robust, strong, rich, malty ale (5.6%) brewed by Clark's of Wakefield, West Yorkshire.

Harrier S.P.A
A light-brown bitter (3.6%) with a light, hoppy taste, from the Cotleigh brewery, Somerset.

Harvest Ale
A staggeringly strong bottled ale (11.5%) that is produced each year from the new season's malt and hops by the Lees brewery in Manchester. This vintage brew can be laid down to mature in the cellar for several years.

Harveys Christmas Ale
A strong warming ale produced annually by the Harveys brewery, Lewes, Sussex.

Harveys Firecracker
This brew was bottled in honour of the emergency services who fought a disastrous fire at the Harveys brewery in 1996. It is a strong, dark pale ale with a smoky flavour (5.8%).

Harveys Sussex Best Bitter
A golden, hoppy bitter (4%) from Harveys of Lewes.

Harveys Sussex Pale Ale
A light, hoppy ale (3.5%) from the Harveys brewery.

Harveys Tom Paine
A strong pale ale (5.5%), from Harveys brewery.

Hatters
A fine, light mild (3.3%) from the Robinson's brewery, Stockport.

Headstrong
A fruity bitter (5.2%) from the Blackawton brewery in Devon.

Heritage
A full-bodied beer (5.2%) with a roast-malt, fruity flavour from the Smiles brewery, Bristol.

Hersbrucker Weizenbier
A light wheat beer (3.6%) from the Springhead brewery, Nottinghamshire.

Hick's Special Draught
Also known as HSD, this full-bodied, fruity cask bitter (5%) is produced by the St Austell brewery, Cornwall.

High Force
A complex, smooth beer (6.2%) with a sweet, malt flavour, from the Butterknowle brewery in Bishop Auckland.

Highgate Dark Mild
A dark-brown, smooth mild (3.2%) produced in this Victorian tower brewery in Walsall, West Midlands. It is fermented using a vigorous four-strain yeast to give a complex flavour.

Highgate Old Ale
A dark, red-brown, fruity ale (5.6%) with a complex flavour, brewed in winter by this Walsall brewery.

High Level
This sweet and fruity, bright, filtered brown ale (4.7%) is brewed for the working men's clubs by the Federation Brewery in the north-east of England. It is named after the bridge in Newcastle which crosses the River Tyne.

Hobgoblin
A robust, red ale (5.5%) sold in the cask and bottle in Britain and also in Europe and North America. It is produced by the Wychwood brewery, Oxfordshire.

Holden's Black Country Special Bitter
A sweetish, full-bodied bitter (5.1%) from Holden's brewery in Woodsetton in the West Midlands.

Holt's Bitter
This uncompromising dry bitter (4%) is sold at a relatively low price and still supplied in huge hogsheads (54-gallon casks) by Holt's brewery of Manchester.

Hook Norton Best Bitter
A dry, hoppy, cask-conditioned beer (3.4%) from this old Oxfordshire village brewery.

Hop and Glory
Complex bottle-conditioned beer (5%) from Ash Vine brewery, Somerset.

HSB
Famous, full-bodied bitter (4.8%) from Gale's of Horndean, Hampshire.

Imperial Russian Stout
A classic beer from Scottish Courage, the dark-brown, smooth brew (10%) has a rich malty flavour.

Indiana's Bones
A rich, dark, cask ale (5.6%) which is sold both as a cask beer and a bottled brew, from the Summerskills brewery, South Devon.

Innkeeper's Special
This smooth, malty brew (4.5%) has a rich, ruby-port hue and a crisp, hop taste. It is produced by the Coach House brewery in Warrington.

Inspired
A dark, malty cask bitter (4%) from the small Lichfield brewery.

Ironbridge Stout
A dark, rich stout (5%) from the Salopian brewery, Shrewsbury.

Jennings Bitter
A light, dry malty bitter (3.5%) from Jennings brewery in Cumbria.

John Smith's Bitter
A dark-amber, sweet, malty cask bitter (3.8%) with a creamy texture, from Yorkshire. One of the most popular beers in England.

Kimberley Classic
A light-coloured premium bitter (4.8%) with a dry, hoppy taste, from Hardys & Hansons brewery, Nottinghamshire.

King Alfred's
A hoppy cask beer (3.8%) from the Hampshire brewery.

Kingsdown Ale
This powerful, fruity, draught beer (5%) is produced by the Arkell's Kingsdown brewery, Swindon.

Lancaster Bomber
A straw-coloured cask ale (4.4%) from the Mitchell brewery in Lancaster.

Landlord
A classic, amber-coloured, premium bitter (4.3%) with a buttery flavour, from Timothy Taylor's brewery in Keighley, Yorkshire. It won the Champion Beer of Britain award in 1994.

Larkins Best Bitter
A full-bodied, fruity bitter (4.4%) from this Kent brewery.

London Pride
Fuller's fine, deep-red best bitter (4.1%) has a rich, dry, malty, hoppy taste.

Lynesack Porter
This is very dark, even for a porter (5%) with a sweet, malty finish. It is produced by the Butterknowle brewery in Bishop Auckland.

Mackeson's Stout
England's best-known bottled sweet stout (3%) from Whitbread is a blackish colour with a sugary, fruity taste. It was originally brewed by the firm of Mackeson in Hythe, Kent, in 1907. At that time it was claimed to be a tonic for invalids because it contained milk sugar or lactose. The sugar does not ferment, so the beer is low in alcohol.

Mackeson's was called milk stout until the British Government banned the term in 1946. However, Whitbread continues the connection through a milk churn on the label. It is still the leading brand in a declining sweet stout market and was once exported to 60 countries, and brewed under licence in Belgium, Jamaica, New Zealand and Singapore.

Above: A 1950s advertisement for Mackeson's before the British Government banned the term "milk stout" as misleading.

Magnet
A nutty-tasting premium bitter from the John Smith's brewery, Tadcaster, North Yorkshire.

Malt and Hops
A lively, seasonal ale (4.5%) made by Wadworth's, in Devizes, Wiltshire. It is one of a range of seasonal brews made using the new season's unkilned fresh hops.

M&B Mild
A reddish, full-bodied cask mild (3.2%) from Mitchells & Butlers brewery in, Birmingham.

Mann's Original
England's best-known bottled, sweet brown ale (2.8%) has a sticky, sugary texture and a fruity taste, and is now brewed by Ushers in Wiltshire.

Mansfield Bitter
This refreshing, sweetish bitter (3.9%) is brewed using traditional Yorkshire squares by the Mansfield brewery, Nottinghamshire.

Marston's Bitter
A light-brown, hoppy cask bitter (3.8%) from Marston's brewery, Burton-on-Trent.

Mauldon Special
A very hoppy cask beer (4.2%) from the Mauldon brewery in Suffolk.

Millennium Gold
This fruity, amber, cask beer (4.2%) is produced by Crouch Vale brewery, Essex.

Ministerley Ale
A complex, pale, cask bitter (4.5%) from the Salopian brewery, Shrewsbury.

Mitchell's Bitter
An amber-coloured, mild-tasting, hoppy bitter (3.8%) from Mitchell's of Lancaster.

Moles Best
A fruity cask bitter (4%), the leading beer from the Moles brewery, Wiltshire.

Monkey Wrench
A smooth, dark, sweetish, potent beer (5.3%) which is produced by Daleside brewery in the spa town of Harrogate, Yorkshire.

Moonraker
A rich, strong, orangey ale (7.5%) from the J.W. Lees brewery, Manchester.

Morocco Ale
This dark, rich, spicy bottled ale (5.5%) is said to be based on a 300-year-old recipe. It is produced by the Daleside brewery, Harrogate, Yorkshire.

Morrells Bitter
A golden-brown cask bitter (3.7%) from the Morrells brewery in the university town of Oxford.

Mutiny
A reddish, full-bodied cask ale (4.5%) from the Rebellion brewery, Buckinghamshire.

Natterjack
An aromatic, golden ale (4.8%), named after the natterjack toad, produced by the Frog Island brewery, Northampton.

Newcastle Amber
This less-well-known cousin of Newcastle Brown was introduced in 1951 as a lighter version. It has a malty, sugary taste.

Newcastle Brown
This pioneering northern brown ale (4.7%) has a nutty, caramel taste. It was first produced by Newcastle Breweries in 1927. Newcastle Brown is strong, dry and light in colour. Drinkers usually expect a small glass so they can keep topping up. This best-selling bottled beer is exported to more than 40 countries. It is now brewed by Scottish Courage on Tyneside.

Nightmare Porter
A smooth, dry porter (5%) with a roast-malt and liquorice taste from the Hambleton brewery near Thirsk, North Yorkshire.

Noel Ale
A Christmas ale (5.5%) from the Arkell's Kingsdown Brewery, Swindon.

Norfolk Nog
The 1992 Champion Beer of Britain. This tasty old ale (4.6%) is produced by Woodforde's of Norfolk.

COMMEMORATIVE BEERS

Brewers often make one-off brews to commemorate special occasions. Harveys of Lewes in Sussex, for example, bottled a special strong pale ale, called Firecracker, in honour of the emergency services who fought to save it from disaster when a fire broke out in the brewery in 1996. Many brewers bottled ales to keep for the Queen's Coronation in 1953 and later royal marriages.

Norman's Conquest

A dark, strong ale (7%) from the Cottage brewery in West Lydford, Somerset. It won the Champion Beer of Britain title at the Great British Beer Festival in 1993.

North Brink Porter

A special, reddish-black winter beer (5%) from the Elgood brewery in Wisbech.

Nut Brown

A nut-brown ale with a nutty, sweet flavour (4.5%) from the Whitby brewery, North Yorkshire.

OBJ

An intense, fruity, winter ale (5%) produced by the Brakspear brewery.

Old Baily

A copper-coloured, fruity, malty bitter (4.8%) from the Mansfield brewery in Nottinghamshire.

Old Bircham

An amber, sweet, malty winter beer (4.6%) from the Reepham brewery, near Norwich.

Old Bob

A dark-amber strong bottled pale ale (5.1%) from Ridleys brewery.

Old Brewery Bitter

A malty, nutty cask bitter (4%) from Samuel Smith's who also brew a distinctive orangey-coloured bottled pale ale (5%).

Old Buzzard

This winter beer (4.8%) is almost black. It has a smooth, rich flavour and is produced by the Cotleigh brewery, Somerset.

Old Ebenezer

A dark, tawny-coloured, rich ale (8%) from Butterknowle brewery in Bishop Auckland, County Durham.

Old Expensive

A strong, fruity winter barley wine (6.7%) brewed by Burton Bridge in Burton-on-Trent.

Old Growler

A complex porter (5.5%) with a sweet fruit and malt taste and chocolatey character, which comes from the Nethergate brewery, Suffolk.

Old Hooky

A strong, reddish-brown beer (4.6%) with a honey, orange and malt flavour. This cask brew is produced by the Hook Norton brewery in Oxfordshire.

Old Knucker

An additive-free rich, dark old ale (5.5%) from the Arundel brewery, Sussex.

Old Masters

A dry, tawny bitter (4.6%), brewed by Morland's of Abingdon.

Old Mill Mild

A dark-red, malty mild (3.5%) from the Old Mill brewery, Snaith, Yorkshire.

Old Nick

A devil of a bottled barley wine (6.9%) with a dark-reddish-brown hue and a pungent, but mellow, fruity flavour from Young's.

Old Original

A premium bitter (5.2%) with a strong, rich, malty character from Everard.

Old Peculier

Theakston's famous, rich, dark old ale (5.7%) with a roast-malt flavour, comes from Masham, North Yorkshire. The odd name refers to the Peculier of Masham, the town's ancient ecclesiastical court.

Old Smokey

A warming, malty dark ale (5%) with a slightly bitter, liquorice taste, brewed by Bunces brewery, Wiltshire.

Old Speckled Hen

A deep-gold, premium pale ale (5.2%) with a good malt, hop balance from Morland's of Abingdon, Oxfordshire. It is named not after a farmyard fowl, but an old MG car made in the town which was speckled black and gold.

Old Spot Prize Ale

A reddish, fruity cask ale (5%) from the Uley brewery in Gloucestershire. The spent grains from brewing go to a local pig herd, and the ales have retained the porky connection. Others include Hogshead, Pig's Ear and Severn Boar.

Old Stockport Bitter

A malty, fruity cask bitter (3.5%) from Robinson's brewery, Stockport.

Old Thumper
A pale-coloured, strong ale (5.8%) with a rounded grain and hops flavour, from Ringwood, Hampshire.

Old Tom
Robinson's rich, fruity, barley wine (8.5%) from Stockport, Cheshire, was originally named after the brewery cat. It was first brewed in 1899.

Olde Merryford Ale
A light-brown, full-bodied, sweet bitter (4.8%), with a good malt and hop balance, from the Wickwar brewery in Gloucestershire.

Olde Stoker
A dark-brown, smooth winter bitter (5.4%) from the Branscombe Vale brewery, Devon.

Original Porter
A ruby-brown porter with a roast-malt and liquorice flavour from the liquorice used in the recipe (5.2%). Produced by the Shepherd Neame brewery, Kent.

Owd Rodger
A rich, strong, creamy winter ale (7.6%) from Marston's brewery, Burton-on-Trent.

Oyster Stout
A creamy, bottle-conditioned stout which, despite its name, doesn't contain oysters, by Marston's, Burton-on-Trent.

Pedigree
A classic, coppery-coloured pale ale (4.5%) with a dry hop and malt taste and woody, spicy overtones, from Marston's of Burton-on-Trent. It is brewed using the traditional Burton Union system.

Pendle Witches Brew
A tasty, full-bodied ale (5.1%) which comes from the Moorhouse brewery in Burnley, Lancashire.

Penn's Bitter
A reddish, sweet bitter (4.6%) from the Hoskins brewery in Leicester.

Peter's Porter
A seasonal porter (4.8%) brewed in autumn and winter by the Arkell's Kingsdown brewery, Swindon.

Phoenix Best Bitter
A light-tawny, hoppy cask bitter (3.9%) from the Phoenix brewery, near Manchester.

Prize Old Ale
This remarkable bottle-conditioned ale (9%) from Gales of Horndean, Hampshire, is intensely warming with a hop and fruit-cake flavour. It is matured for six to twelve months before being put into corked bottles, where it continues to mature for several years.

Progress
A malty ale (4%) from the Pilgrim brewery, Reigate, Surrey.

Rain Dance
A golden, fruity wheat

beer (4.4%) from the Brewery-on-Sea, Lancing, Sussex.

Ram Rod
A full-bodied ale (5%) with a bitter hops and malt flavour, produced by Young's brewery in Wandsworth, London.

Ramsbottom Strong
A tawny-brown, rich and complex bitter (4.5%), brewed using local spring water by the Dent brewery in the Yorkshire Dales.

Rapier Pale Ale
An amber, malty, fruity cask ale (4.2%) from the Reepham brewery, near Norwich.

Rebellion IPA
This refreshing, sweet, malty pale ale (3.7%) comes from the Rebellion brewery in Marlow, Buckinghamshire.

Ridley Champion Mild
A dark cask mild (3.5%) with a fruity, malt flavour and a dry, hops finish, brewed by Ridleys, near Chelmsford, Essex.

Riggwelter
A complex, dark ale (5.9%) with a roasted flavour. It is fermented in traditional Yorkshire stone squares by the Black Sheep brewery, North Yorkshire.

Roaring Meg

A malty, light-brown cask bitter (5.5%) from the Springhead brewery, Nottinghamshire.

Robinson's Best Bitter

A hoppy, amber, malty, fairly bitter beer (4.2%) from this Stockport brewery.

Rooster's Special

A challenging, amber-coloured, malty, hoppy ale (3.9%) from this Harrogate brewery, Yorkshire.

Royal Oak

A red-brown, fruity, sweet ale (5.0%) produced by Thomas Hardy of Dorset.

Ruddles Best Bitter

A characterful cask bitter (3.7%) from this famous Rutland brewery in Langham.

Ruddles County

A full-bodied, malty, strong cask bitter (4.9%) from Ruddles.

Rumpus

A ruby-coloured nutty ale (4.5%) with a fruit and malt flavour, from the Ridleys brewery, near Chelmsford.

Ryburn Best Bitter

A fine, hoppy cask bitter (3.8%) from the Ryburn brewery, Sowerby Bridge, West Yorkshire.

Rydale

A brown, malty cask bitter (4.2%) from the Ryburn brewery.

Salem Porter

A deep, dark porter with a nutty, dry taste (4.7%) from the Bateman family brewery in Wainfleet, Lincolnshire.

Salisbury Best

A sweetish bitter (3.8%) from the Gibbs Mews brewery in the cathedral town of Salisbury, Wiltshire.

Salopian Bitter

A fruity, hoppy cask bitter (3.5%) from the Salopian brewery, Shrewsbury.

Samuel Smith's Imperial Stout

A rich, heavy, bottled stout (7%) from this famous North Yorkshire brewery in Tadcaster, which is best served and enjoyed as a liqueur.

Samuel Smith's Oatmeal Stout

A distinctive stout (5%) with a thick, dark texture and chocolatey, fruity flavour.

SAS

Strong Anglian Special is a dry, well-balanced cask bitter (5%) produced by the Crouch Vale brewery, Essex.

SBA

A malty bitter from the Donnington brewery, Stow-on-the-Wold.

Shakemantle Ginger

A cloudy, ginger wheat beer (5%) produced by the Freeminer brewery, Gloucestershire.

Shefford Bitter

A good, well-balanced, real ale (3.8%) from B&T, Bedfordshire.

Shropshire Lad

A flavoursome bitter (4.5%) produced by the Wood Brewery, next to the Plough Inn, Wistanstow.

Shropshire Stout

A deep-red, rich, dry cask beer (4.4%) from the Hanby brewery, Shropshire.

Single Malt

A powerful, seasonal ale (7.2%), which uses whisky malt in the brewing process, from Mitchell's brewery in Lancaster.

Slaughter Porter

A dark, roasted, malty porter (5%) produced by the Freeminer brewery, Gloucestershire.

Smiles Best Bitter

A rich, brown-coloured, clean-tasting, sweetish bitter (4.1%) with a dry, bitter finish from this Bristol brewery.

Smuggler

A bitter-sweet, hoppy, fruity beer (4.1%) from the Rebellion brewery, Buckinghamshire.

Sneck Lifter

A rich, dark malty premium bitter (5.1%) from the Jennings brewery in the Lake District. Also available in a bottle.

SOS

Shefford Old Strong is a malty, fruity real ale (5%) from B&T, Bedfordshire.

Spinnaker Bitter

This smooth, hoppy ale (3.5%) is one of the Brewery-on-Sea's range of cask beers. Brewed at Lancing, Sussex.

Spitfire

An amber-coloured, mild, smoky malt ale (4.7%) from the Shepherd Neame brewery, Kent.

Stabber's

A brown, strong bitter (5.2%) with a rich, malty flavour from the Ryburn brewery, West Yorkshire.

Stag

A light-brown, malty, sweet bitter (5.2%) from the Exmoor brewery in Wiveliscombe, Somerset.

Steeplejack

A light-brown cask bitter (4.5%) with a fresh, hoppy taste, from the Lichfield brewery in the Midlands.

Stig Swig

A golden, seasonal ale (5%) brewed by Bunces brewery, Wiltshire, using the herb Sweet Gale (bog-myrtle), an old Viking ingredient.

Stones Bitter

This famous straw-coloured bitter (3.9%) with a sweet, malt and hops flavour was introduced by the Cannon Sheffield brewery in the 1940s.

Strongarm

Camerons premium ruby bitter (4%) with a smooth, creamy head from Hartlepool was originally brewed for the steelworkers of Teesside.

Stronghart

A rich, dark, strong beer (7%) produced by the McMullen brewery in Hertford.

Strong Suffolk

An intriguing, unique, complex bottled ale (6%) which comes from Greene King of East Anglia. It is produced by blending an old ale that has been matured in oak vats for at least two years with a fresh brew of dark beer.

Summer Lightning

A striking, strong pale bitter (5%) which comes from the Hop Back brewery, near Salisbury, Wiltshire.

Summerskills Best Bitter

A good, brown-coloured, malt and hops bitter (4.3%) from this South Devon brewery.

Sussex Bitter

A light-coloured, tasty bitter (3.5%) from the King & Barnes brewery in Horsham, Sussex.

Sussex Mild

A dark-brown, malty mild (3%) from Harveys brewery, Lewes, Sussex.

Taddy Porter

A distinctive dark-brown, rich, dry, bottled porter (5%) from Samuel Smith's, Yorkshire.

Tally Ho

A rich, warming barley wine (7%) brewed by Adnams at Christmas. Palmer's of Dorset also brew a dark nutty ale (4.7%) which is sold under the same name.

Tanglefoot

A toe-tingling strong, sweet, amber bitter (5.1%) brewed at the Badger brewery, Blandford St Mary, Dorset, by Hall & Woodhouse.

Tetley Bitter

This pale-amber, hoppy, fruity bitter (3.7%) is traditionally served through a tight tap to give a creamy head. Brewed by Tetley in Leeds, Yorkshire.

Tetley Mild

This amber, hoppy mild (3.3%) with a malt finish, is produced by Tetley, Leeds.

Theakston Best Bitter

A bright-gold, soft bitter (3.8%) with a nutty flavour, which originally came from the North Yorkshire Theakston brewery in Masham. It is now also brewed by Scottish Courage in Newcastle.

Thomas Hardy's Ale

This bottle-conditioned ale (12%) was introduced by Eldridge Pope of Dorset in 1968 to celebrate that summer's Thomas Hardy festival in Dorchester, marking the 40th anniversary of the novelist's death. It was brewed the previous autumn "about as strong as it is

possible to brew" by head brewer Denis Holliday to match Hardy's description of Dorchester strong ale in his novel *The Trumpet Major*: "It was of the most beautiful colour that the eye of an artist in beer could desire; full in body yet brisk as a volcano; piquant, yet without a twang; luminous as an autumn sunset; free from streakiness of taste; but, finally, rather heady." After maturing in casks for six months, the highly hopped ale was filled into bottles, corked, sealed with wax and displayed with velvet ribbons. The brewery said it would continue to mature for up to 25 years. It was only expected to be a one-off special brew, but such was interest and demand that it was repeated, and now drinkers compare different vintages. Each bottle is year-dated and gradually changes from a rich, fruity brew when young to a deeper, mellower flavour, like a spicy Madeira wine.

Three Sieges

A winter ale (6%) flavoured with liquorice, from the Tomlinson brewery in the Yorkshire town of Pontefract.

Thwaites Best Mild

This smooth, dark mild (3.3%) is the best-known brew from Thwaites brewery in Blackburn, Lancashire, which still uses shire horses for local deliveries.

Tiger Best Bitter

A good malt-and-hops-flavoured bitter (4.2%) brewed by the Everard brewery in Narborough, near Leicester.

Tinners Ale

A good, light, hoppy cask ale (3.7%) from the St Austell brewery, Cornwall.

Toby

A light mild (3.2%) brewed by the giant Bass group.

Tolly's Strong Ale

This reddish-coloured, mild, creamy bottle-conditioned ale (4.6%) has a slightly sweet taste. Brewed by the Tolly Cobbold brewery, Suffolk.

Tom Hoskins Porter

A traditional porter (4.8%), brewed using honey and oats by the Hoskins and Oldfield Leicester brewery.

Top Dog Stout

A dark, strongly roasted winter brew (5%) from the Burton Bridge brewery, Burton-on-Trent.

Top Hat

A malty, nutty bitter (4.8%) brewed by Burtonwood near Warrington.

Topsy-Turvy

A dangerously drinkable strong ale (6%) from the small Berrow brewery at Burnham-on-Sea, Somerset.

T'owd Tup

A dark-coloured, strong old ale (6%) from the Dent brewery in the Yorkshire Dales.

Traditional Ale

This light-brown ale (3.4%) is one of a range of cask beers from the Larkins brewery in Kent.

Traditional Bitter

A smooth, hoppy, copper-coloured bitter (3.8%) with a strong malt character and a dry after-taste, produced by Clark brewery in Wakefield, West Yorkshire.

Traditional English Ale

A light-brown, malty, fruity ale (4.2%) from the Hogs Back brewery in Tongham, Surrey. It is commonly known as TEA.

Trelawny's Pride

A light, mild-flavoured cask bitter (4.4%) from the St Austell brewery, Cornwall.

Umbel Ale

A coriander-spiced brew (3.8%) from the Nethergate brewery in Clare, Suffolk. There is also a stronger version, Umbel Magna (5.5%).

Ushers Best Bitter

A golden-brown, hoppy bitter (3.8%) from this Wiltshire brewery.

Valiant

A golden, slightly fruity bitter (4.2%) with a bitter hops flavour, from the Bateman brewery in Lincolnshire.

Varsity

A cask beer with a good balance of sweet and bitter tastes, from the Morrells brewery, Oxford.

Vice Beer

A wheat beer (3.8%) brewed by Bunces brewery, Wiltshire.

Victory Ale

A full, fruity pale ale (6%) first brewed in 1987 to celebrate the Bateman brewery's narrow escape from closure after a family split.

Viking

A hoppy, malty, cask beer (3.8%) with a fruity finish, from the Rudgate brewery, near York.

Village Bitter

A light, hoppy bitter (3.5%) brewed by Archers of Swindon.

Waggle Dance

A golden honey beer (5%) brewed by Ward's of Sheffield for Vaux.

Wallop

A fresh, fruity, light bitter (3.5%) with a hoppy finish, from the Whitby brewery, North Yorkshire.

Ward's Mild

A malty cask ale (3.4%) brewed by Ward's, a traditional Sheffield brewery.

Wassail

A full-bodied draught and bottled beer (6%) from Ballard's, Sussex.

Wherry Best Bitter

The 1996 Champion Beer of Britain. This amber-coloured, hoppy cask bitter (3.8%) is produced by Woodforde's of Norfolk.

Whistle Belly Vengeance

A malty reddish ale (4.7%) from Summerskills of South Devon.

White Dolphin

A fruity wheat beer (4%) from the Hoskins & Oldfield brewery in Leicester.

Willie Warmer

A fruity cask beer (6.4%) produced by Crouch Vale brewery, Essex.

Wilmot's Premium

A strong ale (4.8%) brewed by the Butcombe brewery near Bristol.

Wiltshire Traditional Bitter

This dry, malty, hoppy bitter (3.6%) is produced by the Gibbs Mews brewery in Salisbury, Wiltshire.

Winter Royal

Wethered's famous rich, fruity brew (5%) now brewed by Whitbread at Castle Eden, County Durham.

Winter Warmer

A red-brown seasonal ale (5%) with a rich fruit and malt flavour and a sweetish aftertaste, produced by Young's in London.

Wobbly Bob

A robust cask beer (6%) from the Phoenix brewery, Heywood, near Manchester.

Worthington White Shield

This bottle-conditioned, pale ale (5.6%) has a delicate, yeasty, hoppy, malt flavour. It is now brewed at Mitchells and Butlers in Birmingham. For years White Shield was the only widely available bottled pale ale which retained a sediment of yeast. This meant it was a living beer – a brewery in a bottle. It developed a complex character and required careful handling. Bar staff had to pour the ale steadily into the glass without disturbing the sediment – but some drinkers preferred their glass cloudy and added the yeast anyway. It was not just a beer but a ritual.

Wye Valley Bitter

A bitter, hoppy cask bitter (3.5%) from the Wye Valley brewery in Hereford.

XL Old Ale

A bottled Christmas beer (6.9%) from Holden's brewery in Woodsetton, West Midlands.

XXX

A rare, dark, sweet, mild (3.6%) with a fruity finish, from the Donnington brewery near Stow-on-the-Wold, Gloucestershire.

XXXB Ale

A complex-tasting premium bitter (4.8%) from the Bateman brewery in Lincolnshire.

XXXX Mild

A dark, malty beer (3.6%) from the St Austell brewery, Cornwall.

THE BURTON UNION SYSTEM

In the Burton Union brewing system the beer is fermented in several linked oak casks – in union – with the fermenting beer rising through a swan-neck pipe connecting each cask to a top trough which runs the length of the whole system.

From the trough, the beer then runs back down into the casks, leaving any excess yeast behind in the trough. This constant circulation while the beer is fermenting ensures a vigorous fermentation and fully aerates the beer, giving the yeast enough oxygen to work properly.

The Burton-on-Trent giants Bass dropped the Burton Union system in 1982, claiming that it had become too expensive to maintain. In contrast, however, the traditional Marston's brewery has heavily invested in new unions and still uses the Burton Union system to brew its Owd Rodger and some of its Pedigree. The system is also used to provide the yeast for some of Marston's more conventionally fermented beers.

Yates Bitter

A fruity, straw-coloured bitter (3.7%) from this Cumbrian brewery.

Young's Ordinary

A classic bitter (3.7%) from this traditional London brewery.

2XS

An aptly named strong real ale (6%) from B&T, Bedfordshire.

3B

A draught beer (4%) from Arkell's Kingsdown brewery, Swindon.

4X

A winter warmer (6.8%) from Hydes in Manchester.

6X

Wadworth's premium fruity bitter (4.3%) from Devizes in Wiltshire, which has become well known way beyond the south-west of England. It is also sold in bottles in a stronger export version which clocks in at (5%).

1066

A strong pale ale (6%) which is available in bottle from the Hampshire brewery in Andover, Hampshire.

THE BREWERS

Adnams

This seaside family firm from Southwold, dating from 1872, sprang to fame outside Suffolk in the real ale revival of the 1970s. Adnams is now one of the top quality brewers of Britain. Most production is devoted to its traditional draught beers.

Ansells

This Birmingham brewery, known for its Aston ales, closed in 1981. However its liquorice-tasting dark mild lives on, brewed by Carlsberg-Tetley at Burton-on-Trent.

Archers

Enterprising brewery set up in the old Great Western Railway workshops in Swindon, Wiltshire, in 1979.

Arkell

In 1843 after John Arkell returned from Canada, where his family had founded the village of Arkell near Toronto, he established the Arkell company. Its Kingsdown brewery in Stratton St Margaret, Swindon, is a classic Victorian brewhouse still with its steam engine.

Badger

Hall & Woodhouse's historic Dorset brewery in Blandford Forum, established in 1777, now goes by the popular name of "Badger", after its traditional "Badger" beers.

Ballards

This Sussex country brewery, founded in 1980, is famous for producing an annual bottled beer with a staggering strength to match the date. In 1997 the brewery at Nyewood produced Old Pecker (9.7%). Each new year's beer, with its cartoon label, is launched at a charity walk on the first Sunday of December.

Bass

England's best-known brewery was founded by William Bass in 1777 in Burton-on-Trent. The firm's flagship ale in England, Draught Bass, lost a little of its reputation when the Burton Union system of brewing was abandoned in 1982. Bass's Burton home also houses England's leading brewing museum, which includes a pilot brewing plant used to produce special ales.

Bass is Britain's largest brewing group and if the proposed merger with Carlsberg-Tetley in 1997 is allowed by the Office of Fair Trading, Bass would control 40% of Britain's beer business. Besides Burton, it also owns notable breweries in Birmingham (Mitchells & Butlers), and Sheffield (Stones). Outside England it controls Tennents in Scotland, Hancock's in Wales and the Ulster Brewery in Ireland. In addition to exporting to 70 countries, in the 1990s Bass took over brewing groups in the Czech Republic, notably Staropramen in Prague and launched a joint venture with Ginsberg Brewery in China.

Bateman

This Lincolnshire brewery was founded in Wainfleet in 1874 and narrowly survived a family split in the mid-1980s thanks to the determination of Chairman George Bateman to keep brewing his "Good Honest Ales".

Batham

A traditional Black Country family brewery which was founded at Brierley Hill, near Dudley, in 1877.

Black Sheep

When Paul Theakston of North Yorkshire's famous brewing family lost control of Theakston's Masham brewery, he was determined to start brewing again. The Black Sheep brewery, founded in an old maltings at Wellgarth, Masham, in 1992, is the result. Built on a much larger scale than most new breweries, it installed equipment taken from the former Hartley's brewery in Cumbria. Black Sheep brewery ferments its beer in traditional Yorkshire stone squares and boasts its own visitor centre, making Masham a place of pilgrimage for serious beer drinkers.

Boddingtons

This Manchester brewery, founded in 1778, was once worshipped for the parch-dry bitterness of its straw-coloured bitter. It was taken over by Whitbread in 1989.

Brakspear

A traditional brewery dating back to the 17th century in Henley-on-Thames, Oxfordshire. Its pubs pack the streets of the small town that is famous for its rowing regatta. It is one of the least spoilt breweries in Britain.

Burtonwood

A north-west regional brewery dating from 1867. It built a new brewhouse in Burtonwood, near Warrington, in 1990.

Butcombe

One of the most successful new breweries, set up in the Mendips near Bristol in 1978.

Above: A beautifully decorated English pub with the handpumps for serving traditional draught beer visible on the curving bar.

Cains

This Liverpool brewery has enjoyed a history as elaborate as its towering Victorian brewhouse. After many years as Merseyside's most popular brewery, Higson's, the site is now owned by a Danish brewing group, who restored it to its original title of Robert Cain.

Camerons

The north-east's major brewer of real ales was bought by the Wolverhampton & Dudley Breweries in 1992 as part of their expansion programme. The Hartlepool brewery is best known for its ruby-red ale Strongarm, which once sustained the many steelworkers in the area.

Below: Draught Strongarm from Camerons brewery.

Castle Eden

Whitbread's specialist ale brewery in County Durham produces a wide range of limited-edition brews, often using imaginative flavourings and spices. Formerly Nimmo's Brewery, this County Durham plant also brews beers from breweries closed by Whitbread like Wethered's, Fremlin's and Higson's.

Courage

Originally Courage was a London brewer, founded in 1787. It developed into a national combine before being taken over by a series of multinational companies starting with Imperial Tobacco in 1972 and ending up with the Australian brewers, Foster's. Control of Courage was brought back to Britain in 1995 when Scottish and Newcastle Breweries bought the company from Foster's to form Britain's second largest brewing group, which is now known as Scottish Courage. Courage's traditional cask bitters are today brewed in Bristol.

Donnington

Described as the most picturesque brewery in Britain, time seems to have stood still since the Cotswold stone buildings were first built as a medieval cloth mill near Stow-on-the-Wold, Gloucestershire. Trout rise in the mill pond and ducks nest in the reeds. The brewery was added in 1865 by Richard Arkell. The plant is powered by a waterwheel.

Elgood

This classic Georgian riverside brewery in the Fens at Wisbech has been run by the Elgood family since 1878. It uses open trays for cooling the beers, and also has its own small pilot plant for brewing special beers.

Everard

A family brewery established in 1849 which originally brewed in both Leicester and Burton-on-Trent. Everard opened a new plant in Narborough in 1991 and since then has concentrated its brewing there.

Exmoor

A venture set up in the old Hancock's brewery in Wiveliscombe, Somerset, in 1980, which won the best bitter award at the Great British Beer Festival in its first year.

Federation

The only surviving clubs brewery in England was set up in 1919 in Newcastle by working men's clubs because of a postwar beer shortage. The co-operative opened a brewery at Dunston on the south side of the Tyne in 1980. It brews mainly bright, filtered beers for the clubs.

Flowers

The former Stratford-upon-Avon brewer was taken over and closed by Whitbread. The name is now used for the group's Cheltenham brewery.

Fuller's

This famous family brewer has been in Chiswick, London, since 1845. Fuller's had to boost its brewing capacity in the 1990s to keep up with demand for its traditional ales. The three main brews – Chiswick Bitter, London Pride and ESB – have won more awards at the Great British Beer Festival than the beers of any other brewer.

Gales

Hampshire family brewery at Horndean with an impressive tower brewery built in 1869.

Greene King

The East Anglian regional giant based at Bury St Edmunds, Suffolk, was founded in 1799. In 1995 it added a range of seasonal cask ales to its well-known IPA and Abbot Ale.

Hardys & Hansons

Two Nottinghamshire breweries started in the 19th century in Kimberley, that merged in 1930. The firm is still family controlled.

Harveys
Founded in 1790, this quality family brewer still brews at its attractive riverside site in Lewes, Sussex, despite a damaging fire in 1996.

Highgate
A West Midlands Victorian tower brewery in Walsall, famous for its Dark Mild. Since being bought out by the management from Bass in 1995, Highgate has added a Saddlers Best Bitter to its range of beers.

Holden
Black Country family brewery in Woodsetton in the West Midlands which goes back four generations.

Holt
This Manchester family brewery since 1849 is famous for the uncompromisingly dry bitterness of its bitter. Holt is also known for its low prices. One of the few breweries to still use hogsheads (huge 54-gallon casks) in its pubs.

Hook Norton
This dramatic Victorian tower brewery in a small Oxfordshire village near Banbury still retains much of its original equipment.

Hydes
A traditional family brewer in Manchester since 1863, turning out ales under the Anvil trademark. Unusually, Hydes still brews two milds, light and dark.

Ind Coope
This historic brewing group was originally based in Romford, Essex. It became part of Allied Breweries in 1961, and merged with Carlsberg in 1993 becoming

Above: A 1952 advertisement for Ind Coope's Arctic Ale, a famous rich, strong ale which is no longer brewed.

Carlsberg-Tetley. The proposed merger with near-neighbours Bass is currently awaiting approval from the Office of Fair Trading. It brews a range of specialist beers under the Allsopp name.

Jennings
The only surviving long-standing brewer in Cumbria, dating back to 1828.

J.W. Lees
A well-established north Manchester family brewery since 1828, still committed to delivering its beers in oak casks.

King & Barnes
A Sussex family firm in Horsham, dating back to 1800, which has extensively modernized its brewery.

McMullen
A Hertford family brewer since 1827, located in a fine Victorian brewhouse.

Mann's
This famous east London brewer's Albion brewery was taken over by Watneys in 1958 and closed in 1979. But the name lives on in England's best-known bottled, sweet brown ale, Mann's Original, which is now brewed by Usher's in Wiltshire.

Mansfield
A regional brewery in Nottinghamshire, founded in 1855, which has expanded considerably since opening its new brewhouse in 1984. It still uses traditional Yorkshire squares to ferment its ales.

Marston Thompson & Evershed
This is the last brewery in Britain that still uses the Burton Union system and the last major independent company brewing in Burton-on-Trent. Besides its famous Pedigree, it now brews a range of special cask beers under the Head Brewer's Choice label.

Mauldon
This Suffolk brewing family from Sudbury started brewing in 1795. The brewery closed in 1960 but restarted brewing in 1982.

Melbourn
This brewery in Stamford, Lincolnshire closed in 1974 and became a museum under Samuel Smith. Since 1993 Melbourn have brewed fruit ales in the old brewery, using wild yeasts from Belgium.

Mitchell's
Traditional family brewer in Lancaster since 1880.

Mitchells & Butlers
Often just known as M&B, Mitchells and Butlers are the dominant Birmingham brewers and merged with Bass in 1961. Their Cape Hill brewery in Smethwick, near Birmingham has been heavily modernized.

Morland

The second-oldest English brewery founded in 1711. The Abingdon firm sprang to fame outside Oxfordshire in the 1990s with the success of its strong pale ale, Old Speckled Hen.

Morrells

The only brewery left in the university town of Oxford which has been run by the Morrell family since 1782.

Oakhill

A historic stout brewery founded in 1767 at Oakhill, near Bath, which was badly damaged by fire in 1924, and then closed. In 1984 the brewery was restarted and moved to the Old Maltings, a larger site in 1993.

Palmer

England's only thatched brewery which was founded at Bridport, Dorset in 1794.

Ridleys

This family brewery was established in 1842 by Thomas Ridley at Hartford End, near Chelmsford, Essex.

Ringwood

Set up by Peter Austin in 1978 in the Hampshire town. In 1995 Ringwood moved beyond the micro-brewery stage with the opening of a 125-barrel modern brewhouse.

Robinson's

A major regional family firm from Stockport, near Manchester, founded in 1838.

Ruddles

One of the most famous names in English brewing, Ruddles lost its independence in 1986 when Watneys bought up the Rutland brewery in Langham. Since 1992, it has been owned by the Dutch brewers, Grolsch.

St Austell

Cornwall's only remaining long-established independent family brewery, founded in 1851. The solid Victorian brewery dominates the town.

Shepherd Neame

England's oldest brewery dates back to 1698. It is fittingly to be found in the hop garden of Kent, at Faversham. Shepherd Neame still uses steam engines and two teak mash tuns from 1910. It produces a range of cask and bottled beers.

Smith, John

A magnificent Victorian building in Tadcaster, North Yorkshire, built in 1884, houses the John Smith's brewery. The company is now owned by Scottish Courage. Today the towering stone buildings house a modern brewhouse.

Smith, Samuel

Samuel Smith was the first of the two Smith brewers of Tadcaster and the firm is still brewing in the Old Brewery which dates back to 1758. The family firm has remained fiercely independent. The beer is still fermented in Yorkshire stone squares and racked into wooden casks.

Stones

The Stones brewery has quenched the fire of the steel city of Sheffield in Yorkshire since 1865. It was taken over by Bass in 1968.

Taylor

One of the top quality brewers of England. Timothy Taylor began brewing in Brontë country at Keighley, Yorkshire, in 1858.

Tetley

England's leading brewer of bitter was founded in Leeds, Yorkshire, in 1822. A modern brewhouse was built in the 1980s and more Yorkshire squares for fermenting the beer were added in 1996. It became known as Carlsberg-Tetley in 1993 following the merger with Carlsberg.

Theakston

This North Yorkshire brewer has been at Masham since 1827. Theakston is famous for rich, dark Old Peculier. The family lost control in the late 1970s, and after a succession of takeovers the country brewery is now owned by Scottish Courage. Most Theakston beers are brewed at its Tyne brewery in Newcastle, as well as at the original Masham brewery.

Thomas Hardy

Formerly Eldridge Pope of Dorchester, this grand brewery, founded in 1837, was renamed after their most famous customer, the novelist Thomas Hardy.

Thwaites

A major Lancashire regional brewer founded in Blackburn in 1807 that still uses shire horses for local deliveries.

Tolly Cobbold

A Suffolk brewer since 1746 in a fine Victorian brewhouse in Ipswich which was closed in 1989 – but was then saved by a management buyout. The popular name comes from the merging of Cobbold with another well-known Ipswich brewery, Tollemache, in 1957. The grand Cobbold brewery in Ipswich was built on Cliff Quay on the banks of the River Orwell in 1894–6. It is a classic example of a tower brewery, and still retains many fine old brewing vessels. Following the management buyout in 1990, the brewery has become one of the main tourist attractions in the town, with guided tours. The offices alongside have been turned into the Brewery Tap pub.

Above: A game of cards is a traditional accompaniment to a pint.

Ushers

This Wiltshire brewery was founded in Trowbridge in 1824. After being taken over by Watneys of London in 1960 it lost its local identity. A management buyout in 1991 restored its independence.

Vaux

The giant northern brewery which is based in the town of Sunderland on the River Wear. Vaux also owns Ward's of Sheffield.

Wadworth

A traditional family brewery whose towering brewhouse has dominated the Wiltshire market town of Devizes since 1885. The brewery includes a rare open copper.

Ward's

A traditional Sheffield brewery which was founded in 1840, 15 years before the better-known Stones brewery in the steel city.

Watneys

This once-famous London brewery ruined its reputation by leading the movement to processed keg beers. It is now part of Scottish Courage. Its Mortlake brewery is used by Anheuser-Busch to brew Budweiser. Most remaining Watneys beers are brewed abroad for foreign markets.

Wells

Enterprising Bedford family brewers since 1876 who rebuilt their brewery in 1976. Wells brews various foreign lagers under licence, including Kirin from Japan and Red Stripe from Jamaica.

Whitbread

This famous London brewer since 1742 closed his brewery in the capital city in 1976. Originally Whitbread was known for its porter. It is England's third largest brewing group, brewing foreign lagers under licence, notably a weak version of Heineken and Stella Artois. It also produces a wide range of cask beers under local names such as Wethered, Fremlins and Higsons, now produced at Flowers brewery in Cheltenham, Gloucestershire, and at Castle Eden, County Durham. Whitbread also owns Boddingtons in Manchester.

Wolverhampton & Dudley

Wolverhampton is the home of this brewery, famed for its reddish-amber Banks's mild, a favourite in the industrial West Midlands. It trades as Banks's and Hanson's in the Black Country. It is the largest regional brewing group in Britain, with around 1,100 pubs and in 1992 bought Camerons brewery in the north-east.

Wood

A small brewery behind the Plough Inn in Wistanstow, Shropshire.

Woodforde's

Quality Norfolk brewery since 1980 which has the rare distinction of having twice won the Champion Beer of Britain title.

Worthington

This famous Burton brewing name merged with Bass in 1927. The brewery has since been demolished, but the name lives on in a national bitter brand and more notably in the bottle-conditioned pale ale Worthington White Shield, now brewed at Mitchells & Butlers brewery in Birmingham.

Young's

A firmly traditional London family brewery situated at the Ram brewery in Wandsworth since 1831. Young's is noted for cask beers. Deliveries are still made by horse-drawn drays, a wonderful sight in south London, although these are now under threat from the increased traffic in the area. The Victorian brewery also houses geese, peacocks and a ram (the company mascot). In recent years Young's has added seasonal ales including a summer wheat beer. Its bottled ales are also sold abroad.

Below: Cheers!

SCOTLAND

Once Scotland was famous for its beer, and during the 19th century the capital Edinburgh ranked alongside Burton-on-Trent in England, Munich in Germany and Plzen in the Czech Republic as a notable brewing centre.

A T THE START OF THE 20TH CENTURY Edinburgh boasted 28 breweries, most packed into an area with an excellent water supply known as the "Charmed Circle". Alloa, just across the River Forth, was also a famous beer town.

In 1960, Edinburgh still had 18 breweries and Scottish brewers were vigorous exporters, but as the overseas trade dried up many companies fell into financial difficulties and were taken over and closed down like Robert Younger. Two giants – Scottish & Newcastle and Tennent's – came to dominate the market. This hastened the disappearance of traditional cask beer. Eventually only two breweries were left in Edinburgh. Overall, just three independent breweries survived in the whole of Scotland. A once-thriving industry had almost vanished. Since 1980 there has been a small revival, with the appearance of a number of new breweries bringing back welcome variety to the bar. Scottish beers are darker, more full-bodied, and sweeter than English ales. Perhaps because hops are not grown in the country, there is less emphasis on bitterness. Perhaps the malty warmth helps to keep out the northern cold. Local specialities include strong barley wines known as "wee heavys", as well as "oatmeal stout", made using a local cereal. The English terms of mild and bitter are not generally used north of the border. Instead, beers are traditionally rated in strength according to the invoice price charged per barrel in the 19th century. Under the "shilling system" the weakest beer is 60/-, an average-strength beer 70/-, and a premium brew 80/-. Strong ales are 90/-. These designations usually refer to cask beers. Keg beers are more popularly known as light (this refers to the light alcoholic content, not the colour, which may well be dark); special or heavy indicate mid-strength brews; and export is the name given to premium ales. Scotland also has its own individual dispensing system, which uses tall air-pressure fonts, rather than handpumps, to serve traditional ales.

Above: Traditional ales are still brewed in Scotland, despite its radically reduced brewing industry and the increasing popularity of lager.

THE BEERS

Ale of Atholl
A rich, malty beer (4.5%) from the Moulin brewery, near Pitlochry.

Arrol's 80/-
A fruity, cask-conditioned Scottish heavy (4.4%) with a hoppy aftertaste, brewed by the Alloa brewery.

Auld Alliance
Tart, hoppy refreshing bitter (4%) from the Fife brewery, Kirkaldy.

Bear Ale
This cask ale (5%) is fermented in oak vessels at the historic Traquair House manor brewery.

Black Douglas
This distinctive, dark, winter ale (5.2%) comes from the Broughton brewery.

Borve Extra Strong
A powerful, extra-strong ale (10%), which is matured in oak whisky casks at the Borve home-brew pub.

Broadsword
This golden cask ale (3.8%) with a fruity, malty flavour and bitter finish is brewed at Alloa by Maclay.

Buchan Bronco
This cask beer (4.6%) is produced by the Aberdeenshire brewery in Keith, fermented using Yorkshire squares. The brewery also produces the lighter Buchan Gold (4%).

Calder's
This is the brand name for keg beers made by the Alloa brewery, including Cream Ale (4.5%) and 80/-.

Caledonian
A range of beers from the Caledonian brewery. The weakest is a flavoursome, dark, malty 60/- beer (3.2%) with a refreshing hint of roast barley. Caledonian 70/- (3.5%) is a more tawny coloured, creamy brew and Caledonian 80/- (4.1%) has a complex malt and hops flavour.

Cuillin
Red Cuillin (4.2%) and Black Cuillin (4.5%) are two cask beers produced by the Isle of Skye brewery at Uig on Skye.

Dark Island
A rich, wine-coloured, refreshing beer (4.6%) with a fruity aroma, from the Orkney brewery.

Deuchars IPA
This very pale "pale ale" (4.4%) is late-hopped to produce a refreshing brew. Brewed by Caledonian.

Douglas
See Gordon's.

Dragonhead Stout
This smooth, classic stout (4%) is produced by the Orkney brewery.

Edinburgh Strong Ale
A strong, premium ale (6.4%) with a complexity of malt and hop flavours, but without the usual sweetness of strong beers. It is brewed by Caledonian.

Fraoch
Bruce Williams has been brewing Fraoch (the Gaelic word for heather) at Maclay's Alloa brewery every flowering season since 1993. Instead of adding hops – which are not grown in Scotland – to the boiling wort, he follows the example of the ancient Picts and uses native heather tips and

myrtle leaves. The hot liquid is also infused in a vat of fresh heather flowers before fermentation. The spicy, floral brew that results comes in two strengths – Heather Ale (4.1%) and Pictish Ale (5.4%).

Gillespie's
First introduced in 1993, Gillespie's keg and canned creamy, sweet-malt stout (4%) is named after a closed Dumbarton brewery. It is produced by Scottish Courage in Edinburgh.

Golden Pale
A pale-amber-coloured, aromatically hoppy, organic beer (4%), from the Caledonian brewery.

Golden Promise
The first organic beer from Caledonian, Golden Promise is slightly stronger (5%) than Golden Pale. A quality brew, it is named after Scotland's traditional variety of barley.

Gordon's
This warming range of bottled, strong ales is brewed in Edinburgh by Scottish Courage, mainly for the Belgian market. It includes Gordon's Scotch Ale (8.6%), Christmas Ale (8.8%) and Gold Blond (10%). It is sold in France under the Douglas name.

Greenmantle

This distinctive, smoky, fruity ale (3.9%) is available in bottles and cask. It is produced by the Broughton brewery.

Grozet

First produced in 1996 by Bruce Williams at the Maclay brewery in Alloa, this hazy beer (5%) is a wheat ale to which whole gooseberries are added after fermentation.

Highland Hammer

This powerful, full-flavoured strong ale (7.3%) is a seasonal speciality of the Tomintoul brewery.

Jacobite Ale

This strong brew (8%) is fermented in oak and flavoured with coriander. It comes from the Traquair House brewery.

Kane's Amber Ale

This amber cask beer (4%) with a good malt and fruit flavour is produced in the brewing town of Alloa by the Maclay brewery.

Laird's Ale

The weakest cask ale (3.8%) from Tomintoul is a traditional, dark-mahogany 70/- ale, with a malty flavour and fine hop balance.

McEwan's Export

A sweet and malty Scottish ale (4.5%) produced by McEwan's in Edinburgh.

MacAndrew's

A strong, amber-coloured ale (6.5%) brewed for sale in the US by Caledonian.

Maclay

Maclay brewery's cask beers include a full-flavoured, malty, fruity 70/- ale (3.6%) with a sweet, fresh flavour. The flagship 80/- Export (4%) is a creamy, malty beer with a dry finish. There is also an oat malt stout (4.5%).

Malcolm's

A range of beers, named after King Malcolm III who slew Macbeth, including Malcolm's Ceilidh (3.7%), Folly (4%), and Premier (4.3%), from the Backdykes farm brewery in Fife.

Merlin's

This distinctive, hoppy, golden ale (4.2%) is one of a range of beers produced at the Broughton brewery.

Merman

A mellow, reddish-bronze, malty, fruity, bottled pale ale (4.8%) from Caledonian, based on an 1890 recipe.

Montrose

A tasty, tawny cask beer (4.2%) from the Harviestoun brewery.

Murray's Heavy

An amber-coloured, traditional Scottish heavy beer (4.3%), produced by Caledonian.

Old Jock

A distinctive dark-ruby, sweetish, fruity, bottled strong ale (6.7%). It is produced by the Broughton brewery in the borders.

Old Manor

This old ale (8%) is brewed each winter by the Harviestoun brewery. Molasses gives the beer a good ruby colour and a rich fruitiness. This is one of a range of seasonal brews.

Ptarmigan

An outstanding pale-golden, fruity, premium beer (4.5%) from the Harviestoun brewery. It has a light, refreshing flavour and is brewed using Saaz hops.

Raven Ale

An amber-red, nutty, dry ale (3.8%) from the Orkney brewery.

Red MacGregor

A full-bodied, smooth, red-brown beer(4.1%)from the Orkney brewery,

St Andrew's

A rich, brown, malty cask beer (4.9%) with a fruity butterscotch flavour, brewed by Belhaven.

Sandy Hunter's

A bitter-sweet, roasted-malt, hoppy cask beer (3.6%) from the Belhaven brewery. It was named after a former head brewer.

Schiehallion Lager

A cask-conditioned, Bohemian-style lager (4.8%), brewed using German Hersbrucker hops, from the Harviestoun brewery. It won a Gold Medal at the Great British Beer Festival in 1996. Schiehallion, a local mountain, was once climbed as part of an experiment by Astronomer Royal Neville Maskelyn.

THE OUTWARD-LOOKING SCOTS

Scottish brewers have always been enthusiastic exporters of their wares, partly because of the relatively small size of the home market. The strong, rich, dark brews have been widely drunk throughout Britain for centuries, and in the heyday of the British Empire they also reached the former colonies scattered across the world, from the US to Australia and India. The ales were dispatched overseas in great quantities to quench the thirsts of Scots who had emigrated. The "export" brews became well known and well regarded. They were so popular in parts of Europe that Belgian brewers began to produce their own "Scotch" ales – a style that persists today.

Left: At the beginning of the 20th century, many brewers produced beers for the export market but declining sales spelled the end for most of them.

Skull Splitter
An powerful, strong, dark-amber barley wine (8.5%), from the Orkney brewery.

Stag
A dark, malty ale (4.1%) from the Tomintoul brewery in the Highlands which is sold in cask and bottle.

Stillman's 80/-
This mid-gold, mild beer (4.2%) with a complex flavour is produced by the Tomintoul brewery. Its name reflects the local whisky distilling industry in the Spey valley.

Sweetheart Stout
This very weak (2%), sweet and fruity brew is produced by Tennent's, but bears little resemblance to a real stout.

Tennent's Lager
This fizzy, golden keg lager (4%) is the mainstay of the Tennent's brewery's lager range, which includes a grainy, pale-gold Pilsner (3.4%), a stronger Extra (4.8%), Gold (5%) and a weighty, amber-coloured, sweetish, strong Super (9%). Tennent's are Scotland's dominant lager brewers.

The Ghillie
This distinctive bottled ale (4.5%) is produced by the Broughton brewery.

Traquair House Ale
A dark, strong classic oak-fermented ale (7.2%) from the Traquair House brewery. It has a fruity, malt flavour and a slight dryness. This distinctive ale is exported to the US.

Triple Diamond
This is the special, extra-strong, export ale brand (8.5%) produced by the Alloa brewery.

Wallace IPA
A hoppy, fruity pale ale (4.5%) with a bitter finish, produced by Maclay.

Waverley 70/-
A chestnut-coloured, hoppy, cask beer (3.7%), from the Harviestoun brewery.

Wild Cat
A deep-amber ale (5.1%) with a complex flavour from the Tomintoul brewery.

Young Pretender
A golden, dry ale (4%) from the Isle of Skye brewery named after Bonnie Prince Charlie. It was first produced in 1995 to mark the 250th anniversary of the Jacobite rebellion.

Younger's Tartan
A dark-amber Scottish keg ale (3.7%) with a sweet and fruity flavour from William Younger of Edinburgh.

THE BREWERS

Alloa

Founded in 1810, the Alloa brewery became known in the 1930s for its lager, Graham's, then Skol (3.6%) after becoming part of Allied Breweries. It also produces keg ales under the Calder's name and special export brands such as Triple Diamond. Since 1982 it has brewed cask beer, notably Arrols 80/-.

Belhaven

Scotland's oldest brewery, Belhaven dates back to at least 1719. Built on former monastery land on the coast at Dunbar, its ales were sold way beyond Scotland and found their way to the Imperial Court of Austria, where the Emperor declared them "The Burgundy of Scotland". This claim is still carried by its robust 80/- ale (4.2%). Other malty cask beers include 60/- (2.9%), 70/- (3.5%), St Andrew's and Sandy Hunter's besides a rich, warming 90/- (8%).

Above: The Caledonian brewery in Edinburgh was restored after a fire in 1994. It produces a wide range of cask and bottled beers. Caledonian 80/- was the Champion Beer of Scotland in 1996.

Borve

Originally set up on the Isle of Lewis in 1983, this home-brew pub is now on the mainland at Ruthven.

Broughton

David Younger, a descendant of the George Younger brewing family of Alloa, set up the brewery in 1980 in the Borders region at Broughton. In 1995 it relaunched its distinctive cask and bottled ales as "Beers with Character".

Caledonian

Caledonian is the sole survivor from an era when Edinburgh boasted 30 independent breweries. The Victorian brewhouse still uses direct-fired open coppers, one dating back to 1869 when the firm was founded as Lorimer and Clark. Its wide range of quality cask and bottled beers includes 60/- (3.2%), 70/- (3.5%), 80/- (4.1%), Deuchars IPA, Murray's Heavy, Double Amber, Merman, Edinburgh Strong Ale (6.4%) and two organic beers. The Caledonian 80/- was the first champion Beer of Scotland in 1996.

Harviestoun

A village brewery in an old stone dairy at Dollar, near Stirling, since 1985, Harviestoun produces a prize-winning range of cask beers including Waverley 70/-, Original 80/- (4.1%), Montrose, Ptarmigan and Old Manor.

McEwan's

A famous firm since 1856 which merged with Younger's in 1931 and is now part of Scottish Courage. McEwan's still brews at its Fountain brewery in Edinburgh which has recently been completely rebuilt. Though McEwan's is best known for its keg and canned beers (McEwan's Export is the best-selling canned beer in Britain), it also produces some cask-conditioned beers in the old classic Scottish shilling ratings – 70/- and 80/-.

ALLOA

The town of Alloa at the head of the Firth of Forth has long been a brewing centre, using water from the Ochil hills, local barley and coal from nearby mines. Early in the 20th century it boasted nine breweries, the most famous being George Younger's which closed in 1963. By 1996 only two were left, Alloa (now part of Bass) and the independent Maclays.

Maclay's

The last independent family-owned brewery left in Alloa was founded in 1830. The traditional tower brewhouse was built in 1869. Maclay's still uses bore-hole water drawn from 300ft (100m) below ground for its brewing. Cask beers include 70/- (3.6%), the flagship 80/-Export (4%), Maclay's Oat Malt Stout (4.5%), Wallace IPA and also a strong, golden Scotch Ale (5%).

Orkney

Britain's most northerly brewery is located on the Orkney's main island off the north coast of Scotland. It was set up at Quoyloo in 1988 by Roger White. Its cask and bottled beers are Raven Ale, Dragonhead Stout, Red MacGregor, Dark Island and the powerful Skull Splitter.

Scottish Courage

This is Britain's second-largest brewing group. It is based in Edinburgh and was formed in 1995 when Scottish & Newcastle Breweries bought the Courage brewing group of England. It has only one brewery in Scotland, located in Edinburgh. Its beers are still marketed under the McEwan's and William Younger names.

Tennent's

Founded in Glasgow around 1776, the Wellpark Brewery became famous as Scotland's first lager brewers in 1885. Today, the brewery produces a range of lagers for the British and overseas markets. It also brews keg ales and bottled stout.

Tomintoul

This brewery in the heart of the Highlands malt whisky country, just a couple of miles from the Glenlivet distillery, claims to be the highest brewery in Britain. It was set up in 1993 in an old watermill by Andrew Neame, a member of the brewing family in Kent, England. Its cask beers include Laird's Ale (3.8%), Stag (4.1%), Stillman's 80/- (4.2%), Wild Cat (5.1%) and Highland Hammer (7.3%).

Traquair House

A rare survivor from an age when all great manor houses had their own breweries. Traquair House at Innerleithen, near Peebles, dates from the 12th century and is said to be the oldest

Scotland boasts a handful of home-brew houses, most established in the mid-1990s:

- Aldchlappie Hotel, Kirkmichael, Perthshire.
- Harbour Bar, Kirkcaldy, Fife.
- Lugton Inn, Lugton, Ayrshire.
- Mansfield Arms, Sauchie, Alloa.
- Moulin Hotel, Moulin, Pitlochry.
- Rose Street, Edinburgh.

Above: Stirring the brew in modern shiny coppers.

inhabited building in Scotland. Its beer was first recorded in an account of a visit to the house by Mary Queen of Scots in 1566. The present brewery, dating back to the 1730s, was revived in 1965 by the Laird, Peter Maxwell Stuart. A second brewhouse has since been added to keep up with demand. All the beer is fermented in oak vessels.

Younger's

William Younger founded his brewery in 1749. It is now part of Scottish Courage. The Holyrood brewery closed in 1986, and production moved to McEwan's Fountain brewery. Younger's is best known for its Tartan ale. Its cask ales, Younger's Scotch and Younger's IPA, are the same as McEwan's. Younger's No. 3 is McEwan's 80/- with added caramel.

DENMARK

*Perhaps because it is further south and much more firmly attached to mainland
Europe than its northern neighbours in Scandinavia, Denmark has always
enjoyed a relatively relaxed attitude to beer and to its brewing industry.*

WHEN DRINKERS THINK of Denmark, one name stands a thick foaming head
above all others – the famous Carlsberg. Besides having
a worldwide reputation, the Carlsberg group controls the
domestic market. It absorbed its main rival Tuborg in
1970, and it also holds stakes in the other leading
brewing groups. This domination by one brewery has
restricted choice. Drinkers in Copenhagen have to
look hard in their bars to find anything apart from
Carlsberg and Tuborg.
The variety of beer
styles is also on a tight
rein with Pilsners reigning supreme.

Denmark has played a major role in spreading
the popularity of bottom-fermenting lagers and a
malty, mild style of Pilsner is by far the most
widely available beer today. Before this most
brewers once produced top-fermenting wheat
beers. Carlsberg, more than any other brewery, has
popularized the golden lager style, devised in
central Europe, around the world. In 1993 its
worldwide sales were more than five times larger
than its home sales. So profound has this
company's contribution been to the development of
lager, that the classic bottom-fermenting yeast used
by brewers, *Saccharomyces Carlsbergensis*, has
been named after the Copenhagen brewery.

As well as golden lagers, however, there are some
seasonal brews and darker beers to be found in Denmark. You may even come
across the occasional porter – a reminder of the days when English ale was sold in
the Baltic. There is also a tradition of brewing an extremely weak, dark, top-
fermented table beer called hvidtol, which is so low in alcohol that it escapes the
tax levied on other beers. Despite the lack of variety and relatively high taxes on
alcohol, the Danes certainly enjoy their beer – drinking more per head of
population than any other nation, apart from the Czech Republic and Germany.

*Above: There are occasional
unusual brews to be found in
Denmark, such as this red beer
from Ceres. However it is
Carlsberg's world-famous golden
lager, that is associated with
Danish beer, and lagers that
dominate brewing and drinking.*

THE BEERS

Albani Porter

A strong, smooth all-malt porter (7.8%) from the Albani brewery in Odense.

Bering

Bering is an unusual cross between a strong spicy stout and a lager blended with lemon and rum (6.3%), brewed by Ceres.

Bjørne Bryg

A bright-gold, strong lager (8.3%) with a bitter hops after-taste from Harboe. The name means "Bear Beer".

Buur

A deep-gold, strong, sweet, hoppy, Dortmunder-style beer (7.6%) from Thor, part of the Ceres brewing group.

Carlsberg Let

A light, golden, weak table-beer (2.7%) with a malty and bitter hoppy taste, from Carlsberg.

Carlsberg Master Brew

A highly alcoholic, strong, beer (10.5%) created for the firm's 150th anniversary.

Carlsberg Pilsner

Also known as Carlsberg Lager Beer (or sometimes as Hof after the royal court), this lager (4.6%) with the green label has a clean, soft flavour.

Ceres Royal Export

This strong golden lager (5.8%) produced by Ceres, has a ripe, malty flavour with a hoppy finish.

Dansk Dortmunder

A strong, malty, golden lager (7.7%) brewed by Ceres that is widely exported under the name Ceres Strong Ale.

Dansk LA

This low-alcohol beer is probably the best-known beer made by Wiibroe, a Carlsberg subsidiary at Elsinore, founded in 1840, which mainly produces lower-priced products.

Elephant

A rich golden lager (7.5%) in the German bock style, from Carlsberg. It is named after the brewery's elephant gates.

Faxe Premium

A malty lager with a soft, malt finish (5%) from the Faxe brewery.

Gamle Special Dark

This dark lager (4.2%) from Carlsberg recalls the brewery's original malty, Munich-style lager.

Gammel Porter or Imperial Stout

This strong, Baltic-style stout from Carlsberg (7.5%) is bottom-fermenting, and has a rich, roasted flavour. "Gammel" means old.

Giraf

A pale, strong lager (6.8%) with a long-neck label, produced by Albani of Odense. It was first brewed to help sponsor the purchase of giraffes for the local zoo.

Grøn

Tuborg's main brand is known as Grøn after the green colour of the label, with a premium Guld (gold) and a dark lager Rod (red).

Hof

See Carlsberg Pilsner.

The dominant bottle

One peculiarity of the beer market in Denmark is that the vast bulk is sold in returnable bottles and relatively little is available on draught. The litter-conscious Danes are vehemently opposed to the can, and they have banned its use for the sale of drinks on environmental grounds. This has brought the country into conflict with the European Union's free-market directives.

Kongens Bryg

This low-alcohol golden lager (1.7%) is produced by Tuborg.

Red Erik

This lager from Ceres is named in honour of the Viking who discovered Greenland and began brewing there.

Silver Pilsner

This tasty Pilsner is the selling beer from the Harboe brewery.

Sort Guld

Sort Guld or "Black Gold" is a malty, dark beer (5.8%) produced by Carlsberg.

The Brewers

Albani

One of the larger independent breweries in Denmark was founded in Odense in 1859. It is best known for its tall-necked pale, strong lager Giraf, and it also brews a porter, Albani Porter (7.8%), an Easter brew, Albani Påske Bryg, Albani Christmas Jule, as well as a range of Pilsners.

Apollo

A home-brew pub in Copenhagen near the famous Tivoli Gardens. This establishment first appeared in 1990 at the Hereford Beefstouw restaurant in co-operation with the Wiibroe brewery of Elsinore. It produces a range of unfiltered lagers.

Carlsberg

See panel opposite.

Ceres

After a merger with the Thor and Faxe breweries, Ceres of Aarhus in Jutland is now part of the second-largest brewing group in Denmark. The brewery was founded in 1856, and is named after the goddess of grain. Besides a range of Pilsners, it brews a strong, dark Ceres Stowt (stout, 7.7%) and a range of stronger golden lagers that are widely exported.

Faxe

This brewery at Fakse gained cult status in the 1970s with its Faxe Fad beer. "Fad" means draught, and the bottled brew was unpasteurized. The brewery has linked up with Ceres to form Brewery Group Denmark, the second largest combine in the country.

Harboe

The independent family-owned brewery was founded in Skaelskor on Zealand in 1883. It initially brewed the non-alcoholic hvidtol before starting to brew lager in 1890. Its modern brewery, built in 1960, is best known abroad for its powerful Bjørne Bryg ("Bear Beer") but its best-selling brew is its Silver Pilsner. It also brews a premium Harboe Guld (5.9%) and a range of seasonal beers. Harboe is the sole Danish producer of malt extract and still produces low-alcohol malt brews.

Danish dynasty

Some have said that the Carlsberg story is like a dynastic blockbuster. Danish television agreed and in 1996 made its most expensive production, a 12-part series based on the remarkable life of J. C. Jacobsen. It is simply called *The Brewer*.

Tuborg

Although Tuborg is less well known on the international market than its sister brewery Carlsberg, this Copenhagen brewery outsells Carlsberg in the home market and in the other Nordic countries. Tuborg was founded in Tuborg, to the north of Copenhagen, in 1873 by a group of bankers.

At first it sold the same dark Munich-style lagers that had been introduced by Carlsberg, but in 1880 the Tuborg brewer Hans Bekkevold launched Denmark's first Pilsner. The Tuborg brewery was also one of the first in Denmark to bottle its beers and the green-labelled Pilsner proved a major success with consumers – so much of a success in fact that in 1903, a new seven-storey brewhouse was built to keep up with demand. A clock looked down on the new shiny coppers, with the financiers' favourite words below the dial, warning slack workers, "Time is Money".

One of the odder features of the Tuborg brewery in Copenhagen which, like Carlsberg, has a large visitor centre, is a massive 26-metre (85-foot)-high beer bottle. This city landmark was originally built for the Great Nordic Industrial Fair in Tivoli Park in 1888, and was fitted with Denmark's first ever hydraulic lift. At its centenary in 1988, the towering bottle was shipped back to the town centre to stand alongside the city hall.

Throughout the 20th century Tuborg and Carlsberg co-operated closely, and finally in 1970 the two major brewers merged, and the combined company now accounts for about 80% of domestic beer sales. Each still retains its own independent management and takes control of its own marketing. Tuborg has also maintained production at its own brewery in Copenhagen. The company has made its mark on the international scene, being sold and brewed in more than 130 countries.

The Tuborg range of beers is similar to Carlsberg's, although its Pilsners tend to be a little lighter and hoppier. The main Tuborg brand is known as Grøn after the green colour of the label. There is also a premium Guld and a dark lager, Rod. Like Carlsberg, Tuborg also produces some seasonal brews and a dark, rich, creamy porter.

THE CARLSBERG STORY

Since 1901, four stone elephants have stood guard at the gates of the Carlsberg brewery in Copenhagen. They symbolize the enduring power of one of the most famous names in brewing and signify that this is no ordinary company. The story of Carlsberg is an epic tale.

The Carlsberg brewery was founded in 1847 by Jacob Christian Jacobsen on a hill at Valby just outside Copenhagen. He named it after his five-year-old son Carl and the Danish word for a hill – "berg". At the time, many small Danish breweries (including one run by his father) were producing top-fermented wheat beers, but Jacobsen was determined to brew on a grand scale – and to brew the new bottom-fermented lagers, which were then being pioneered in Bavaria.

Jacobsen travelled to Munich to study under the famous Gabriel Sedlmayr of the Spaten brewery and, according to legend, returned from one trip in 1845 with 2 litres (3½ pints) of the vital bottom-fermenting yeast, which he kept cool throughout the long stagecoach journey by frequently dousing it with cold water and covering the

containers with his stovepipe hat. After successful experiments to produce the dark, Munich-style lager, using the cellars under the city ramparts while his new brewery was being built, he began to brew the first batch at his plant at Valby on November 10 1847.

Jacobsen became one of the leaders of the new science of brewing and built a famous set of laboratories. It was here in 1883 that Emil Hansen isolated the first single-cell yeast culture *Saccharomyces Carlsbergensis*. This major development allowed brewers to control the quality of their beers by eliminating bad yeast strains. Jacobsen also established the Carlsberg Foundation in 1876, to promote scientific research. After his death in 1887, this foundation became the owner of the brewery. Jacobsen's son Carl, often in dispute with his father, set up his own brewery on an adjoining site to brew Pilsners. His interest lay in

the arts, and in 1901 he designed a new brewhouse on an elaborate scale, complete with Florentine flourishes and elephant gates. The Carlsberg Foundation took over this cathedral of beer in 1902. Today the company is uniquely run as a charity for the benefit of the sciences and, following Carl's intervention, for the arts. Its huge trust fund donates vast amounts of money. Carl Jacobsen helped develop Copenhagen as a city of soaring spires. In 1913, he donated the Little Mermaid statue, which has become the symbol of the city. Carlsberg first became known outside Denmark when its beer was shipped to Scotland in 1868. The other Scandinavian countries

and the West Indies soon followed. Carlsberg is a particularly big brand in the Far East. The first brewery outside Denmark was built in Malawi in Africa in 1968. In 1970, Carlsberg merged with Tuborg to form United Breweries, which in 1987 became Carlsberg.

Today, Carlsberg has about 100 subsidiary and associated companies, mostly abroad. More than 80% of its sales are outside Denmark. Its beer is sold in 150 countries and brewed in 40. In Denmark, where it serves four out of every five glasses of beer, it also owns Wiibroe of Elsinore, and in 1979 opened a new brewery at Fredericia to serve western Denmark.

Above: The imposing Carlsberg brewery in Copenhagen

NORWAY

The frozen lands of northern Europe might conjure up images of hard-drinking, ale-quaffing Vikings, but the truth is that few regions have done more to try to curb alcoholic drinks.

FEW COUNTRIES SQUEEZE THEIR DRINK into a tighter strait-jacket. Norway levies the highest and most punitive rate of duty on beer in the world. One result of this is that home-brewing is a potent tradition in Norway, with some rural recipes still incorporating home-grown juniper berries. The styles and strengths of commercial beers are strictly regulated by the State. The positive side of this strict regulation has meant the introduction of a beer purity law along German lines, which gives the all-malt Norwegian beers a smooth, clean taste.

Since 1995 there have been seven tax bands in operation, known by letters of the alphabet. The biggest leap is between the third level (for beers with an alcohol content of 2.75–3.75%) to the fourth level, (3.75–4.75%). Despite this price hike, the fourth level, (band D), is by far the most popular, accounting for more than three-quarters of all sales. Virtually all of this is Pilsner-style beer. A dark variety of Pilsner is also brewed, called baierol or bayer. The three stronger bands, up to a maximum 7%, include export-style lagers or gullol (gold beer) and some darker, seasonal brews, such as bokkol or juleol, at Christmas. Lower-alcohol beers are called brigg or lettol. All are bottom-fermented. There are few nationally sold brands. Instead, regional beers tend to dominate in their local areas. Dahls Pils rules Trondelag for instance; Tou Pils is pre-eminent in Stavanger; and Arendal Pils reigns supreme in the Sorlandet region. In the mid-1980s there were around 15 independent breweries. Since then the largest company, Ringnes, has been taking over its rivals and now controls all the dominant brands mentioned. This concentration in the industry has inevitably led to the closure of some plants.

Above: Norway taxes its beer heavily, and the variety of brews available is limited. The most popular beers tend to be light lagers, and the main brewery is Ringnes, founded in 1877.

THE BEERS

Aass Bock

A creamy, copper-coloured, malty bock beer (6.1%), from the Aass brewery.

Aass Classic Special Brygg

An aromatic, dark-gold lager (4.5%) with a crisp, clean hop taste from the Aass brewery in Drammen.

Akershus Irish Stout

This uncompromisingly black stout (4.6%) from Akershus has a smooth, rich chocolatey flavour.

Akershus Pale Ale

A copper-coloured, hoppy pale ale (4.6%) from the Akershus brewery.

Akershus Weissbier

This filtered, German-style wheat beer (4.6%) is brewed using wheat and barley by the Akershus brewery.

Arctic Pils

This golden, hoppy Pilsner (4.5%) is brewed by Mack.

Christmas Juleol

A seasonal celebration brew from Aass, Drammen. It has a deep-caramel colour and a toasted-malt flavour.

Frydenlund Pilsener

A well-hopped, traditional Pilsner now brewed by Ringnes following the closure of the Frydenlund brewery in Oslo in 1995.

Hansa Bayer

A tasty, dark, Bavarian-style brew (4.5%) from Hansa.

Hansa Eksportol

A tawny-gold lager (4.5%) with a salty, malt flavour. It is brewed for export.

Hansa Premium

A light-tasting wheat beer (4.5%), brewed by Hansa in Bergen, which is very popular in western Norway.

Lauritz

This Dortmunder-style beer is named after the founder of the Aass brewery Lauritz Aass.

Ludwig Pils

A golden, hoppy Pilsner from the Hansa brewery.

Lysholmer

Ringnes-owned Dahl's brewery in Trondheim produces this range of nationally popular brews which includes the golden special and an ice beer.

Mack Bayer

A Bavarian-style, dark chocolatey brew from the Mack brewery.

Mack Polar Bear

A hazy, amber lager with a malty taste, from Mack.

Pilsener Mack-Ol

This malty, golden Pilsner from the Mack brewery in the far north of the country is reputedly the best brew with which to wash down a local delicacy – seagulls' eggs.

Ringnes Pils

A golden Pilsner-style lager with a fresh, mild hop and malt flavour. This is the flagship brand for Ringnes.

THE BREWERS

Aass

Norway's oldest brewery was founded in Drammen in 1834. A medium-size independent company, it generates tremendous loyalty among local drinkers with its own beer club boasting more than 8,000 members. It also offers one of the widest range of beers, with more than ten different brews.

Akershus

This firm was founded in the Oslo suburb of Enebakk in 1992. It brews a variety of top-fermenting styles.

Hansa

The large Bergen brewery was founded in 1891 and is best-known for its Ludwig Pils, but it brews a large range of beers. It also runs a traditional farmhouse brewery for tourists and makes a juniper beer. The firm regained its independence in 1996, following the merger of Ringnes and Pripps.

Mack

The world's most northerly brewery at Tromsø, inside the Arctic Circle, was founded in 1877. As well as its flagship Pils, Mack also brews hoppier Mack Norges and Arctic Pils, besides other beers which have a more Bavarian accent.

Mikro

Norway's first home-brew pub, the aptly named Mikro Bryggeri, in Oslo, has brewed top-fermented English-style draught bitters and stout since 1990.

Ringnes

Norway's major brewery, founded in Oslo in 1877, also owns many other brands and breweries. Its main national beers are Ringnes Pils and Lysholmer Ice from Dahl's brewery in Trondheim. In 1995 it merged with Pripps of Sweden to form Pripps Ringnes.

SWEDEN

Brewers in Sweden have long struggled to keep their heads above water due to the strict laws that govern alcohol consumption. However, in recent years the rules have been relaxed and there has been a revival of small-scale brewing.

Above: Swedish brewers have long struggled against a strong temperance movement. Spendrup's is one of the few hardy survivors.

LIKE ITS NEIGHBOURS, Sweden has had to contend with a powerful temperance movement. Both politicians and church leaders regularly hold up alcohol as the source of the nation's moral ills. The production and sale of beer is tightly controlled, including strict demarcation according to strength. Beers are sold in three different strengths (Class I to 1.8%; Class II to 3.5%; Class III to 5.6%) – often with the same label. Only Class I and Class II beers can be sold in bars or food stores. Laws were introduced that severely restricted the sale of stronger, Class III beers. Under the legislation, stronger beers could only be bought in restaurants or from State shops (which are closed in the evenings and at weekends) and large taxes were levied on their consumption.

In 1960 there were 85 breweries in the country, but this strait-jacket on sales proved to be the final straw for many struggling companies, who went out of business in the years that followed. Many of the other brewers switched to producing medium-strength beers. At one stage, the State owned some breweries, including the leading brewer Pripps.

However, since Sweden's entry into the European Union in 1995, some of the State monopolies and restrictions have had to be relaxed, to conform with rules on free trade within the union. A ban on beer stronger than 5.6% was dropped, and the country is now adopting a uniform rate of duty on alcohol instead of the three-class system, which heavily favoured the brewing and sale of weaker brews. A licence has been granted for a brewpub in Stockholm, and a growing number of new, small, local breweries has begun to spring up, mainly devoted to brewing the stronger Class III beers.

THE BEERS

Dart
This English-style copper-coloured, hoppy bitter is brewed by Pripps.

Falcon Export
This gold Pilsner has a bitter, hop taste and a light-malt finish. It is produced by Falcon, Falkenberg.

Gorilla
This new extra-strong beer (7.6%) is one of the potent brews that have arrived on the Swedish market since the relaxing of the beer laws. It is produced by the speciality Abro brewery, Vimmerby.

Pripps Bla
The best-selling Swedish beer in all three strength classes. It is a honey-gold sweetish Pilsner. There is also a new Extra Strong Pripps Bla (7.2%) in the strongest beer class.

Royal Pilsner
This is the brand name for a range of hoppy, all-malt Pilsners from Pripps, whose label was designed by Prince Sigvard Bernadotte of Sweden.

Spendrup's Old Gold
This deep-gold, hoppy, all-malt Pilsner-style lager (5%) comes in a distinctive, ridged brown bottle. It is produced by the Spendrup's brewery in Grangesberg.

Spendrup's Premium
This flavoursome, full-bodied, all-malt premium Pilsner comes from the Spendrup's brewery in Grangesberg.

Tom Kelley
This is a potent and flavoursome brew (7.5%). Tom Kelley was introduced by Pripps when the regulations on strong beers were relaxed.

CARNEGIE PORTER – A SCOTTISH BREW IN SWEDEN

Many Swedish beers carry English names, but one of Pripps' more distinctive brews poured out of Scotland. A Scot called David Carnegie emigrated to Gothenburg in the early 19th century, setting up his own brewery there in 1836 to produce the popular porters of the day. The company was eventually absorbed by Pripps, but they never stopped brewing the top-fermented dark drop. Today, Carnegie Porter is brewed in Stockholm in two strengths – a richly roasted 5.6%, and a thin shadow of the full-bodied version at 3.6%. It has also introduced a vintage, year-dated stark (strong) porter, which is matured for a full six months. In 1992, the heavy, aromatic brew returned home to Britain to win a gold medal at the International Brewing Exhibition in Burton-on-Trent.

THE BREWERS

Abro
A family brewery at Vimmerby since 1856, Abro is known for its speciality products, notably a powerful Gorilla (7.6%) in the new extra-strong sector. Other brews include Abro Guld and a darker Abro Bayerskt.

Falcon
This large Falkenberg firm has been brewing since 1896. Besides a range of Pilsners, it also offers a malty Falcon Guldol, and a dark, Munich-style Falcon Bayerskt.

Gamla Stans
Sweden's first brewpub opened in Stockholm in 1995 brewing a fresh, unfiltered lager, Faerskoel (5%).

Gotlands
A small brewery in Visby on the island of Gotland which was revived by Spendrups in 1995. Besides a dry Munkeol lager, it also brews two Scottish-style beers, a creamy Oat Malt Stout (4.5%) and Scotch Ale (4.2%) plus the unfiltered, fruity Klosteroel (6%).

Pripps
The dominant force in Swedish brewing has absorbed many smaller breweries. It was founded in Gothenburg in 1828 and merged with Stockholm Breweries in 1963. At the time of the merger the combined company boasted 30 breweries. Its main plant is now at Bromma near Stockholm and the leading brand is the sweetish Pilsner Pripps Bla ("blue").

In 1995, Pripps merged with Norway's major brewer Ringnes. Pripps also has a stake in Hartwall of Finland, and the two companies have expanded heavily eastwards into the new Baltic states.

Spendrup's
In the difficult and restricted trading conditions that have prevailed in Sweden for many years, it seemed that this local brewery in Grangesberg, like a large number of others, was in danger of closing. The brewery, which was then trading as Grangesbergs, revived its fortune when it restored the old family name of Spendrup's and launched a range of all-malt Pilsners in distinctive bottles.

FINLAND

Finland has, more than any other Scandinavian country, managed to retain its ancient brewing traditions, and despite a vigorous anti-alcohol movement in the country, the modern industry is also thriving.

SUCH IS THE POPULARITY of the traditional Finnish beer *sahti* that it has moved out of remote rural farms into more commercial production. Many Finns like to drink sahti after a traditional sauna, and some households even make it in the sauna. The country also has a long history of more conventional brewing, but the development of the industry was heavily disrupted by anti-alcohol legislation. Like the United States, Finland endured a long period of Prohibition from 1919 until 1932. However, unlike its Scandinavian neighbours, the dry grip of the temperance movement shows little sign of relaxing in Finland and taxes on beer have remained high (as much as 40% on the strongest brews, with an additional value-added tax of around 16%).

Beer is divided into classes according to strength for regulation of sales and for tax purposes. Only the weakest, Class I (beers below 2.8% alcohol by volume), are allowed to be sold through ordinary shops, and may be advertised freely. The popular Class III (3.7–4.7%) is more restricted, through higher taxation and State-regulated distribution. Almost all Class III beer is of the Pilsner style.

As strength climbs, so the State's grip tightens, and sales of stronger beers (to 5.7%) are closely controlled by the State-owned retail monopoly, Alko. These export lagers can only be legally sold through Alko's shops and licensed restaurants. There are also a few speciality brews containing up to 7.8% alcohol. Despite these severe restrictions, the Finnish brewing industry has managed to remain quite vigorous, with two main groups, Hartwall and Sinebrychoff, dominating the tightly controlled market, and a growing number of small "restaurant-brewers" are now springing up all the time.

Above: Hartwall, Finland's biggest brewer, produces a golden lager Lapin Kulta, which, in its strongest form (5.3%), may only be sold in restricted outlets.

THE BEERS

Cheers

A copper-coloured, bottom-fermented ale, produced by one of the Finnish giants, Sinebrychoff.

Jouloulot Christmas Beer

A reddish-coloured, rich-flavoured, seasonal winter brew (5%), produced by Sinebrychoff.

Karhu 3

A dark, brownish lager (4.6%), with a strong, full flavour. This is one of a range from the Sinebrychoff's second brewery at Pori.

Karjala

This tawny-coloured, richly flavoured, spicy, hoppy Pilsner is brewed by Hartwall and is their best-selling brew after Lapin Kulta. The company have recently added Hartwall 1836 Classic, a full malt ale to their range, first produced in 1996.

Koff

Koff is the abbreviated name which is given to the beers from the Sinebrychoff brewery, these include a popular, light-brownish, pleasant-tasting Pilsner (4.5%), a powerful pale Extra Strong (7.5%) and an export lager (5.2%).

Koff Porter

The Sinebrychoff brewery still brews one of its oldest beers (7.2%), a dense dark ale which was only revived after the Second World War, using a top-fermenting yeast cultured from a bottle of Guinness. Centrifuged but not filtered, it has a rich, roasted flavour. Four different malts are used in the mash, and the beer is conditioned for six weeks before it is pasteurized. It was once exported to the US under the name Imperial Stout.

Lammin Sahti

The best-known commercial sahti producer sells the Finnish speciality in a container resembling a wine box. The reddish, hazy drink (8%) has a spicy, tart taste.

Lapin Kulta

Hartwall's leading Pilsner from its most northern brewery trades on its fresh image using the icy waters of Lapland. Its strongest form (5.3%) is smooth and malty.

Leningrad Cowboy

This unusually named, golden export lager (5.2%) is brewed by Sinebrychoff and reflects the brewery's Russian connections.

Pilsner Nikolai

A sweetish, premium Pilsner (4.5%) brewed by the Sinebrychoff brewery. It is named in honour of the brewery's founder.

Postin Oma

Michael Jackson (*The Beer Hunter*) described this dark brew from the small Ravintola Wanha Posti brewery very favourably when he visited in 1995, saying, "It has a very attractive copper-brown colour and a good, dense head. The flavour has some nuttiness and some dark chocolate with a good development of malt flavours. It is very easily drinkable and soothing." The brewery was so pleased that it has immortalized Mr Jackson's complimentary write-up of their brew on the back of its beer mats!

Sahti

This is the traditional beer style of Finland. It is strong (usually around 8%), unfiltered, hazy, reddish-amber in colour and quite flat, with a spicy, bittersweet flavour. Rye, rather than barley, is used as the main component in the mash. This, combined with the main seasoning of juniper (rather than hops), gives the finished product a refreshingly tart tang. Juniper twigs are also traditionally used to strain the brew, and saunas are sometimes used to kiln the grains. Sahti production was originally a domestic enterprise, and the fact that baking yeast is often used in the recipe reflects its homely origins.

Sandels

Olvi's lightly hopped, light brown, traditional Finnish lager which has a smooth, malty taste. It is named after Colonel Sandels, a famous soldier in the Russian-Finnish War.

Vaakuna

This dark, golden, malty, toffeeish, Bavarian Märzen-style lager (4.5%) is produced by the Olvi brewery.

Sowing the seed

Finland's cold climate is well suited to cereal production, and it is one of the major barley growers of the world. Its malted grain is exported widely and may even end up in brews as far afield as Japan.

Above and below: The colours of Lapin Kulta's label are inspired by Finland's midnight sun.

THE BREWERS

Hartwall

The Hartwall company controls more than half of the beer market in Finland, with breweries in Helsinki, Lahti and Tornio. The brewery in Tornio was founded in this trapping and gold-rush town in 1873 and the Lapin Kulta name, meaning "Lapp Gold", was taken from an old mine. This brewery is one of the few breweries in the world to take its water from rivers.

Hartwall was a soft drinks manufacturer until 1966 when it bought its first brewery. Its main Pilsner brand is Lapin Kulta. but it also produces Karjala and Hartwall 1836 Classic. In 1991, Hartwall set up a joint venture with Pripps of Sweden, Baltic Beverage Holdings (BBH), to expand into the Baltic states, buying into breweries in Estonia, Latvia, Lithuania and Russia.

Kappeli Brasserie

The Kappeli Brasserie in Helsinki produces unfiltered lagers and seasonal specials.

Olvi

The third-largest brewing group in Finland is based in Iisalmi. Besides a range of Pilsners it produces a malty export lager, Vaakuna and the light brown Sandels.

Sinebrychoff

Finland's oldest brewery was established by a Russian merchant, Nikolai Sinebrychoff, in 1819 in Helsinki. Originally the brewery made porter, mead and top-fermenting beers, then it introduced lager to its range in 1853. It still trades on the Russian connection. The beers are mainly sold under the abbreviated Koff name, but there is also a premium Pilsner Nikolai and oddities such as an export lager called Leningrad Cowboy.

A northern industry

There are thousands of local sahti producers, churning out about four million litres (900,000 gallons) each year. The majority is made in the region the Finns call "the north" – the area stretching 150 km (100 miles) or so to the north-east and north-west of Tampere. The best-known commercial producers are Joutsa, Sysmä and Honkajoki.

ICELAND

The small, northerly island of Iceland has a tradition of producing very weak beers as a result of prohibitive legislation that placed an effective brake on normal beer production for 74 years.

IN 1989, ICELAND finally came in from the cold when it ended a 74-year ban on beer imposed in 1915. Previously, companies such as the family-run Egill brewery of Reykjavík, produced only soft drinks and low-alcohol beers, but since the relaxation of the ban they have added a number of stronger brews for the country's tiny population of 250,000, half of whom live in the capital, Reykjavík. Since the repeal of the ban on beer, Reykjavík is fast gaining the reputation of being a fun-loving town, and an increasing number of well-heeled younger Europeans now visit to experience the hedonistic nightlife, particularly during the summer months. At the same time alcoholism is a growing social problem, which perhaps can be partly attributed to the long, dark winters during which there can be as little as four hours' daylight.

Above: Viking is a new beer that has appeared in Iceland since the repeal of the beer ban.

A Viking toast

Iceland is the home of the oldest "parliament" in the world – the Thingvellir. The ancient sagas handed down from Viking times tell of the annual meeting there to make laws, resolve disputes and strike deals. It was a great occasion accompanied by feasting and of course copious beer drinking.

THE BEERS

Dökkur
This stronger (in Icelandic terms) beer (3.8%) was introduced by Egill after the ban on producing alcoholic drinks was lifted in 1989. The name means dark.

Egils Malt
This old-fashioned style of low-alcohol beer (1%) is still brewed by Egill of Reykjavík.

Egils Pilsner
The weak, pale-gold Pilsner (2.25%) is produced by Egill brewery of Reykjavík. The refreshing beer is brewed with pure Icelandic water and is the most popular light beer in Iceland.

Gull
This golden, Pilsner export lager (5%) was introduced by Egill brewery following the repeal of the ban on strong beers. It is now the most popular beer in the country.

Viking Bjór
This pale-gold, clear Pilsner-style lager (5%) is produced by Viking.

THE BREWERS

Egill
Run by the Tomasson family since 1913, Egill concentrated on the production of low-alcohol beers such as Egils Malt until 1989. It still markets these, but since the repeal of the beer ban it has added the stronger Dökkur and Gull to its range, besides brewing Tuborg under licence.

Viking
Originally a soft drinks producer called Sanitas. Viking built a new brewery at Akureyri in 1988 to meet the demand for stronger beer when the ban was lifted in 1989.

BELGIUM

Belgium is the land of beer. No country offers such a rich variety of styles – from wild, spontaneously fermenting brews and fruit beers to spiced beers and blessed Trappist ales still produced in monasteries.

ON ONE LEVEL the Belgian beer market has become concentrated over the last century. The number of breweries has declined from around 3,000 in 1900 to little more than 100 today. Pilsner-style beers, such as Stella Artois and Jupiler, from the major brewers Interbrew and Alken-Maes, dominate domestic consumption, and while they are fine brews, they do not match the top-quality lagers available in the Czech Republic and Germany.

However the joy of Belgian beer lies not in its pils but in the fascinating range of other beers which can be found in its bars. What France is to wine, Belgium is to beer. It may be a small country, but it is vast in what it has to offer those thirsting after new tastes. For the adventurous, Belgium is heaven on earth, a beer drinkers paradise.

There are monasteries still producing strong, richly favoured, Trappist ales such as Chimay and Orval, which are now copied by some commercial breweries and sold as abbey beers. Near Brussels a region creates wild lambic beers which are allowed to ferment spontaneously. Some breweries add fruit to these ancient wheat brews to produce beers such as the deliciously dark kriek made using cherries, while others add spices or sour their beers in special ways.

It is in this colourful and complex speciality section that Belgium has earned its reputation. The speciality beers can be divided into seven main groups – lambic (sometimes spelled lambik), white beer, brown beer, red beer, ales, Trappist and saison. Within these categories the range of flavours, styles and strengths is bewildering and some brews are unique and defy categorization. Many cafés and bars offer a staggeringly long beer menu for the customer to choose from, and each beer is often served in its own special glass.

Above: Belgium's speciality beers have earned acclaim throughout the world. Cherry-flavoured kriek beers, with their luscious dark, red colour, are usually made using whole fruit.

THE BEERS

Abbaye d'Aulne
This is the name used by the de Smedt family brewery in Opwijk for some of its commercially produced abbey-style beers.

Abbaye de Bonne Espérance
This bottle-conditioned, cloudy golden tripel (7.5%) is better known as Floreffe tripel from the Lefebvre brewery in Quenast.

Adler
The third largest lager producer in Belgium, Haacht brews this strong, golden, premium lager (6.5%).

Affligem
The abbey beers from the De Smedt brewery of Opwijk are brewed according to original recipes from the ancient Benedictine Affligem Abbey in the region of Aalst. It produces a brown, dry Affligem Dubbel, a golden blonde (both 7%) and a fruity, amber tripel (8.5%).

Agnus Dei
A complex, strong, pale tripel (8%). This abbey-style beer is sold under the Corsendonk name. The brew, which dates from 1982, is brewed at the Du Bocq brewery. It is the brainchild of Jozef Keersmaekers.

Augustijn
The strong abbey-style beers from the Van Steenberge brewery of Ertvelde include Augustijn (8%) and a Grand Cru (9%).

Avec les Bons Voeux de la Brasseries
A strong, gold, spicy (9.5%) New Year beer with a long title. This brew comes from Dupont in Hainaut. An organic (biologique) version is also available.

Bel Pils
Considered one of Belgium's better Pilsners, Bel Pils (5.3%) is pale gold with a hoppy flavour. It is produced by the independent family brewery Moortgat, which also makes Duvel and Maredsous abbey beers.

Belle-Vue
Gueuze, kriek and frambozen (5.2%) from this large-scale brewer of lambic beers are pleasant but a little undemanding.

Blanche de Namur
This pale wheat beer (4.3%) with a spicy, fruity flavour is brewed in Namur province by the family brewery Du Bocq.

Blanche des Honnelles
A cloudy wheat beer (6%) that incorporates malted oats in the mash and is spiced with juniper, coriander and orange peel. Produced by Abbaye des Rocs.

Block Special 6
Brewed in Peizegem, Block produces this unique sour beer, Block Special 6 (6%), which is a blend of lambic and young and old pale ales. It also brews the range of Satan ales.

Bokkereyer
A strong (5.8%) Vienna-style lager from a Limburg family brewery, St Jozef, on the Dutch border at Opitter.

Bourgogne des Flandres
Lambic brewer Timmermans of Itterbeek produces this lambic-based, plummy, sour, red ale (6.5%).

Brigand
A robust, bronze-coloured ale (9%) with a sweetish taste. It is served in corked bottles by the Van Honsebrouck brewery of Ingelmunster, West Flanders. Brigand has gained a cult following.

Brugs Tarwebier
Also known as Blanche de Bruges, this cloudy wheat beer (5%) is the best-known brew from Gouden Boom in Bruges. Tarwe means wheat.

Brugse Straffe Hendrik
See Straffe Hendrik.

Brugse Tripel
This strong, golden beer (9.5%) comes from the small Gouden Boom brewery in Bruges (the brewery also boasts its own beer museum).

Right: Transferring casks of craft-brewed Belgian ale from the lorry to the bar earlier this century.

Bush

The strongest beer in Belgium, Bush (12%) is an amber-coloured, English-style barley wine from the Dubuisson brewery in Pipaix, Hainaut. Originally brewed in 1933, this dry, warming brew with a mellow, oaky taste, became the family firm's only regular beer. It is sold as Scaldis in the US in order to avoid confusion with brewing giant Anheuser-Busch. Dubuisson also brews a dark amber Bush Noël (12%) at Christmas. In 1994, the brewery marked its 225th anniversary with the launch of a weaker hoppy Bush Beer (7%).

Celis White

This wheat beer (5%) is now brewed by De Smedt under licence from the original producer of Belgian wheat beer, Pieter Celis, who now brews in America.

Chapeau

This range of weak, lambic fruit beers, including banana, strawberry and pineapple, is produced by De Troch.

Charles Quint

This strong, sweetish brown ale (7%) is produced by Haacht.

Chimay Blanche

See Chimay Cinq Cents.

Chimay Bleu•

See Chimay Grande Réserve.

Chimay Cinq Cents

A golden, amber Trappist tripel with a malty flavour (8%). It is the hoppiest, driest offering from the Abbaye de Notre-Dame de Scourmont, near Chimay. In the smaller bottle size it is known as Chimay Blanche, and is so called after the white colour of the bottle cap.

Chimay Grande Réserve

This rich, fruity Trappist ale (9%) is the strongest and most complex ale from the Abbaye de Notre-Dame de Scourmont. The bottle has a blue cap and label. It was originally introduced as a Christmas beer, but has been brewed regularly since 1958. It is vintage-dated and benefits from being laid down for a few years. In the smaller size it is known as Chimay Bleu.

Chimay Première

A rich, red-brown Trappist ale (7%) with a spicy, fruity flavour from the Abbaye de Notre-Dame de Scourmont. The bottle has a red label and top. In the 33cl bottle is called Chimay Rouge.

Chimay Rouge

See Chimay Première.

Cochonne

An annual ale (9%) from the small Vapeur brewery in Pipaix in Hainaut.

The Antwerp brewery De Koninck was founded in 1833. It uses a traditional Flemish brick-clad kettle with a hop sieve that is removed by a pulley system. The recipe is all malt (using no adjuncts) and incorporates Saaz hops. The best way to enjoy a glass of De Koninck is on draught in the Pilgrim café opposite the brewery, where locals often add an extra shot of yeast to their glass.

Corsendonk

These two abbey beers in their stylish brown bottles date from as recently as 1982. They are named after the former Corsendonk Augustinian priory near Turnhout, which was established in the 15th century and recently restored. The brews are the brainchild of a member of the well-known brewing family, Jozef Keersmaekers. The dark, chocolatey dubbel, Pater Noster, is brewed by the Van Steenberge brewery. The stronger, pale tripel, Agnus Dei (8%), is brewed at the Du Bocq brewery.

Cristal Alken

This unpasteurized beer is generally regarded as the hoppiest of the main Belgian Pilsners (4.8%). Brewed by the Alken-Maes group, it is the best-selling beer in its home province of Limbourg.

Cuvée d'Aristée

Unusual honeyed ale (9.5%) from the tiny Praille brewery in Peissant near Mons.

Cuvée de l'Hermitage

Cuvée, like the terms luxe and spéciale, has largely become a meaningless title, but this rich, russet ale (8%) from the Union brewery in Jumet deserves the accolade.

De Koninck

This all-malt, top-fermenting ale (5%) has been described as a cross between an English bitter and a German alt. It is matured in the cask, then pasteurized in the bottle. There is also a stronger version available, called Cuvée de Koninck (8%).

Delirium Tremens

This aptly named, notoriously strong, golden, spiced ale (9%) from the Huyghe brewery near Ghent is served in a glass painted with pink elephants.

Dentergems Wit

The Riva brewery of Dentergem launched this, one of the first rival white beers to Hoegaarden, in 1980. The pale, cloudy brew (5%) is more in the German wheat-beer style, with a delicate, wheaty, lemony taste.

Doppelbock Bugel

This is one of the strongest (8%) bottom-fermented beers in Belgium. A heavy Christmas brew, it is produced by Domus, the first home-brew house in Belgium, set up in Leuven in 1985 by a former Cristal Alken brewer. Other beers include a tasty, fresh lager and a cloudy wheat beer, Leuvens Witbier (5%).

Double Enghien Brune

This interesting, creamy, walnutty, strong, dark ale (8%) and the amber blonde come from the Silly brewery in the town of Silly.

Duivelsbier

An unusual beer (6%), produced by the Vander Linden brewery by blending a conventional pale ale and a lambic.

Duvel

This is a beer with a devil of a reputation, one of the best-known and most celebrated drinks in Belgium. A golden ale with a frothy white top, it appears attractive but unremarkable in its balloon goblets apart from its surging lines of bubbles. However, just one sniff of its heady hop aroma and one taste of its complex fruity flavour, together with its sustaining strength

(8.5%), make the beer drinker appreciate that this is a glass apart.

Duvel is brewed by the Moortgat brewery in Breendonk. After the First World War, the brewery attempted to brew a Scotch ale. The Moortgat brewers examined bottles of McEwan's ale from Edinburgh and made a dark ale using the McEwan's yeast. "It's a devil of a brew," claimed one taster, and the name Duvel was born in 1923. In 1968 Moortgat perfected a golden version.

Today, the devil appears in two guises: the delicious bottle-conditioned brew has a red-lettered label; a blander, filtered version has green letters. Other Belgian brewers have tried to copy the beer, but none can match the original.

Ename

A range of abbey beers brewed by the Roman brewery in East Flanders which includes a dark Dubbel (6.5%) and a golden Tripel (8%).

Felix

The Clarysse brewery of Oudenaarde produces this range of sweetish East Flanders brown ales. Beers include Felix Oud Bruin (5.5%), Special Oudenaards (4.8%), plus two kriekbiers (6% and 5%).

Floreffe

This range of quality bottle-conditioned abbey beers from the Lefebvre family brewery at Quenast, south-west of Brussels, is named after the Norbertine abbey at Floreffe.

The best, a mahogany-coloured spicy ale, is simply called La Meilleure (8%). A golden tripel (7.5%) is also sold as Abbaye de Bonne Espérance. Additional beers include a tasty dubbel and a blonde (both 7%).

Gildenbier

This strong, sweetish brown ale (6.6%) is produced by Haacht.

Goudenband

See Liefmans Goudenband.

Gouden Carolus

A distinctive, smooth, dark ale (7%) from the family-run Anker brewery of Mechelen, its name derives from a gold coin of the Holy Roman Emperor Charles V who grew up in the city. There is also a lighter, less spicy Mechelsen Brune (5.5%) and a yellow, pale ale, Toison d'Or Tripel (7%).

Grimbergen

This range of abbey beers from the large Alken-Maes group is brewed at its Union brewery in Jumet. They include a warming Optimo Bruno (10%), a sweet, winey, golden tripel (9%) and blonde (7%) and a dark,

fruity dubbel (6.5%). The beers are named after the abbey of Grimbergen in the northern suburbs of Brussels.

Hapkin

The Louwaege brewery of West Flanders produces this strong, bottle-conditioned golden ale (8.5%), which seeks to rival Duvel.

Het Kapittel

The Van Eecke brewery of Watou produces this range of quality abbey beers. Brews include a strong abt (10%) and darkly delicious prior (9%), plus a dubbel (7%) and pater (6.5%).

Hoegaarden

The renewed interest in cloudy wheat beers began with this beer, first brewed by Pieter Celis at his De

Kluis Brewery in Hoegaarden in 1966. It revived the art of brewing "white" beers spiced with coriander and curaçao. Hoegaarden's chunky glasses have become a familiar part of Belgian bars. Besides the refreshing cloudy, lemon-coloured Hoegaarden (5%), the brewery also produces a stronger, golden Grand Cru and a spicier orangey-coloured Julius (both 8.7%), plus a rich, fruity brown ale, Verboden Vrucht (8.8%). All are bottle-conditioned.

Horse-Ale

This is an English-style pale ale (4.8%), with an aromatic hop character brewed by Interbrew.

Ichtegems Oud Bruin

A refreshing, Flemish red ale, with a sweetish, malt taste from the Strubbe brewery of Ichtegem.

Jacobins

This range of sweetish lambic beers – Jacobins amber, sweet-and-sour gueuze, the red, cherry-flavoured kriek and raspberry frambozen (all 5.5%) – comes from the Bockor brewery of Bellegem.

Jupiler

Belgium's best-selling beer, the popular malty Pilsner (5.2%) comes from Jupille

near Liège. Founded in 1853, the brewery is now part of Interbrew.

Kasteel

A very strong, amber-coloured, bottled, rich dark ale (11.5%). It is laid down to mature by the Van Honsebrouck brewery in the cellars at Ingelmunster Castle, an 18th-century moated mansion owned by the brewing family. The taste is rich, almost like a port.

La Chouffe

This golden ale (8%) from the Achouffe brewery is spiced with coriander.

La Divine

This interesting, strong, dark, amber-coloured ale (9.5%) with a full, spicy flavour, is brewed by the Silly brewery.

La Gauloise

The distinctive strong ales from the Du Bocq brewery of Namur include an ambrée (6.5%), blonde (7%) and dark, red-coloured brune (9%). The larger-size bottles are corked.

La Meilleure

This mahogany-coloured, bottle-conditioned spicy ale (8%) is, as the name implies, the best brew from the Floreffe range of abbey ales.

Leffe

Interbrew produces this range of abbey beers, named after the Leffe abbey at Dinant, near Namur. Besides an amber-coloured blonde and a dark-brown, malty, fruity brune (both 6.5%), there's a golden tripel (8.4%) and two brown ales, Vieille Cuvée (7.8%) and Radieuse (8.2%).

Liefmans Frambozenbier

This pale-pink, sour, raspberry fruit beer (5.7%) can be served as an aperitif in place of champagne.

Liefmans Goudenband

An acidic, chocolate-brown-coloured, sweet-and-sour Belgian brown ale (8%) that is brewed by Liefmans using four different hop varieties and a 100-year-old yeast strain. Part of the brew is matured for six to eight months, then it is mixed with a younger version to make the distinctively flavoured finished product.

Liefmans Kriekbier

This traditional tart, cherry fruit beer (6.5%), produced by the Liefmans brewery in Oudenaarde, is a deep, cloudy red-brown colour. It is suitable for keeping for up to four years and will age and mature with time.

Limburgse Witte

This tasty wheat beer (5%) is produced by the family-owned Martens brewery.

Lucifer

This is one of the rival brews to Duvel. It is a strong, golden ale (8%) brewed by the Riva brewery in Flanders.

McChouffe

A complex, copper-coloured, creamy, malty Ardenne strong ale (8.5%) with a vague Scottish ancestry, from the Achouffe brewery.

McGregor

A dark, whisky-malt brew (6.5%) from the Huyghe family brewery in Melle.

Maes Pils

This popular, mass-market, deep golden Pilsner with a big hoppy flavour (5.1%) comes from the Maes brewery near Antwerp.

Marckloff

A hazy Walloon pale ale (6.5%) which comes from the homebrew café La Ferme au Chêne in Durbuy.

Maredsous

The range of abbey ales from the Moortgat brewery in Breendonk includes a strong, black quadrupel (10%), a dark tripel (8%), a mild-tasting blonde dubbel (6%) and a dark dubbel (6%) and a golden ale with an orange colour. These beers are identified by degree numbers, 10, 8 and 6. They are named after a Benedictine abbey at Denée, south of Namur.

Moinette

These strong ales from the Dupont brewery in Hainaut include a spicy, complex blonde and brune (both 8.5%) and an organic biologique (7.5%).

Mort Subite

These sweet, commercial lambics from the De Keersmaeker brewery include the gentle, amber Mort Subite gueuze, a sweet, cherry-flavoured kriek (both 4.5%), sweet framboise and pêche (both 4%) and a cassis (4%) made with blackcurrant juice. The name means "sudden death" after a card game.

Oerbier

This popular, dark, hazy amber, Scottish-style ale (7.5%) was the first brew produced by De Dolle Brouwers.

Op-Ale

This pale, sweetish, malty ale (4.8%) is produced by the De Smedt family brewery in Opwijk.

Optimo Bruno

This warming Grimbergen abbey beer (10%) comes from the Alken-Maes group's Union brewery.

Orval

This Belgian classic Trappist ale (6.2%) is the only brew made by the Abbaye d'Orval. It is orange, with a heady, hoppy aroma and an intense, dry flavour. Its complex character is in part due to three separate fermentations and dry-hopping.

Oud Beersel

These traditional unfiltered lambics, from the tiny Van-dervelden brewery at Beersel, near Brussels, include Oud Beersel Lambik (5.7%), gueuze (6%) and kriek (7%).

Oud Kriekenbier

This is the only non-lambic cherry beer (6.5%) to be made completely with whole cherries rather than using juice. It is produced by the small Crombe brewery.

Oudenaards Wit Tarwebier

This white wheat beer (4.8%) is produced by Clarysse at Oudenaarde in East Flanders.

Palm

Palm Spéciale (5.2%) is the biggest-selling ale in Belgium. It is brewed by the independent Palm brewery of Steenhuffel. It is an amber, fruity, refreshing beer. A darker version called Dobbel Palm (5.5%), is produced at Christmas. The village brewery, which dates back to 1747, also brews a more powerful, copper-coloured, bottle-conditioned ale, Aerts 1900 (7%), and a wheat beer, Steendonk (4.5%).

Pater Noster

A dark brown, smoky, malt-tasting dubbel (7%) from the Van Steenberge brewery sold under the Corsendonk name.

Pauwels Kwak

This warming, garnet-coloured ale (8%), named after an innkeeper, is served in a distinctive round-bottomed Kwak glass which has to be supported on a wooden stand.

Petrus

The top-fermented beers from the Bavik brewery include a dark imitation of Rodenbach which is matured in oak casks (5.5%). Bavik also brews a golden spéciale (5.5%) and tripel (7.5%).

Poperings Hommelbier

A creamy, hoppy, amber ale (7.5%), this seasonal drink is brewed by the Van Eecke brewery of Watou to celebrate the hop harvest in nearby Poperinge.

Primus Pils

A highly regarded, dry, yellow, hoppy Pilsner (5%), produced by Haacht.

Rodenbach

This distinctive ale (5%) is made by blending a vintage brew, which has been matured in oak casks for over a year, with fresh, young beer, which has only been matured for five to six weeks. A quarter of the old ale is mixed with three-quarters of the new. The resulting beer is so tart that it is sweetened with sugar to produce a refreshing sweet and sour taste. Some of the vintage brew is bottled

unsweetened and undiluted to create the much-bolder Grand Cru (6.5%). There is also a sweeter version, blended with cherry essence, called Alexander (6.5%).

Rose de Gambrinus

The most celebrated lambic frambozen (5%), which comes from the Cantillon brewery in Brussels. It contains a small proportion of cherries and a dash of vanilla, as well as raspberries. It is blood-orange-coloured, wih a tart, fruity flavour.

St Benoît

The fine abbey beers from the Du Bocq brewery of Namur include a yellow, wheaty St Benoît Blonde and amber-brown brune (both 6.5%) with a fresh, dry, woody flavour, besides a hoppy golden tripel (8%), which is also sold as Triple Moine.

St Idesbald

These unusual, sour abbey beers come from the Damy brewery in east Flanders and include a licht and dubbel (both 6%), as well as a dark tripel (8%).

St Louis

The Van Honsebrouck brewery produces this range of sweet commercial lambics, including a gueuze, kriek, framboise and cassis (all 5%). There is also a more characterful, unfiltered Gueuze Fond Tradition (5%).

THE LAMBIC HELPER

Thousands of tiny yeast organisms are carried on cool evening air currents through the open windows of lambic breweries. Inside the dark, dusty interiors (for lambic brewers know better than to remove the cobwebs and moulds from the brewery walls) the yeasts settle on cobwebs and into damp nooks and crannies. Some find their way into the open vats of cooling beer, where they begin to feast on the sugars and ferment the brew. These untamed, wild helpers produce an ale that is tart and refreshing. Trusting to the action of wild yeasts borne invisibly in the air is the oldest fermentation method in the world, and their effect was once regarded by brewers as nothing short of magical. The lambic brewers of Belgium, though they now understand the source of their help, have maintained this ancient tradition.

St Sebastiaan

These abbey beers from the Sterkens brewery of Meer, close to the Dutch border, are sold in distinctive pottery bottles. The beers include a Grand Cru (7.6%) and a dark (6.9%) which is also sold as Poorter.

St Sixtus

See St Bernardus.

Saison de Pipaix

The small Vapeur brewery produces this refreshing spicy saison (6.5%).

Saison Régal

A spicy, hoppy saison-style, amber-coloured beer (6%) from Du Bocq in the province of Namur.

Saison de Silly

A fruity saison beer (5%) produced by the Silly brewery in Hainhaut.

Satan

Strong red, gold and brown ales (all 8%) from the Block brewery of Peizegem.

Sezuens

A hoppy, sunny, gold-amber, saison ale (6%) which comes from the Martens brewery of Bocholt. It follows the saison style of thirst-quenching beers, which are brewed during the winter for drinking in summer.

Martens also brews a stronger, amber-red Sezuens Quattro (8%) and the less-powerful Sezuens Europe (6.5%).

Silly Brug-Ale
This fruity beer (5%) comes from the Silly brewery in the town of the same name.

Sloeber
The Roman brewery produces this rich, malty, strong, golden ale (7.5%) in the Duvel style. The name means "joker".

Steenbrugge Dubbel
This abbey ale (6.5%) comes from the small Gouden Boom brewery in Bruges.

Steenbrugge Tripel
This creamy, golden abbey beer (9%) from Gouden Boom is less heavy than the brewery's Brugse tripel.

Stella Artois
Belgium's best-known, golden lager is the flagship Pilsner (5.2%) of the brewing giant Interbrew.

Stille Nacht
Dolle Brouwers produces this strong, orangey, seasonal, bottle-conditioned ale (9%) in winter. The name comes from the German title for the popular carol, "Silent Night".

Straffe Hendrik
This heavily hopped pale ale (6.5%) is the only beer produced by Straffe Hendrick, Bruges.

Titje
A distinctive, cloudy, gold wheat beer (5%) with a fruity, spicy flavour from the Silly brewery.

Tongerlo
Abbey beers from Haacht brewery include a double blonde (6%), brune (6.5%) and amber tripel (8%).

Unic Bier
A characterful, weak table beer (3.2%) from Gigi, a fine example of this style.

Verboden Vrucht
The name of Hoegaarden's distinctive, strong, orangey-coloured dark ale (9%) means "forbidden fruit", and it is also sold as Fruit Défendu in France. When customs officials in the United States saw the sexy label of Adam and Eve, based on a Rubens painting, they tried to ban bottles of the revealing brew.

Vieille Provision
An excellent, hoppy, saison-style ale (6.5%) which comes from the farmyard Dupont brewery. It is also known as Saison Dupont and Vieille Réserve. This classic country beer has a complex, refreshing taste and a solid creamy head.

Vieux Temps
Interbrew's malty, pale ale (5%) from Leuven, is popular in the south of the country. Its name means "old times".

Vigneronne
A tart lambic (5%) made from green grapes and blended lambic beers, from the Cantillon brewery.

Westmalle
Both the dark dubbel (6.5%) and the golden tripel (9%) from this monastic brewery have a secondary fermentation. They are then primed with sugar and given a dose of yeast before being bottled. The dubbel is complex and surprisingly dry. The tripel has many imitators. It is extremely pale with a delicious citric and honeyed flavour.

Westvleteren
A range of much-sought-after beers produced by the small Westvleteren monastery, including a dark, fruity special (6.2%) and a similar and stronger extra (8%) leading up to a stern but rotund abt, which at 11.5% is one of the strongest beers in the country. All are on the sweetish side for Trappist ales. The bottles are identified by the colour of their crown corks – red for special, blue for extra and yellow for abt.

Witkap
This range of quality abbey ales, named after the monk's cowl, come from the Slaghmuylder brewery in Ninove, which was founded in 1860. The Witkap beers include the hoppy pale Stimulo (6%), a rich Dubbel Pater (7%) and a golden, bitter, fruity tripel (7.5%).

Yperman
A robust pale ale (6%), from the Leroy family brewery near Ypres.

THE BREWERS

Abbaye d'Orval

Abbaye d'Orval is the most attractive of the Trappist monasteries, set in woodland above a lake in the rolling hills of the Ardennes. Though an abbey has stood on this site near Florenville since 1070, it was repeatedly sacked and the present stone buildings were only planned in 1926. Five years later, construction was still not finished, so, to provide funds to complete the grand scheme, the community decided to add a brewery, the outside of which is designed like a chapel. It opened in 1931, and drinkers have been giving thanks for this brew ever since.

Orval means "Vale of Gold", and the true treasure of the Orval monastery is its one precious beer. Unlike the other Trappist breweries, Orval does not brew a range of beers, but produces one delicious, intensely dry ale. The monks at the monastery also produce a crusty bread and a fine cheese which go well when eaten as accompaniments to a bottle of Orval.

Abbaye des Rocs

This commercial brewery in Montignies-sur-Roc has been producing strong Walloon ales since 1984. It is best known for its dark, spicy Abbaye des Rocs and golden La Montagnarde (both 9%).

Achouffe

This farm brewery in the Ardennes uses its own spring water for brewing. Its bearded gnome symbol has been a familiar sight in this holiday area since 1982.

Alken-Maes

The Belgian arm of the French brewing giant Kronenbourg controls a fifth of the Belgian beer market through its Cristal Alken and Maes Pilsners, as well as other brands such as Grimbergen abbey ales and Mort Subite lambics.

Artois

Best known for its international Pilsner brand, Stella Artois (5.2%), Artois was founded in Leuven in 1366. Now it is part of Interbrew, the second-largest brewing group in Europe. A massive new brewery opened in Leuven in 1995, alongside the huge original plant.

Bavik

A regional brewery in Bavikove in West Flanders, Bavik was founded in 1894. It produces a range of Pilsners and a witbier, plus top-fermented ales under the Petrus name.

Belle-Vue

The largest brewer of lambics, Belle-Vue has two breweries on the edge of Brussels – a traditional plant at Molenbeek and another operation at Zuun. The Molenbeek brewery has more than 10,000 wooden casks filled with maturing lambic. The quality of these brews is largely unknown because they are diluted with immature young lambics which have been brewed in steel cylinders at Zuun. Since 1990, the Molenbeek plant has also produced an excellent, unfiltered Séléction Lambic (5.2%). Belle-Vue exports its beers to France under the Bécasse brand name.

Binchoise

This small Hainaut brewery was founded in 1989 in an old maltings. It produces a range of strong, spiced ales, notably the citric blonde, which is also sold as Fakir (6.5%) and a honey beer, Bière des Ours (9%).

Block

Brewers at Peizegem in Brabant since 1887 who are best known for their wide range of Satan ales.

Bockor

This regional brewery in Bellegem, West Flanders, founded in 1892, is best known for its Pilsner and Jacobins range of lambic beers. It also brews a brown beer, Bellegems Bruin (5.5%), in which corn is added to the mash and mixed with a lambic brew.

Boon

The pioneering brewer, Frank Boon, helped to revive interest in the ancient lambic style when he started to brew and blend in Lembeek in 1975. His beers include a sweetish Boon gueuze, kriek and frambozen, plus a sourer range which is sold under the Mariage Parfait label. He also brews a weak table beer (2%) called Lembeek and a heavy mix of lambic, pale ale and sugar called Pertotale Faro (6%).

Bosteels

The Bosteels family brewery has been operating in Buggenhout, East Flanders, since 1791. It is famous for its garnet-coloured Pauwels Kwak beer (8%) drunk from its distinctive round-bottomed glass. Bosteels also brews Prosit Pils (4.8%).

Brunehaut

A former African brewer, Guy Valschaerts, established this brewery in 1992 at Rongy in the Hainaut region of Belgium. Brunehaut's beers include an organic wheat Blanche de Charleroi (5%), a juniper brew Abbaye de St Amand (7%) and a golden Bière du Mont St Aubert (8%), besides its original blonde and ambrée ales.

Cantillon

This working brewery museum produces true lambics in the back streets of Brussels. Run by the Van Roy family since 1900, it is famous for its brewing open days. Its uncompromisingly sour beers include a Cantillon lambic, kriek, super gueuze and a gueuze matured in port casks, called Brabantiae (all 5%).

Caracole

A small brewery in Falmignoul, near Namur, Caracole produces a wide range of Walloon strong ales under the sign of the snail, including Caracole ambrée and brune (both 6.5%), an annual Cuvée de l'An Neuf for the New Year, and a good wheat beer called Troublette (5%).

Clarysse

Clarysse has been brewing in East Flanders at Oudenaarde since 1946. It produces mainly brown ales under the Felix name, and is a local rival to the neighbouring Liefmans Brewery. It also brews a wheat Oudenaards Wit Tarwebier (4.8%).

Crombe

A small village brewery in Zottegem near Ghent which dates back to 1798. Crombe is best known for its Oud Kriekenbier (6.5%), the only non-lambic cherry beer to be made completely with whole cherries rather than juice.

De Dolle

See panel opposite – *The Mad Brewers*

De Keersmaeker

This lambic brewery in Kobbegem mainly brews commercial lambics under the Mort Subite brand, but also produces a more traditional gueuze (5%) which is marketed under its own name.

De Koninck

The De Koninck brewery was founded in 1833 in Antwerp. It stuck to producing ale when most of its rivals switched to brewing Pilsners, and it has thrived.

CHIMAY

Chimay is the largest and most internationally famous of the Belgian Trappist breweries. It has been brewing beer on a commercial scale at the Abbaye de Scourmont near Chimay since 1862. The brewery is located behind the walls of the abbey and uses its wells, but the work, as at other Trappist breweries, is carried out largely by secular staff under the monks' supervision. Bottling is handled at a modern plant in nearby Baileux. Chimay brews three distinctive ales, each known by the red, white or blue cap on the bottle. Chimay Rouge, or red (7%), was the original beer produced at the monastery, and was the only product for almost a century.

The quality of the beers owes much to a Belgian scientist, Professor Jean De Clerck of Leuven University, who helped the monastic brewery get back on its feet, after the disruptions of the Second World War, by developing its distinctive yeast strain. When he died in 1978, he was buried at the abbey.

The monastery also produces a range of foods, including some excellent cheeses, which go well with Chimay beer. One, called Chimay à la Bière, has a rind steeped in hops.

De Smedt

A wide range of abbey beers, notably the Affligem range but also Abbaye d'Aulne, are produced by this enterprising family brewery which has been based in Opwijk since 1790. Other beers include a pale Op Ale and the wheat beer Celis White.

De Troch

One of the oldest lambic brewers, De Troch dates back to 1820 in Wambeek. It produces a rare orangey-coloured, sour gueuze and a sweet, fruity kriek (5.5%), but concentrates on a range of weak lambic fruit beers under the Chapeau brand.

Du Bocq

This family brewery, located at Purnode in Namur province since 1858, brews an excellent, if confusing, range of ales, often under a variety of labels. Best known for its La Gauloise beers, it also produces abbey ales under the St Benoît name, a wheat beer Blanche de Namur (4.3%) and a spicy, hoppy Saison Régal (6%).

Dupont

This family farmhouse brewery at Tourpes in Hainaut has been operating since 1850. It produces an excellent saison Vieille Provision (6.5%) and a range of Walloon strong ales under the Moinette label. It also brews organic (biologique) versions of these beers, as well as a strong New Year beer.

Eupener

An old brewery in the border market town of Eupen which has its roots firmly in Germany. This small German-speaking area east of Liège was taken over by Belgium after the First World War. Besides a pleasant pils (4.7%), Eupener brews a sweetish, tawny bock called Klosterbier (5.5%) and two dark, low-alcohol, table beers in the German Malzbier style.

Facon

A family brewery at Bellegem in West Flanders since 1874, which until recent years concentrated on Pilsners and weak table beers. Today it also brews specialist ales, including a dark Scotch Ale (6.1%) and an Extra Stout (5.4%).

Friart

An attractive, old, red-brick Hainaut brewery in Le Roeulx, which was closed in 1977 but reopened in 1988, Friart mainly brews abbey beers under the St Feuillien name. These include a heavy, roasted Cuvée de Noël brewed for Christmas. Some beers are sold in huge six-litre Methuselah bottles.

THE MAD BREWERS

When three brothers rescued an old brewery from closure in 1980 in Esen, near Diksmuide in West Flanders, their bank manager thought they were insane, but the success of their dark Scottish-style ale, Oerbier (7.5%), proved otherwise. De Dolle Brouwers now produce a range of strong and seasonal bottle-conditioned ales including the strong Christmas brew, Stille Nacht (9%), Ara Bier, Boskeun and Oeral.

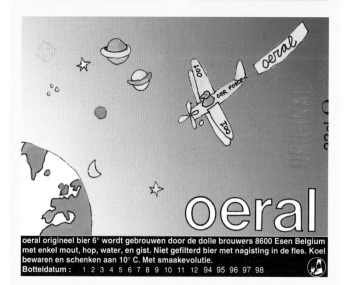

Gigi

This old Gérouville brewery in Luxembourg province produces the best weak table beers in Belgium, notably the lightly hoppy Double Blonde (1.2%) and the characterful Unic Bier (3.2%). It also sells pale and brown ales (5%) under the La Gaumaise label.

Girardin

This small traditional farm brewery at St Ulriks Kapelle produces fruity lambics from its own wheat, notably Girardin lambic, gueuze and kriek (all 5%). It also produces an aromatic Framboos using raspberries in the brew.

Haacht

The largest independent brewery in Belgium has been operating in Boortmeerbeek in Brabant since 1890. It mainly produces a range of lagers, notably Primus Pils (5%) and a premium Adler (6.5%). It brews a wheat beer Haacht (4.7%), two strong, sweetish brown ales – Charles Quint (6.7%) and Gildenbier (6.6%) – plus a range of abbey beers under the Tongerlo name.

Interbrew

The Belgian brewing giant was formed in 1988 by the merger of Artois and Jupiler. It has bought up several smaller Belgian brewers and produces a large range of brews on home soil. Following the takeover of Canadian brewers Labatt in 1995 and expansion into Eastern Europe after the fall of the Iron Curtain, it is now one of the largest brewing groups in the world, with interests around the globe.

Lefebvre

Brabant brewery in Quenast since 1876 which produces a wide range of ales, notably the Floreffe abbey beers.

Liefmans

Liefmans is the classic producer of East Flanders brown ales. Its stronger beers are sold in corked bottles, tissue-wrapped for laying down in the cellar to improve with age. All the beers are matured for three months in the bottle before leaving the brewery.

Lindemans

A farmhouse lambic brewer in Vlezenbeek since 1816, Lindemans now sells its beers as far from home as the US. The demands of the world market have led to a range of sweetish lambics including Lindemans faro, gueuze, kriek and framboise. It has recently launched a more distinctive range called Cuvée René, named after the owner.

Martens

This is one of the largest independent breweries in Belgium, but it is still family-owned. Martens has brewed at Bocholt in Limburg since 1758 and is best known for its Sezuens beer, though it also brews a wheat beer, Limburgse Witte (5%), a range of Pilsners and a tafelstout.

Moortgat

A family-owned brewery in Breendonk, north of Brussels, famous for its delicious flagship ale, Duvel.

Riva

Ambitious Flanders brewing group based in Dentergem which includes Liefmans. Best known for its Lucifer ale (8%) and Dentergems witbier.

Rochefort

The least known and most secretive of the Trappist breweries is situated deep in the Ardennes, at the Abbaye de St Rémy near the town of Rochefort.

The first brewery at the abbey, which used its own hops and barley grown in the grounds, dated from 1595, but the present one was built in 1960. More of the monks are involved in day-to-day brewing than at other blessed breweries, and three typically rich, dark Trappist beers are produced. These are all in the same basic style, but increasing in strength from the 6 (7.5%) through the 8 (9.2%) to the ultimate 10 (11.3%), and are known by their degree numbers.

Until quite recently, labels were not used; instead, the three beers were identified by the colour of their bottle caps – red for the 6, green for the 8 and blue for the 10. The chestnut-coloured and powerfully fruity 8, a complex, richly textured and richly rewarding beer is the most popular by far. The lighter, drier 6 is sold only locally, while the near-black 10 is overpowering in its heavy intensity.

KWAK

The story of Kwak is a marketing lesson in how to make your beer stand out at the bar. In a land where every brew seems to have its own distinctive glass, the Bosteels brewery of Buggenhout went one

better and designed a glass which could not stand up on its own. Every time a customer asks for a Kwak, it is served in a tall glass with a round bulbous bottom held erect by a wooden stand. Everyone in the bar knows at a glance when you order a Kwak. Pauwels Kwak (8%) is a warming, garnet-coloured ale named after a famous innkeeper who used to serve beer in stirrup cups to horsemen, for drinking in the saddle.

Roman

A large, family brewery near Oudenaarde, Roman dates back to 1545. It brews a range of East Flanders brown ales including Oudenaards (5%), the soft, bitter special (5.5%) and bottle-conditioned Dobbelen Bruinen (8%). It also brews a Christmas ale and various Pilsners mainly under the Romy brand, a wheat beer, Mater, and abbey beers under the Ename name.

St Bernardus

This West Flanders brewery, founded in 1946 at Watou specializes in producing abbey beers, both under its own name and that of St Sixtus, after the nearby brewing monastery at Westvleteren. The beer is matured for three months and then bottled without filtering. At one time the monastery used to licence the brewery to produce imitations of its own beers. St Bernardus brews a dark pater (6%), prior (8%), a golden tripel (7.5%) and a strong abt (10%).

St Jozef

Limburg family brewery in Opitter which produces a strong reddish lager Bokkereyer (5.8%).

Silly

Brewery in the Hainaut town since 1950 which brews a vast range of beers including Saison de Silly (5%).

Slaghmuylder

Ninove brewery best known for its quality abbey beers sold under the Witkap label.

Straffe Hendrik

This small brewery in the centre of the city of Bruges brews one ale, Brugse Straffe Hendrik (6%), the classic, hoppy Belgian pale ale.

Timmermans

Lambic brewers in Itterbeek since 1888, their range of lambics includes a fine kriek and Gueuze Caveau (both 5%), plus lighter, aromatic framboise, pêche and cassis (all 4%). They also brew a refreshing lambic wheat beer (3.5%) and a red Bourgogne des Flandres (6.5%).

Vander Linden

A small lambic brewer in Halle since 1893, Vander Linden brews a stronger than average range of lambics, which include a frambozenbier (7%), and the Vieux Foudre gueuze and kriek (both 6%). It also produces Dobbel Faro (6%) and an unusual Duivelsbier.

Westmalle

This Belgian monastic brewery, more than any other, has influenced and defined the abbey style. The monastery near the village of Westmalle, close to the Dutch border near Antwerp, was founded in 1794 by monks from the La Trappe monastery in France. It has been brewing since 1836, but only on a commercial scale since the 1920s. It is now the second largest of the five Belgian Trappist breweries. The brothers brew the defining dark dubbel and tripel. There is also a single, but this everyday drinking beer (4%), also known as Extra, is kept mainly for the monks themselves. The monks also produce a range of cheeses for sale.

Westvleteren

The St Sixtus abbey at Westvleteren, near Ypres in West Flanders, has been brewing since 1839. It is the smallest of the Trappist breweries. Its old brewery is small and its brews are much sought after, partly because they are difficult to obtain. The local beer drinkers queue at a hatch when they hear that a batch of bottles is ready for sale.

In order to meet growing public demand after the Second World War, the Westvleteren abbey for a time licensed the commercial St Bernardus brewery in nearby Watou to brew imitations of its St Sixtus beers. This licensing arrangement has now ceased, but St Bernardus still brews Sixtus beers for the nearby St Sixtus abbey.

RODENBACH

Rodenbach is one of the most remarkable breweries of Belgium. When you walk down the lines of upright old oak tuns, it is like stepping back into another age. The great porter breweries of England once looked like this, but only in Rodenbach have the imposing vessels survived to this impressive extent. There are 300 altogether, filling several halls. Some hold as much as 60,000 litres (13,198 gallons) and are over 100 years old.

The brewery, in Roeselare in West Flanders, was founded in 1820 and came to specialize in the region's sour red beers. A reasonably conventional ale is brewed, using Vienna crystal malt to impart a red colour. Rodenbach's distinct character arises from the way it is then matured. After a second fermentation, the beer is left in huge oak tuns for at least 18 months. During this time, it ages and sours. The inside of the tun is bare and uncoated, so the beer is also flavoured through direct contact with the wood.

Rodenbach only produces three beers – Rodenbach, Grand Cru and Alexander – sometimes called the Burgundies of Flanders. Other more conventional breweries have attempted to imitate these classic ales, but rarely use the same demanding craft.

THE NETHERLANDS

Wedged between the quality brewing found in Germany and the rich variety of Belgium, Dutch beer has always been a little flat in comparison. The country is best known for its international brands.

THE NETHERLANDS has suffered more than most countries from the concentration of its brewing industry into just a few hands. In the late 19th century over 1000 breweries existed, mainly concentrated in the south of the country due to the influence of the anti-alcohol Protestant church in the north. Now only about 30 breweries remain. The standard product of the early breweries was a traditional sweet, weak, brown table lager called oud bruin and brown dark boks (a Dutch style in its own right), but these styles were mostly usurped in the 20th century by a ubiquitous, rather bland, golden lager beer.

The international giant Heineken now dominates the beer market, closely followed by the Belgian giant Interbrew which in 1995 took over Oranjeboom. The Netherlands is also the home of one of the largest privately owned breweries in the world, Bavaria, which produces own-brand lagers for supermarkets around Europe. However, as the Dutch interest in speciality beers grows, small brewers producing more interesting varieties appear all the time, influenced by both the Belgian and German traditions.

Ales are the main area of interest in the Dutch micro-brewery movement, with many new alts, Kölsch-style ales and the occasional wheat beer. Some major producers have also added meiboks and dark boks to their product lines. Abbey-style beers are brewed by some secular breweries, either under licence or independently. The Netherlands is also the home of the Koningshoeven "Schaapskooi" brewery – the sixth Trappist brewer (the other five are in Belgium) producing top-fermented ales.

Above: Dutch lager brands such as Amstel have become familiar in many countries. Their fame is mainly a product of the companies' effective marketing .

The Beers

Alfa

A range of all-malt beers from the brewery of the same name, including a full-flavoured Edel (Noble) Pils, which is lagered for two months (5%), and two of the better Dutch boks – Lente Bok, brewed in the spring, and the darker Alfa Bokbier, (both 6.5%), brewed in the autumn. Alfa also produces an unfiltered midzomerbier (3.9%) in June.

Amber

This amber-coloured, top-fermented, alt-style ale (5%) from Grolsch has a good bitter, hoppy flavour.

Amersfoorts Wit

This spicy wheat beer (5%) is brewed by Drie Ringen in Amersfoort.

Ammeroois

A strong, bottle-conditioned ale (7%) from the Kuipertje brewery in Heukelum.

Amstel

Heineken's second-string brand name covers a range of beers, including a light lager, a hoppy Amstel 1870 (5%), the stronger Amstel Gold (7%), a robust dark, malty Amstel bokbier (7%) and the pale Amstel Lentebok (7%).

Arcener

See Arcen.

Bavaria 8.6

The numbers in the name refer to the strength of the beer (8.6%). It is brewed by the independent Bavaria brewery.

Bethanien

The Kölsch-style Bethanien (4.5%) is brewed by the Maximiliaan brewpub.

Brand Dubbelbok

A ruby-red, bottom-fermented, bok-style beer from the Brand brewery. A gold, top-fermented meibok (7%) is also brewed.

Briljant

A malty, mellow dort (6.5%) produced by the Kroon brewery of Oirschot.

Budel Alt

A deep-amber, smooth, strong, German-style ale (5.5%) with a nutty, malt flavour from the Budel brewery.

Buorren

This copper-coloured, sourish ale (6%) is produced by Us Heit.

Capucijn

This opaque-amber, fruity, smoky, abbey-style beer (6.5%) is brewed by Budel. The name – meaning a monk's cowl – is a reference to the religious connection of the abbey beer style.

Casper's Max

A tasty, copper-coloured, malty, sweet tripel (7.5%) produced by the Maximiliaan brewpub in Amsterdam.

Château Neubourg

This "luxury" brew (5%) is the top Pilsner from the Gulpener brewery near Maastricht.

Christoffel Blond

This quality all-malt, bottom-fermented beer (5%) is dry and heavily hopped. It is unfiltered and unpasteurized, and is available in bottle-conditioned form, including 2-litre (3.5-pint), swing-stopped jugs. The brewery also produces a good Munich-style lager.

Columbus

A strong, blond ale (9%) brewed by the home-brew house t'IJ in Amsterdam.

Dominator

A rich, fruity dort (6%) from the Dommelsch brewery. It is also sold under the brand name Hertog Jan Speciaal.

Drie Hoefijzers

See Oranjeboom Pilsner.

Drie Ringen Hoppenbier

A powerfully hoppy, rich fruit and malt-flavoured beer (5%) from the "Three Rings" brewery.

Egelantier

A copper-coloured, full-bodied, Munich-style lager (5%) which is produced by the Kroon brewery of Oirschot.

Enkel

See La Trappe.

Frysk Bier

This bitter, pale ale (6%) is brewed by Us Heit.

Gladiator

This strong, golden brew (10%) from the Gulpener brewery was launched in 1996.

Gouverneur

A bronze, sweetish Vienna-style lager from the Lindeboom brewery of Neer.

Grand Prestige

This powerful, dark, barley wine (10%) is produced by the Arcen brewery.

Grolsch Bokbier

This sweet, dark bok (6.5%) is a less well-known, but fine brew from Grolsch. There is also a dry, golden meibok.

Grolsch Pilsner

A fresh, hoppy Pilsner (5%), which is brewed using only malt, hops, yeast and water, and left unpasteurized in the bottle. (The canned premium lager is pasteurized.)

Gulpener Dort

A mellow, malty strong lager brewed using maize and caramel (6.5%) in the mash, which comes from the Gulpener brewery.

Heineken Oud Bruin

This smooth, lightly hopped weak table beer (2.5%) for easy drinking was first brewed over 50 years ago. There is also a stronger Heineken Special Dark (4.9%) for export.

Heineken Pilsner

A universally popular but rather bland Pilsner (5%). This is the Dutch giant's flagship brand.

Imperator

A quality all-malt, amber bokbier (6.5%), brewed using pale, chocolate and Munich malts by the Brand brewery of Wijlre.

Jubileeuw

An all-malt Pilsner (5%) from the Leeuw brewery.

Koningshoeven

See La Trappe.

Korenwolf

An aromatic, spicy, white beer (5%) from the Gulpener brewery. Korenwolf is made not only from wheat and barley but also oats and rye. It is named after the grain-loving hamster.

Kylian

Heineken's newly introduced top-fermented red ale (6.5%) with a smooth, gentle hops flavour, is based on the George Killian's Bière Rousse based on the old Irish recipe that is produced by its French subsidiary company, Pelforth.

La Trappe

A range of four Trappist top-fermenting, bottle-conditioned ales from the Koningshoeven Trappist monastery. The beers rise in strength starting from the pale-amber, fresh, fruity enkel (5.5%). Enkel is one of the few "single" strength Trappist ales brewed for the monks' everyday consumption that is available commercially. The dark, deep-red, dry dubbel (6.5%) is the next strongest brew, followed by a paler, bronze-coloured, spicier tripel (8%). The rich, reddish-coloured, vintage, heavyweight brew quadrupel (10%) makes an ideal nightcap for the dedicated beer drinker.

Lente Bok

One of the better Dutch boks, Lente Bok (6.5%) is brewed by Alfa.

Lingen's Blond

A weak table beer (2%) produced by Heineken.

Maltezer

A strong, malty dort lager (6.5%) from Ridder of Maastricht.

Maximator

A strong, spicy wheat beer (6.5%) produced by Maximiliaan, an Amsterdam brewpub opened in 1992, with the plant actually in the bar.

Maximiliaan Tarwebier

A sweetish tarwebier (5%) is brewed at the Maximiliaan brewpub. "Tarwebier" means "wheat beer".

Mestreechs Aajt

A refreshing sweet-and-sour, low-gravity summer brew (3.5%) from the Gulpener brewery. Mestreechs Aajt is a blend of oud bruin and a wild, spontaneously fermented beer, which has been aged in wooden tuns for a year.

Mug Bitter

This English-style Mug Bitter (5%) is brewed by the t'IJ micro-brewer.

Natte

This dark, abbey-style double ale (6%) is another beer brewed by the t'IJ micro-brewery.

Oranjeboom Pilsner

This mild, golden Pilsner (5%) is the main brew from the Drie Hoefijzers brewery in Breda.

Parel

A flavoursome, pale-gold, creamy, Kölsch-style beer (6%) from the Budel brewery of North Brabant.

Quintus

Rare old brown ale (6.5%) from the tiny Onder de Linden brewery in Wageningen.

Robertus

This reddish, malty bottom-fermenting beer (6%) from Christoffel is sold in bottle-conditioned form, unfiltered and unpasteurized.

Schele Os

This outstanding Belgian-style pale ale (7.5%) is an aromatic, orange ale made from barley, wheat and rye, by Maasland in Oss.

Sjoes

Some Dutch drinkers like to mix their dry Pilsner with a sweet oud bruin. Gulpener produced Sjoes (4.5%) with the two beers ready-mixed in one bottle.

Struis

This spicy, fruity dark brew (10%) is another strong ale from the t'IJ brewpub. The name means "ostrich" which is the brewpub's symbol.

Super Dortmunder

As strong as the name implies, this is the strongest Dutch dort available. At 7%, it is a ripe, fruity, export-style lager, brewed by the small Alfa brewery.

Superleeuw

This strong, rich, malty dort (6.5%) is brewed by the independent Leeuw brewery.

Sylvester

A strong, fruity, copper-coloured, top-fermented, winter ale (7.5%), from the Brand brewery of Wijlre.

Tarwebok

One of Heineken's new, more adventurous range of beers. This rich, dark wheat bok (6.5%) was introduced in 1992.

Urtyp Pilsner

This all-malt Urtyp Pilsner, also known as UP (5%), is brewed by Brand.

Valkenburgs Wit

A fruity, unfiltered wheat beer (4.8%), introduced in 1991, it comes from the Leeuw brewery of Valkenburg.

Van Vollenhoven Stout

Described as a stout, this full-bodied bottom-fermenting beer with added caramel and sugar is really a creamy, dark lager (6.5%). It is brewed by Heineken, and named after a brewery the giant company took over and closed down.

Venloosch Alt

A malty alt (4.5%) from the Leeuw brewery near Maastricht.

Volkoren Kerst

A Belgian-style, malty-brown winter ale (7%) from the Maasland brewery in Oss.

Wieckse Witte

Wieckse Witte is a softly spicy, lemony-tasting cloudy wheat beer (5%) from the Heineken subsidiary brewery, Ridder of Maastricht.

Witte Raaf

A tart, fruity wheat beer (5%) from the Raaf farmhouse brewery in Gelderland. The name Raaf means "raven".

Zatte

This abbey-style tripel (8%) with a spicy, hoppy taste is brewed by the home-brew house t'IJ.

Trading tradition

It should come as no surprise that the world's biggest beer exporter, Heineken, is a Dutch company. The Netherlands has a long history of vibrant overseas trade. It is one of the great maritime nations of the world, and its merchants have been shipping goods across the high seas for centuries.

THE BREWERS

Alfa

This independent family brewery at Schinnen has a reputation for quality all-malt beers, brewed using its own spring water.

Amstel

This Amsterdam brewery was bought by Heineken in 1968. Its name lives on as a Heineken brand.

Arcen

A pioneer of speciality beers in Limburg since 1981, Arcen's early emphasis on ales has recently switched to more mainstream lagers. Its beers appear under both the Arcener and Hertog Jan labels, including an abbey-style dark dubbel (7%) and an amber tripel (8.5%).

Bavaria

The large, independent Bavaria brewery has been brewing at Lieshout since 1719. It has flourished by brewing own-label Pilsners for supermarkets.

Brand

The Brand brewery at Wijlre, with its individual range of beers, claims to be the oldest in the country, dating back to the 14th century.

Budel

The small independent brewery at Budel near the Belgian border has been operating since 1870. It brews a Budel Pilsner and an unusual range of strong ales.

Christoffel

The small brewery was established by Leo Brand of the Dutch brewing family in Roermond in 1986 to brew quality all-malt beers. It is named after the town's patron saint. Its Pilsners are regarded as some of the best in the world.

De Kroon

The small independent brewery at Oirschot dates back to 1627. "The Crown" produces a range of full-flavoured lagers: light and dark bokbiers (all 6.5%), a brown Egelantier and a dort called Briljant.

Dommelsch

The brewery at Dommelen produces mainly Pilsners. Its Pilsner (5%) is also sold as Hertog Jan Pilsner. Dommelsch also brews a darker bokbier (6.5%).

Drie Ringen

"Three Rings" beers have been brewed in Amersfoort since 1989. It is now one of the larger of the new ventures. Its brews include a wheat beer, a pale ale, a meibok and an amber tripel.

Grolsch

Probably as well-known for its bottle as its beer, this large independent brewery in Groenlo was founded in the 17th century by Peter Cuyper. It stuck by its distinctive, swing-stoppered bottles, which date from 1897, when other breweries were phasing them out, claiming that they had become too expensive. However, the old-fashioned container became the company's most well-known characteristic. Grolsch's bottled Pilsner is sold unpasteurized, even in the export version. The company has been expanding into other countries since the early 1990s.

Gulpener

Brewing in the southernmost tip of the Netherlands, near Maastricht, since 1825, Gulpener is probably one of the most innovative of the country's more established companies. It produces a range of Pilsners, an oud bruin, and a dort. Gulpener has also developed two Dutch versions of Belgian-style beers.

Koningshoeven

The Gospel and the glass have never been more intimately connected than in the birth of the only Trappist brewery outside Belgium, established in 1884 in Koningshoeven, near Tilburg. The beer came first – the Schaapskooi (Sheep's pen) brewery was originally set up by the monks in order to fund the building of the monastery. Fortunately for the holy community, the blessed beer proved popular. The monastery's initial brews were lagers, thanks to a Bavarian brewmaster. The monastery introduced top-fermenting, bottle-conditioned ales in the 1950s. Today, there are four beers produced under the La Trappe brand, and also sold under the Koningshoeven label.

Leeuw

The independent Lion brewery was established in Valkenburg near Maastricht in 1886 on the site of a former gunpowder factory with a giant waterwheel. Today it brews a range of lagers including an all-malt Pilsner Jubileeuw brewed in honour of the centenary celebration in 1986, as well as an alt, an oud bruin, a winter wit, a meibok and a bokbier (6.5%).

Lindeboom

The small independent Linden Tree brewery was founded in 1870 in Neer, north of Roermond.

Today the brewery produces a variety of lagers including a Vienna-style Gouverneur, a quite bitter, dark, dry Lindeboom bokbier and a sweetish meibok (both 6.5%), as well as a dryish Pilsner (5%) and an oud bruin.

Maasland

This brewery was set up in 1989 in Oss and has been described as the Netherlands' best brewer of spiced ales. Besides the Belgian-style beers, there are two tasty boks.

Oranjeboom

The Orange Tree brewery, founded in Rotterdam in 1671, was once one of the largest breweries in the Netherlands. However, it was closed in 1990 and production moved to the Drie Hoefijzers (Three Horseshoes) brewery in Breda.

Oudaen

A grand brewpub in Utrecht, Oudaen is known for its wheat beers, including a strong tarwebok (6.8%).

Raaf

The Raven farmhouse brewery in Gelderland was revived in 1983, brewing a wide range of beers, including a tasty tripel (8.5%).

Ridder

The Knight brewery was founded in 1857 on the banks of the River Meuse in Maastricht. It brews a cloudy wheat beer, Wieckse Witte, a malty dort, Maltezer, a dark Ridder bokbier (7%) and a Ridder Pilsner (5%).

t'IJ

Probably the most striking home-brew house in the world. t'IJ, situated on Amsterdam's waterfront, is topped by a windmill. Established in 1984, the beers include two abbey-style beers and two strong ales – the blond Columbus and dark Struis. The last name means "ostrich", which is the brewpub's symbol. t'IJ also brews an English-style Mug Bitter.

Us Heit

Founded in a cowshed in Friesland in 1985, the Our Father brewery produces a good range of sourish ales. It also brews a bokbier (6%) and two Pilsners both (5%).

THE HEINEKEN STORY

Heineken's giant strides through the world of brewing began on December 16, 1863, when 22-year-old Gerard Adriaan Heineken bought the Haystack brewery (founded in 1572) in Amsterdam. His intention, he told his mother, was to tackle the staggering problem of alcoholism by offering the public a light beer as an alternative to the widely consumed strong spirits like gin. He found a ready market. Haystack was the largest brewery in the city, but he soon outgrew it and five years later a larger brewery was opened in Amsterdam. By 1874 the ambitious brewer

was already exporting, and in 1886 Heineken employed Dr Elion, a pupil of Louis Pasteur, to help develop a consistent Pilsner.

Heineken began to export its beers as far as Indonesia after the First World War. In 1933 the brewery made the first legal beer shipment to the United States after Prohibition ended, and today Heineken is the leading imported brand in the United States.

Heineken has acquired stakes in local breweries around the world and built foreign plants, so that Heineken now has over 100 breweries throughout the world.

Only the American giant Anheuser-Busch brews

more beer, but while Anheuser is primarily a US brewer, Heineken is an international force. The vast bulk of its business is outside the Netherlands. It sold 6.7 million hectolitres (147 million gallons) in 1996 in its native land, compared to 1,553 million worldwide. Heineken beer is sold in 170 countries; its second brand Amstel is available in 85.

Heineken in the Netherlands operates two vast plants at 's Hertogenbosch and Zoeterwoude, as well as

owning Brand and Ridder. Its old city brewery in Amsterdam is now a visitor centre.

Heineken concentrates on producing beers which appeal to the widest possible taste. However, since the early 1990s it has started to produce all-malt beers, rejecting the cheaper adjuncts like corn used by many major brewers. It has also extended the variety of its beers.

LUXEMBOURG

The Grand Duchy of Luxembourg, despite its position in the heart of Europe's brewing lands, is not famed for its beers. However, this tiny country has a proud brewing history and rolls out a surprisingly large quantity of beer each year.

ALTHOUGH IT IS BORDERED by Germany and Belgium Luxembourg's brews are more similar to those of its other neighbour, France. Luxembourg beers have neither the exciting variety of Belgium nor the purity of Germany, (brewers often use adjuncts in the mash). Nevertheless, Luxembourg has a long brewing tradition that can be traced back to the abbey at Altmünster in 1083. The abbey is the site of Les Brasseries Réunies de Luxembourg Mousel et Clausen, one of Luxembourg's leading brewers.

This small country has two other large brewing companies, Bofferding, which merged with Funck Bricher in 1975 to form Brasserie Nationale, the largest group, and Diekirch, which has brewed in the city of the same name since 1871. These breweries mainly brew a mild Pilsner and an export lager, and offer interesting specialities, such as strong seasonal Christmas beers or German-style dunkels.

A major family in the history of brewing in Luxembourg was the Funcks, in particular Henri Funck, whose name is commemorated on the lager Pils produced today by the Mousel group. The Brasserie Henri Funck, which he founded, was in the forefront of brewing technology for years and was among the first brewers to use refrigeration equipment and steel tanks. It became part of the Brasseries Réunies group in 1982.

Above: At the beginning of the 19th century Luxembourg had about 60 breweries. Diekirch is one of the handful of brewers that have managed to survive into the 20th century.

Two of the most interesting small breweries in Luxembourg are the Brasserie Battin, founded by Charles Battin in 1937, which produces four beers sold under the Battin label, and the Wiltz brewery, which has been owned by the Simon family since 1891. This was totally destroyed in the Ardennes offensive at the end of the Second World War and was rebuilt in 1954.

The domestic market in Luxembourg is small, and the main groups survive by concentrating on the export markets, particularly Belgium and France. Almost a third of all the beer produced is exported.

THE BEERS

Altmünster
A firm-bodied, Dortmunder-style beer (5.5%) from Brasseries Réunies.

Bofferding Christmas Béier
This brown, seasonal ale (5.5%) is produced annually by Bofferding.

Bofferding Lager Pils
This refreshing, Pilsner-style lager (4.8%) is brewed using pale malt and corn (maize) and is lagered for a month.

Diekirch Exclusive
A strong, Pilsner-style lager (5.2%) produced by one of the largest brewers in Luxembourg.

Fréijoers
A refreshing, unfiltered beer (4.8%) produced by Bofferding.

Hausbeier
A tasty, all-malt beer (5.5%) brewed by Bofferding.

Henri Funck Lager Beer
This Pilsner (4.8%) is brewed by Mousel to a similar recipe to Mousel Premium. Both use 10% rice in the mash, producing a light, refreshing, bright gold beer.

Luxembourg
Two beers are produced under this brand name, Luxembourg Lager (3%) and the stronger Luxembourg Export (4%). Both are brewed by Mousel.

Mansfeld
A malty Pilsner (4.8%) from Mousel.

Régal
The export-style beer (5.5%) from the Wiltz brewery.

Simon Noël
A rich, dark, Christmas beer (7.5%) from the small brewery in Wiltz, run by the Simon family. They also produce Simon Pils (5.8%) and Simon Régal (5.5%).

THE BREWERS

Battin
This is the smallest of the Grand Duchy's breweries which, along with the similar-sized Wiltz brewery, produces arguably the best beers. Founded in 1937 in Esch-sur-Alzette, it brews an Edelpils, Gambrinus, a fuller-bodied urtyp and darker Battin Dunkel.

Bofferding
The brewery in Bascharge dates back to 1842, and it merged with Funck-Bricher in 1975 to form the country's largest brewing group, Brasserie Nationale. Its main beer is a Bofferding Lager Pils (4.8%), but it also brews an all-malt Hausbeier, a brown Bofferding Christmas Béier (both 5.5%) and the unfiltered, refreshing Fréijoers.

Below: Bofferding, part of Brasserie Nationale, dates back to 1842.

Diekirch
One of Luxembourg's biggest three breweries, this company has brewed in Diekirch since 1871. Besides Diekirch Light (2.9%) and the pale Diekirch Premium Pilsner (4.8%), it brews a mellow, lager, Diekirch Exclusive (5.1%), the amber Diekirch Grande Réserve (6.9%) and a brune (5.2%).

Mousel
Les Brasseries Réunies de Luxembourg Mousel et Clausen brew two similar Pilsners, Mousel Premium and Henri Funck (both 4.8%), and a malty Mansfeld.

Wiltz
This small brewery, founded in 1824, was bought by the Simon family in 1891, who have run it since then. The buildings were totally destroyed during the Second World War.

GERMANY

Drinkers across the world tend to regard Germany as the land of lager, the country where bottom-fermenting beers reign supreme. There is, however, much more to German beer than overflowing steins at the Munich Beer Festival.

No country takes more pride in the quality of its beer, and although the rules of the beer purity law the Rheinheitsgebot, mean that German brewers cannot indulge in the wilder flights of fancy of the Belgian brewers, there is still plenty of variety to be found, and excellent quality.

Top-fermenting ales are still brewed, notably the alts of Düsseldorf and kölsches of Cologne. There has also been a revival in demand for wheat beers. Within the lager market, beers vary – from sharp, hoppy Pilsners in the north to the softer, maltier brews of Bavaria. The glasses shimmer with all the colours of the ripening barley field, from pale golden helles through copper-coloured marzens and darker dunkels and bocks to black beers. There are even a few exotic types, such as the smoked beers of Bamberg. All of these brews comply with the rules that prohibit the use of cheap adjuncts and inferior materials.

No people are more loyal to their local beers. The beer marketplace is fragmented, regionally oriented and highly conservative. Unlike most other countries, there are few national beer brands. People stick to their home-town brews. This has meant that many more breweries have survived in Germany than in other European countries, with around 1,200 still steaming away. Cologne, a city of only one million people, has 23 breweries, and there are some 700 in the Bavarian countryside, where the clock appears to have stopped in another era altogether and almost every village has its own brewhouse. Some local breweries have closed, but since the late 1970s a new wave has sprung up, with over 150 brewpubs opening in the last 20 years, catering for a wide range of tastes. About 30% of all the breweries in the world are in Germany.

Above: Much of the revival in the popularity of wheat beers has been due to the perceived health-giving properties of the cloudy, yeasty brew.

THE BEERS

Abtstrunk
The word "Abt" (abbot) reveals the monastic links of the makers of this thick, potent, liqueur-like beer, (11.5%) which is brewed in a former abbey guesthouse at Irsee near Munich.

Achd Bambarcha Schwarzla
The name of this dark, mellow beer (5.3%) means "true Bamberg black". It is produced by the Klosterbräu in Bamberg, the oldest brewer of rauchbier, dating back to 1533. Its small plant was once run by monks.

Aecht Schlenkerla Rauchbier
This is a classic smoked beer (4.8%) from the Bamberg region. It has a light, fresh, smoked flavour and a dry malt aftertaste. It is produced by the Heller Brauerei in Bamberg for the Schlenkerla tavern.

Alt Franken
See Urfrankisch Dunkel.

Altstadthof Hausbier
A fruity, unfiltered but quite flat, dark lager (4.8%) produced by the small Altstadthof brewery in Nuremberg.

Alt Wetzlar
This is not an Altbier in style, but a dark lager, brewed by Euler in Wetzlar, north of Frankfurt.

Apostulator
A dark, ruby-coloured Doppelbock (7.5%) with a fruity, malt taste. This brew is produced by the Eichbaum brewery of Mannheim.

Arcobräu Coronator Doppelbock
An auburn-coloured Doppelbock (7.5%) with a strong malty flavour, from Graf Arco of Bavaria.

Arcobräu Dunkel Weisse
A cloudy, amber-brown wheat beer (5.2%) with a clean, citrus flavour, from this family owned company.

Arcobräu Urweisse
A refreshing, apple-tasting, unfiltered, cloudy, gold Bavarian wheat beer (4.8%) from Graf Arco.

Astra
A range of gold, hoppy Pilsners from the Bavaria St Pauli brewery of Hamburg. The Astra label also has a gold Bock with a light malt flavour.

Aventinus
This classic, extra-strong wheat beer (8%) or Weizen Doppelbock comes from the specialist wheat beer brewers Schneider of Bavaria. Conditioned in the bottle, Aventinus has a deep reddish-brown colour, a creamy head and a warming, rich, fruity taste.

Ayinger Altbayerische Dunkel
A deep-red lager with a malty flavour and pleasant aftertaste, produced by the quality Ayinger brewery.

Ayinger Bräu-Weisse
A pale wheat beer (5.1%) with a tart, fruity taste, produced by Ayinger.

Ayinger Maibock
A pale-gold, traditional maibock with a complex hop flavour, from the Privatbrauerei Franz Inselkammer in Aying.

Beck's
One of Germany's best-known beers on the international market, this crisp, dry Pilsner (5%) has been brewed in the northern port of Bremen since 1874. It is Germany's leading export beer, with more than six million hectolitres sold every year in more than 100 countries. It accounts for more than 85% of German beer exports to the United States. Beck's also brews a deep-amber, dark beer and a dry, malty Oktoberfest brew.

Bernauer Schwarzbier
This is a very dark, creamy, chocolate-tasting, smooth Schwarzbier from the Berliner Bürgerbräu. It is named after the town of Bernau, once known for the black beer style.

Bitburger
Bitburger (4.8%) is a dry, aromatic and hoppy Pilsner from Bitburg in the Rhienland. It is allowed to mature for a three months, making it a classic of its style, and the second-best-selling Pilsner in Germany.

Brauhernen Pilsner
A pale-gold, dry, bitter Pilsner with a hoppy aftertaste (4.9%), produced by Einbecker.

Braumeister
This bright-gold Bavarian Pilsner is produced by the leading Munich brewer Hacker-Pschorr. It has a pleasant, toasted-malt and hop flavour.

Bremer Weisse
This refreshing summer beer with only 2.7% alcohol is a Bremen variation of a Berliner Weisse. The producer, Haake-Beck still delivers its beers locally by horse-drawn drays.

Brinkhoff's No. 1
A smooth, bright-gold, premium Pilsner from DUB of Dortmund, this beer is named after an early brewer.

EINBECKER BEER – A MEDIEVAL TRADITION

The reputation of Einbecker beer is said to have been built on a remarkable communal operation. The Lower Saxony town of Einbeck was once the major brewing centre for the medieval Hanseatic League of north German trading towns. It developed a style of strong beers – bocks – brewed to survive long journeys.

In the Middle Ages, every citizen in the town brewed, using a communal copper which was wheeled around 700 homes. The door arches of the old buildings had to be high to accommodate the vessel. The citizens then sold their beer to the town council, which traded it through the Hanseatic League. The strong beer gained a widespread following – even Martin Luther praised it. Its reputation caused the Bavarian dukes to entice an Einbeck brewmaster to Munich, so spreading the brewing of bock – or beck – beer to southern Germany, where it is mainly brewed today.

Broyhan Alt

A strong, malty Altbeer (5.2%) in the Düsseldorf style. This beer is produced by the Lindener Gilde brewery of Hannover and it is named after a famous Hannover brewer.

Busch Golden Pilsner

A golden Pilsner-style beer produced by the local Busch brewery in Limburg near Koblenz. Despite its name the brewery has no connection with America's brewing giant Anheuser-Busch.

Carolus

This very deep, ruby-brown-coloured strong Doppelbock (7.5%) has an unusual, complex, fruity taste. It is brewed by Binding of Frankfurt.

CD

A popular, brilliant-gold, sweetish Pilsner, named after Carl Dinkelacker, who founded the brewery in Stuttgart in 1888.

Celebrator

This export name is mainly used in the US for the classic, dark-red, velvety Doppelbock, Fortunator (7.2%), from the Ayinger brewery.

Clausthaler

This pioneering non-alcohol lager (0.5%) took Binding of Frankfurt years to develop before it was launched in 1979. It virtually created a whole new beer sector on its own.

Cluss Bock

This malty, dark-copper-coloured Bock is brewed by the Cluss brewery.

DAB Original

This is the premium version of Meister Pils from DAB in Dortmund. It is a golden, grassy, hoppy beer (5%).

Dampfbier

Dampfbier is an unusual top-fermented reddish ale (4.9%) from the Maisel brewery of Bayreuth in Bavaria, which is not unlike a fruity English bitter. The word "Dampf" means steam.

Delicator

This dark, fruity Doppelbock (7.5%) is brewed by the famous Hofbräuhaus of Munich.

Diebels Alt

A brown, biscuity Altbier (4.8%) from the Privatbrauerei Diebel in Issum Weidernhein.

Dom Kölsch

A leading kölsch beer in Cologne named after the cathedral.

Dom Pilsner

This dry Pilsner is brewed by the Euler brewery of Wetzlar.

DUB Export

Dortmunder Union Brewery brews this smooth, malty Export (5%). DUB also produces Pilsners, most notably its hoppy Siegel Pilsner and the premium Brinkhoff's No. 1.

Duckstein

An unusual, fruity, amber ale, matured over beechwood chips. It is produced by the Feldschlösschen Brewery of Brunswick.

Echt Kölsch

This delicate beer, regarded as the true Kölschbier, was originally produced at a home-brew pub, P. J. Früh's Cölner Hofbräu, near Cologne Cathedral. Demand became so great, however, that Echt Kölsch is no longer brewed behind the tavern, but at a brewery outside the city centre.

Einbecker Maibock

A deep, golden-amber-coloured, malty, seasonally brewed spring Bock (6.5%) produced by the Einbecker brewery.

Einbecker Urbock

This bright-gold, smooth, strong, hoppy Bock beer (6.5%) is produced by the Einbecker brewery.

EKU Pils

A soft creamy Bavarian Pilsner (5%) brewed by the Erste Kulmbacher Union of Kulmbach, a brewery best known for its heavy, extra-strong lager, Kulminator 28.

Erdinger Weissbier

This range of top-fermented wheat beers from the Erdinger brewery is brewed strictly according to the Bavarian purity law. It includes a cloudy Hefe (5.3%), a sparkling Kristallklar (5.3%) and a reddish-brown, strong, spicy, dark Dunkel (5.6%).

Euler Landpils

This Pilsner comes from the independent Euler brewery in Wetzlar.

Feldschlösschen

Feldschlösschen Pilsner is a leading Pilsner brand for Holsten. The large north German Feldschlösschen brewery in Brunswick is part of the Holsten group. Feldschlösschen also produces the distinctive Duckstein amber ale and Brunswick alt.

Fest-Märzen

This marzen-style beer (5.8%) is produced by Ayinger of Bavaria.

Feuerfest

This dark, fruity, warming "fire festival" Doppelbock (10%) is produced in limited-edition, wax-sealed bottles by Schäffbräu of Treuchtlingen, near Nuremberg in Bavaria.

First

A popular, pale-gold Pilsner (4.8%) with a grainy flavour, produced by Ritter of Dortmund.

Fortunator

This rich, dark-red, velvety Doppelbock (7.2%) is brewed by Ayinger.

Franz Joseph Jubelbier

This strong, dark lager (5.5%) is named after the monarch. It is brewed by the south Bavarian Altenmünster brewery near Augsburg.

Franziskaner

A range of wheat beers from the famous Spaten brewery of Bavaria. The wheat brews, which now account for more than half of Spaten's production, include the cloudy but refreshing hefe-weissbier, a filtered, grassy Kristallklar and a Dunkel (all 5%).

Freiberger Pils

This hoppy Pilsner is the best-known beer from the sizeable Freiberger Brauhaus in the old colliery town of Freiberg.

Fürstenberg Pilsner

The widely available, bright-gold, hoppy, dry premium Fürstenberg Pilsner (5%) is the best-known beer of the Fürstenberg brewery, which also produces a range of other brews including three wheat beers.

Gatz Alt

The brown, fruity Gatz Alt (4.8%) is produced by Gatzweiler, the family brewers of Alt, in Düsseldorf. There is also a non-alcohol version. The original Düsseldorf brewery was in the brewpub Zum Schlüssel and still brews.

Gilde Pils

This pale-gold Pilsner with a dry finish (5%) comes from Hannover's Lindener Gilde brewery. As its name implies, the brewery was once run by a city guild.

Hacker-Pschorr Edelhell

This is one of the stronger speciality beers (5.5%) from the Hacker-Pschorr brewery in Munich, which dates back to 1417. Its more popular lagers are fruity Hell (5%) and Dunkel (5.2%).

Hacker-Pschorr Oktoberfest Märzen

This Märzen beer (5.8%) is brewed in Munich for the famous Oktoberfest, by Hacker-Pschorr.

HB Hofbräuhaus München

The premium lager (4.9%) brewed at the former Bavarian Royal Court brewery in Munich.

Holsten Pils

The widely available premium Pilsner (5%) from the Holsten brewery is one of that firm's famous dry, hoppy range from Hamburg.

Hopf Dunkler-Bock

This unusually rich and tangy Dunkler-Bock wheat beer (6.3%) comes from the small Hopf family brewery in the Bavarian Alps at Miesbach that specializes in wheat beers.

Hopf Weisse Export

The fruity, but not hoppy, Weisse Export (5.3%) is a wheat beer from Hopf.

Hubertus

Hubertus is a robust, copper-coloured Bock (6.8%) from Hacker-Pschorr of Munich. The brewery's doppelbock is called Animator (7.5%).

Jahrhundert

A golden, export-style beer (5.5%) from Ayinger of Bavaria. It was originally produced to celebrate its centenary in 1978.

KALTENBERG CASTLE

Once upon a time, almost all aristocratic families brewed their own beer, and this tradition continues in the fairy-tale Kaltenberg Castle in the village of Geltendorf, 50km from Munich. The spires of Kaltenberg tower over the cellars where the beer is lagered. However, most Kaltenberg beers, including its Pilsner and Prinzregent wheat beers, are now produced at a modern brewery in Fürstenfeldbruck.

Jever

This is probably the most bitter beer produced in Germany. Jever Pilsner underlines the general German rule that beers become drier as you travel north. The town of Jever is in Friesland. The brewery of the same name, dating back to 1848, is famed for its Pilsner (4.9%), which has a heady, hoppy aroma and an intense bitterness. Owned by Bavaria St Pauli of Hamburg since 1923, a modern brewery was built in 1992 in this old North Sea resort. Its other brews include Jever Light (2.7%) and the alcohol-free Jever Fun.

Kaiserdom

The most widely available Rauchbier (4.8%) (smoked beer) from Bamberg has been brewed by the Bavarian town's Bürgerbräu brewery since 1716. Although it is not the most intensely smoky beer of its type, it will still surprise the unsuspecting drinker with its fume-filled flavour. The Bamberg brewery also produces more conventional lagers, Extra-Dry (4.9%) and Pilsner (4.8%), as well as a delicious apricot-coloured Weissbier (5.3%).

Kaiser Pilsner

The black-labelled bottles of this premium Pilsner (4.8%) from Henninger of Frankfurt have become familiar around the world.

Kaltenberg

See König Ludwig.

Kapuziner

A range of wheat beers from the Mönchshof brewery of Kulmbach in Bavaria which has monastic origins. The name means "monk's hood" and the beers include two heady, unfiltered brews, Kapuziner Dunkel and Hefetrub (both 5.2%).

Kindl Berliner Weisse

The pale, sour, refreshing wheat beer (2.5%), once called "the champagne of the north" is a speciality of Berlin. It is often laced with fruit juices. The large Kindl brewery was founded in Berlin in 1872 and brews several conventional beers, including Kindl Schwarzbier. The main rival brewer of Berliner Weisse is Schultheiss.

Kloster-Urtrunk

The tasty, unfiltered marzen Kloster-Urtrunk (5.6%) is brewed by Irseer Klosterbräu near Munich.

Kloster Urweisse

Kloster Urweisse (5.2%) is a tasty wheat beer from Irseer Klosterbräu near Munich. The name means "original white".

König Ludwig

König Ludwig Dunkel (5.1%) is named after "mad" King Ludwig II of Bavaria. The Dunkel is one of the beers still brewed by Prince Luitpold, heir to the throne of Bavaria, at his Kaltenburg Castle brewery in Geltendorf.

König-Pilsener

A pleasant, dry Pilsner (4.9%), with a faintly appley flavour, from the König brewery, Duisberg.

Korbinian

This dark-amber Doppelbock (7.4%) with a rich, malt flavour, is produced by the Weihenstephan brewery, a former monastery brewery at Freising.

Köstritzer Schwarzbier

Köstritzer Schwarzbier (4.6%) is a smoothly chocolatey, bitter, bottom-fermented beer with a 450-year-old reputation as a sustaining drink for invalids. Goethe drank the revered drop while recovering from illness. It comes from the Köstritz black beer brewery in the former East German spa town of Bad Köstritz in Thuringia.

Kräusen

Kräusen is an unusual, unfiltered, cloudy version of the standard Pilsner, brewed by Haake-Beck of Bremen. It was introduced to the north German market in 1985.

Kronen Classic

This is the golden premium Pilsner (5.3%) with a slightly sour, hoppy taste, from the popular independent, family-owned Kronen brewery in Dortmund. It also brews a robust, malty export.

Kulminator 28

One of the strongest beers in the world, the threateningly named Kulminator 28 has an alcohol content of more than 12% – the highest gravity of any bottom-fermenting beer. The brew is matured for nine months, including a short period of freezing, to produce this intensely malty, heavyweight, amber beer.

There is a less threatening and darker conventional Kulminator Doppelbock (7.6%) without the number. Both of the beers are brewed by EKU in the Bavarian town of Kulmbach, and are widely exported.

Küppers Kölsch

This deep-gold sweetish kölsch comes from the largest brewer of kölsch in Cologne.

Kutscher Alt

A malty, copper-coloured Alt (5%) that is smooth and gently warming. This beer is brewed by Binding of Frankfurt. It is top-fermented, then cold-conditioned in the classic Altbier style.

Lammsbräu Pils

Lammsbräu's pale, amber, delicately fresh and citric organic Pilsner (5%) was introduced in the late 1980s. It is brewed by the small Lammsbräu brewery at Neumarkt, near Nuremberg, using barley and hops grown without artificial fertilizers or pesticides. Some claimed that it was purer than the requirements of the Rheinheitsgebot – much to the annoyance of larger brewers, although this did not prevent others trying their own "bio beers".

Leichter Typ

This light, low-calorie beer from Eichbaum has a strength of just 2%.

Löwenbräu Hefe Weissbier

An unpasteurized, unfiltered, slightly cloudy, wheat beer (5.0%) which comes from the best-known of the Munich breweries. The Hefe Weissbier is produced using Löwenbräu ale yeast, malted wheat, spring barley and Hallertau hops. A filtered version of the Hefe style, which is clear, is also available, called Klares Weissbier. This version has a distinctive flavour rather like a wheaty lager.

Löwenbräu Oktoberfest

A subtle, light, bottom-fermented Reinheitsgebot beer (6.1%) that is specially brewed each year for the Munich Oktoberfest.

Löwenbräu Premium Pils

This light, refreshing, golden lager is made in Munich under the Bavarian purity law, with Hallertau hops, spring barley and yeast.

Maisel Pilsner

This pale-gold, aromatic Pilsner with a good malt and hops taste (4.8%) is brewed by the Maisel brewery, the largest brewery in the famous Bavarian opera town of Bayreuth, which also produces a good range of fruity wheat beers.

Meister Pils

This gold Pilsner with a fresh, zesty taste, comes from DAB of Dortmund. The name, which means champion, is also used by the Schwaben brewery of Stuttgart for its Pilsner.

Mönchshof Kloster Schwarzbier

This deep-copper-coloured Schwarzbier with a smooth, malt flavour comes from the old Mönchshof brewery in Kulmbach, Bavaria. The brewery has monastic origins and is known for its strong, dark lagers.

Oberdorfer

This is a range of wheat beers from the Franz-Joseph Sailer brewery in Marktoberdorf in Bavaria, one of which is sold mixed half and half with lemonade.

Optimator

An orangey-coloured, strong Doppelbock (6.8%) with a smooth, roasted, malt flavour, brewed by Spaten of Munich.

Pikantus

This strong, russet-coloured Weizenbock (7.3%) is brewed by wheat-beer specialists Erdinger of Bavaria.

Pilsissimus

This hoppy Pilsner (5.2%) is very highly thought of by the patrons of the Forschungs brewpub in the Perlach

Pinkus Hefe Weizen
This cloudy, gold, unfiltered wheat beer (5%) with a citrus and wheat flavour is an organic beer which is produced by the Pinkus Müller home-brew house in Münster.

Prinzregent
This range of wheat beers, named after Prince Luitpold, includes an unfiltered hell,and a brown, spicy, malt-flavoured Dunkel Weissbier (both of them 5%). They are brewed by Kaltenberg in Bavaria.

Radeberger Pilsner
This bright-gold, hoppy Pilsner is the flagship brew of the Radeberger brewery near Dresden in the former East Germany. It was once supplied to the King of Saxony.

Ratsherrn
A brand name that is applied to a hoppy, dry Pilsner and malty Bock from the Elbschloss brewery of Hamburg on the River Elbe. Both beers are unpasteurized.

Ratskeller Edel-Pils
This bright-gold, hoppy, premium Pilsner is brewed by the Lindener Gilde brewery of Hannover.

Rauchenfelser Steinbier
This unique speciality is brewed using an ancient process. When all brewing vessels were made of wood, it was risky to use direct flames to heat them, so instead rocks were fired to high temperatures and then placed in the wort to bring it to the boil. In 1983, Gerd Borges revived this process at Neustadt near Coburg. The white-hot stones not only make the brew bubble, but also cause sugars to caramelize on their surface. The top-fermented beer is then matured for two to three months with the sugar-coated rocks. The result is a tawny-coloured Steinbier (4.8%) that is both smooth and smoky. There is also a Steinweizen made using the same process. In 1993, as part of the Franz Joseph Sailer group, the brewing was moved to Altenmünster in southern Bavaria.

Reichelbräu Eisbock
This is a Bockbier (10%) that is strengthened by freezing for two weeks and removing the ice. The dark, warming brew is then matured in oak casks for two months. It is brewed by Reichelbrau in Kulmbach, Bavaria.

Romer Pilsner
A popular, yellow-gold, dry Pilsner (5%) with a classical image, brewed by the giant Binding brewery of Frankfurt. It is a quality brew with a dry, hop finish.

St Georgen Keller Bier
This is the speciality of the St Georgen brewery, an unfiltered lager (4.9%) bursting with hops, which is even exported in bottle to the United States. The small Bavarian village brewery in Buttenheim brews some of the hoppiest beers in the region, including a very dry marzen (5.6%).

St Jakobus
This quality pale Bock (7.5%) is produced by the Forschungs brewpub in the Perlach suburb of Munich. The brewpub is only open in summer.

Salvator
The pioneer of the Doppelbock style from the famous Paulaner brewery of Munich. This rich, ruby brew (7.5%) is overpowering with its fruit-cake aroma and deep, warming flavour.

Sanwald
The wheat beers from the Dinkelacker brewery of Stuttgart include a bright-gold, light, dry hefe weiss and a sparkling, tawny-amber Weizen Krone.

Schierlinger Roggen
This rare, red-amber rye (Roggen) beer (4.7%) is brewed by the local brewery in Schierling, Bavaria. Launched in 1988, it is similar to a dark wheat beer, but with a more tangy, grainy taste. The mash contains 60% rye. The brewery was once part of a convent.

Schlenkerla
The classic and most uncompromising Rauchbier (4.8%), this smoked speciality of Bamberg in Bavaria is brewed from malt kilned over beechwood fires. The result is a pitch-black brew with a pungent flavour of burnt malt. This dry, smoky beer used to be brewed on the premises at the Schlenkerla tavern in Bamberg, but is now produced at the nearby Heller brewery dating back to 1678.

Schneider Weisse
A refreshing, yeasty wheat beer (5.4%) brewed by the Schneider brewery. This is the classic example of the Weisse style. Besides the Original Hefeweizenbier the brewery also produces a filtered Kristall, a weaker Weizen-hell (4.9%), and a light (2.9%).

OKTOBERFEST

Mention Germany and beer, and many people envisage Munich's famous Oktoberfest, when in just 16 days, around six million litres (1,319,814 gallons) of beer will be drunk in huge canvas beer halls by thousands of visitors. It is the world's biggest beer festival – though it is not in October, but in the last two weeks of September. This mad annual party began when the Bavarian Prince Ludwig married Princess Theresa in 1810, and the city threw a huge celebration. It was such a success that it has been repeated ever since. Only the six major breweries in Munich are allowed to supply beer – to the annoyance of many other Bavarian brewers. In 1882 Spaten created the amber-coloured, Oktoberfest beer which caused such a sensation that it has been served ever since!

Above: A happy participant of the Munich Oktoberfest at the end of the 19th century, complete with his stein of beer and tobacco pipe.

Left: The Hacker-Pschorr beer tent at the Oktoberfest. Only the six main breweries of Munich are allowed to supply beer at the festival.

Below: One of six million litres of beer being drunk at the Oktoberfest. In fact, the festival takes place at the end of September.

SPATEN AND THE LAGER REVOLUTION

Spaten is a Munich brewery whose name means "spade". It was at the heart of the bottom-fermenting lager revolution, which swept the world in the 19th century. Brewer Gabriel Sedlmayr pioneered the production of dark and amber lagers in the 1830s and later developed the use of refrigeration and steam power. Spaten is still justly proud of its lagers today, notably its malty Münchner Hell (4.8%) and dunkel (5%) and its classic, full-bodied Ur-Märzen (5.6%). It also brews a dry Pilsner (5%), a golden maibock (6.5%) and a strong Doppelbock called Optimator (6.8%). Its range of wheat beers under the Franziskaner label now accounts for more than half of all production.

Schöfferhofer
The range of Bavarian-style wheat beers from Binding of Frankfurt includes a tasty and lively Hefeweizen, a filtered golden, yeasty kristall and a dark dunkel (all around 5%).

Schultheiss Berliner Weisse
This is one of the most distinctive examples of the Berliner Weisse style, the pale, sourish, weak type of wheat beer that is favoured in the north. Major Berlin brewer Schultheiss blends fresh and more mature brews in order to create its bottle-conditioned Weisse (3%).

Schultheiss Pilsner
This hoppy Pilsner is the best-known brew in Germany from the Berlin Schultheiss brewery.

Starkbier
This strong, brown Starkbier (6.8%) has a dry, malty flavour. It is brewed by Irseer Klosterbräu just outside Munich.

Stauder TAG
This is a strong, dry, hoppy Pilsner (5.3%). The initials stand for Treffliches Altenessen Gold. It is brewed by a family brewery in Essen, which was founded in 1867. It also brews a soft standard Pilsner (4.6%).

Stephansquell
An amber, full-bodied Doppelbock (6.8%). This beer is brewed in Freising by the Weihenstephan brewery.

Triumphator
A seasonal, strong Doppelbock brewed by Löwenbräu of Munich.

Ureich Pils
This dry, gold Pilsner (4.8%) with a strong hop taste is the flagship brew from the Eichbaum brewery of Mannheim.

Urfrankisch Dunkel
This dark, malty Dunkel (4.4%) is bottled as Alt Franken. It is produced by the large Nuremberg Tucher brewery, which brews a wide range of traditional Bavarian beers.

Ur-Krostitzer
This crisp Pilsner (which should not be confused with Köstritzer Schwarzbier) comes from the former East German Krostitz brewery in the town of Krostitz near Leipzig.

Urstoff
This heavy, reddish-brown Doppelbock with a smooth, malt flavour, is produced by the Mönchshof Kloster brewery in Kulmbach.

Ur-Weisse
A wheat beer, Ur-Weisse (5.8%) uses 60% wheat in the mash and is bursting with flavour. It is slightly darker and more full-flavoured than the other wheat beers brewed by the Ayinger brewery.

Warsteiner
This bright, pale-gold Pilsner (4.8%) is the best-selling beer in Germany. The family brewery in Warstein has had to double its output over five years to six million hectolitres (13,19,814,000 gallons) in 1995, in order to keep up with demand.

Weizenhell
A slightly hazy, light-coloured wheat beer (4.9%) brewed by Schneider of Kelheim near Regensburg.

Witzgall Vollbier
A sweetish, copper-coloured lager from Schlammersdorf in Franconia.

Würzig
The name, meaning "spicy", is applied to two distinctive bottom-fermenting beers from the Hofmark brewery: Würzig Mild and Würzig Herb (meaning dry), both with a strength of 5.1%.

The former is a malty brew and the latter is sharply hoppy. Known for its distinctive swing-stoppered bottles, the traditional east Bavarian Hofmark brewery dates back to 1590. It still uses beechwood chips to clear its beers.

THE BREWERS

There are so many brewers in Germany that it is impossible even to list every German brewery of note. The following firms are worthy of honourable mention.

MAJOR BREWERIES

Augustiner

This is the least known brewery outside Munich, but possibly the most popular inside the town, probably because it produces lagers most faithful to the Bavarian city's malty tradition. This is especially true of its pale, smoothly soft hell (5.2%). It was once a monastic brewery dating back to 1328. Its connections with the holy order were broken in 1803. Its grand 19th-century brewhouse, built in 1885, is now a protected building. It has its own maltings in cellars beneath. Locally, some of its beers are still served from wooden casks.

Ayinger

"The most beautiful thing about Munich is the road to Aying", claims this well-respected country brewer, and it is not far wrong. This family brewery lies at the heart of a picturesque Bavarian village on the edge of the Alps, with its own guest house and beer garden. The beer matches the surroundings. The brewery produces a wide range of specialities: a Hell, an Altbairisch Dunkel, a Pilsner, three Bocks, a golden export-style beer called Jahrhundert-Bier, a Fest-Märzen, three Ayinger wheat beers, and a standard Hefe Weisse Bräu-Weisse (5%).

Beck's

An innovative brewer, Beck's of Bremen has been brewing its famous Beck's Pilsner in the northern port since 1874. Early in the 20th century it was one of the first breweries to invest in ice machines and to cultivate a pure yeast culture. In 1917 it merged with its main export rival in Bremen, St Pauli. Between the wars the company also built two overseas breweries in Singapore and Djakarta in Malaya, these were lost in 1945 but Beck's licensed a brewery in China in 1992. Its sister company Haake-Beck brews a range of beers for the local market.

Binding

Binding is Germany's second-largest brewing group. The company is based in Frankfurt, where it celebrated its 125th anniversary in 1995.

The large brewing group includes DAB of Dortmund, Kindl of Berlin, and the Radeberg and Krostitz breweries in the former East Germany.

Binding has the distinction of having virtually created the alcohol-free beer market in Germany with its dominant Clausthaler brand, which it launched successfully in 1979. This now contains (0.45%) alcohol. German law specifies that non-alcoholic beer should not contain more than (0.5%) alcohol which is about the same percentage as apple juice.

The company also brews Romer Pilsner, two Binding Exports, a Doppelbock Carolus, a range of popular wheat beers under the Schöfferhofer brand name and Kutscher Alt.

PROTECTING THE CONSUMER

The German beer purity law, the Rheinheitsgebot, was first introduced in Bavaria in 1516 by Duke William IV, only gradually spreading to the rest of the country this century. The ruling – one of the world's first consumer protection laws – insisted that beer should only be made from malt, hops and water (yeast was not at first mentioned, as its working was not understood). It ensured that cheap adjuncts and sugars were not used, and that no beer was as wholesome as German beer. In 1987, the European Court ruled that the law was a trade barrier, preventing foreign beers being imported. Although the German government could not then stop beers which did not conform to the purity law crossing the border, German brewers resolved to stick to the ruling. It was a wise decision, as drinkers voted with their glasses to stay loyal to their pure beer. The Rheinheitsgebot is now seen as giving German beer a vital marketing edge in a competitive world.

THE ROYAL BREWERS

World-famous for its beer hall in the heart of Munich, the Hofbräuhaus (HB) has the distinction of being the royal brewery. The royal connection dates back to 1589, when the Duke of Bavaria, Wilhelm V established the brewery.

Now owned by the state, it has only started to market its beers in recent years, cutting the number of brands down to two main ones – a wheat beer and its golden lager Hofbräuhaus Original München (4.9%), besides a number of seasonal specialities such as a maibock, marzen and Christmas Doppelbock called Delicator (7.5%).

Today, the HB brewing plant is located outside the city, next to the old airport. It is the smallest of the big six breweries in the beer capital.

Hofbräuhaus means "court brewhouse", and since Germany was once divided into many dukedoms and principalities, there are a number of royal breweries. The Hofbräuhaus Freising, originally owned by a bishop, is now run by Count von Moy. Located north of Munich, it claims to be the oldest brewery in Germany, dating back to 1160. It is best known for its wheat beers. Bavaria also boasts a Hofbräu Abensberg and a Hofbräu Berchtesgaden. Hofbräuhaus Wolters of Brunswick, now owned by the Lindener Gilde Brewery of Hannover, brews a hoppy Pilsner.

Brau und Brunnen

Germany's leading brewing group includes DUB of Dortmund, Küppers of Cologne, Bavaria St Pauli of Hamburg, and Einbecker and Schultheiss of Berlin.

DAB

Dortmunder Actien Brauerei, incorporated in 1868, is one of the north German city's three main breweries, all famous for their big, bold Export (or Dortmunder) beers. Dortmund is Germany's largest brewing centre and only beers brewed there are allowed to be called Dortmunder. DAB's Export is malty and dry, but the firm now concentrates more on its DAB Meister Pilsner. It also brews an altbier, a maibock and a DAB Tremanator Doppelbock. Local rival Hansa is now part of DAB.

Diebels

The largest brewer of Alt beers is based not in Düsseldorf but in the village of Issum near the Dutch border. Diebels is still a family firm. Founded in 1878, the brewery also produces light and low-alcohol versions of its well-known Diebels Alt.

DOM

One of the larger Kölschbier brewers in Cologne. The name of the brewery means "cathedral".

DUB

Dortmunder Union Brewery, the main rival to DAB with a towering brewhouse in the centre of the industrial city, was formed from the merger of a dozen breweries in the late 19th century. It brews a smooth, malty DUB Export but recently has concentrated on brewing Pilsner, notably Siegel Pilsner and the premium Brinkhoff's No.1.

Erdinger

Germany's biggest brewer of wheat beers was founded in 1886. The company buys much of the wheat it uses locally and even supplies local farmers with seed to ensure it receives the right kind of wheat. It brews a range of popular, light wheat beers, including Erdinger Kristall, Hefe and Dunkel (all 5.2%) and a stronger Weizenbock, Pikantus (7.3%).

Eichbaum

One of Germany's oldest brewers, established in Mannheim in the heart of the Rhineland in 1679, Eichbaum produces a wide range of beers, including a very dry Ureich Pilsner, Eichbaum Export Altgold (5.3%) and three wheat beers, and range in strength from a light, low-calorie Leichter Typ to a powerful dark Apostulator Doppelbock. Part of the third-largest brewing group led by Henninger, Eichbaum (the name means oak tree) also owns the Freiberger Brauhaus of Freiberg.

Hacker-Pschorr

Late in the 18th century, Joseph Pschorr built huge underground beer stores in Munich, making it possible for beer of consistent quality to be brewed all year round. The brewery was the first to export draught beer to the US in the 19th century. Since 1976, Hacker-Pschorr has been linked to Paulaner. The brewery brews a Hell (4.9%) and a Dunkel (5%).

Henninger

This Frankfurt brewery has an international reputation and its beers are sold in over 60 countries. It is the fifth-largest brewery in Germany. The brewery's 110-metre (361ft) high silo tower, containing 16,000 tonnes of barley, is one of Frankfurt's dominant landmarks.

Holsten

This internationally well-known Hamburg brewery was founded in 1879, and is famous for its dry, hoppy range of Pilsners, including Holsten Pils, the local Edel Pilsner and more widely available Premium Bier. Holsten also brews an export and a maibock (which is exported under the name Urbock).

The company owns a number of other German breweries, including Sächsische in Dresden. Holsten rivals Beck's as the leading beer exporter of Germany.

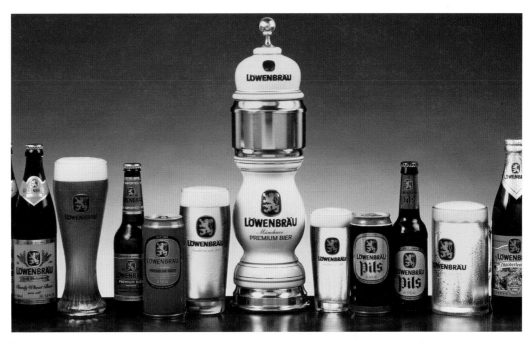

Above: Löwenbräu beer is famous the world over. The brewery produces wheat beers as well as Pilsners.

Klosterbräu

The name means "monastery brewery". Some German abbeys do still brew, such as the Benedictine Kloster brewery at Andechs in Bavaria, but they do not produce their own distinctive beers like the Trappists in Belgium. The Andechs abbey brews beers in the style of its home region, notably a pale Spezial and a Doppelbock. The Kloster title is also adapted by many commercial breweries with monastic connections, such as Irseer Klosterbräu and the Klosterbräu at Bamberg, which is the oldest producer of smoky Rauchbier.

Krombacher

This prominent specialist Pilsner brewer in Kreutzal-Krombach produces more than four million hectolitres (21,996,900 gallons) a year of its hoppy Krombacher Pils, one of the best-selling brand in Germany.

Löwenbräu

The Munich brewery with the highest international profile. Its beers are brewed around the world. In Bavaria, it brews malty lagers, from a Hell and a Dunkel to a hoppy Pilsner and strong Oktoberfest (6.1%). It also produces a range of wheat beers and runs the largest beer hall in Munich (the Mathäser holds 5,000 drinkers). Löwenbräu means "lion brew" and there are a number of other lesser-known Löwenbräu scattered around the country.

Paulaner

The largest brewery in Munich is also credited with having created the Doppelbock style. First established as an abbey brewery in 1634 by the community of St Francis of Paula, it became known for its powerful Lenten beer. Commercial brewers took over in the early 1800s and developed this rich, ruby brew, calling it Salvator (saviour). Other brewers copied this Doppelbock, using similar names, and a new style was born. This complex dark beer became the standard-bearer of the brewery. Paulaner's firm, dry beers include Münchner Dunkel, an original hell, a pale Pilsner, and a Hefe Weissbier.

Schneider

The most celebrated specialist wheat beer brewers in Bavaria since 1872, Schneider offers the classic example of the cloudy, yeasty style in the spicy Schneider Original Hefe Weizenbier. There is also a sparkling kristall and a light (2.9%). Schneider is still a family-owned company, that brewed first in Munich and then in Kelheim, near Regensburg, from 1928.

Spaten-Franziskaner-Bräu

The famous brewery in Munich, founded in 1397, was originally named after the Späth family. In 1922 it merged with Franziskaner-Leistbräu .

OTHER OUTSTANDING BREWERS

Bavaria St Pauli

This brewery is in the St Pauli area of Hamburg in northern Germany. It brews mainly Astra Pilsner.

Bitburger

This Pilsner specialist was founded in the town of Bitburg in the Rhineland in 1817 and brewed one of the first Pilsners in 1883.

Einbecker

Part of the Brau and Brunnen group, the Einbecker Bräuhaus brews three malty Urbock-style beers – Hell, Dunkel and Maibock (all 6.5%). It also brews a Brauherren Pilsner (4.9%).

Above: The immaculate Schneider Weisse brewery in Kelheim near Regensburg. This family firm of specialist wheat brewers moved to Kelheim from Munich in 1928.

Füchschen

Im Füchschen (The Fox) is one of four home-brew pubs in Düsseldorf brewing its own malty Altbier.

Fürstenberg

The aristocratic family of the Fürstenbergs were first granted the right to brew by King Rudolf of Habsburg in 1283. Based in the Black Forest at Donaueschingen, their brewery uses water from a spring in the grounds of Fürstenberg Castle.

Gaffel

Founded, it is claimed, in 1302, this brewery in the centre of Cologne is known for its kölsch.

Garde

Some believe this brewery produces the definitive, fruity kölschbier at Dormagen-bei-Köln.

Hannen

Hannen, founded in 1725, is one of the leading brewers of Alt in Düsseldorf. It also brews Carlsberg in Germany.

Hansa

The light beers, including an export and Pilsner, of this famous Dortmund brewing name are now made mainly for supermarkets by DAB.

Herforder

Predominantly a Pilsner brewery in Herford near Hannover. As well as its full-bodied Pilsner (4.8%), it brews a malty export, a maibock and sommerbier.

Hopf

The family-owned brewery of Miesbach brews only wheat beers.

Irseer Klosterbräu

The village of Irseer, south-west of Munich, is dominated by the former monastery. Irseer Klosterbräu is a grand guest house with its own brewery, a small beer museum and vaulted Keller.

König

The name means "king". The large family-owned König brewery of Duisburg in the Rhineland hopes to be crowned king of the premium Pilsner. In 1995 its aromatic Pilsner (4.6%) was the fifth-best-selling brand in the country.

Below: The modern plant of Bitburger, the Pilsner specialist brewer. Bitburger Pils is exceptionally dry with a clean finish.

Above: The Pinkus Müller Altbierhaus in Munster in 1928.

Königsbacher

The brewery was founded in 1689 in the city of Koblenz where the Rhine and Moselle meet. It is best known for its hoppy Pilsner, but also produces an Alt and a powerful Urbock (7.3%).

Küppers

This is the largest brewer of kölschbier in Cologne. Besides a sweetish kölsch, it also brews an unfiltered version called Wiess.

Moravia

The name of this brewery in Lüneberg pays tribute to the Czech origins of the Pilsner style. It produces a hoppy, dry Pilsner.

Pinkus Müller

This historic home-brew pub has been brewing and serving beer in Münster since 1816. Pinkus Müller is now run by the fifth generation of the Müller family. Despite its small size, the brewery ships its beers around the world. Since 1990, all Pinkus beers have been produced organically.

The brews include an unusual pale alt beer (5%) brewed using wheat in the mash, which is matured for six months, developing a distinctive sourish, lactic taste. The brewery also produces a bottom-fermenting special (5%) and a golden Pilsner.

Rhenania

This independent family brewer in Krefeld, near Düsseldorf, was founded in 1838. It produces one of Germany's more widely available alts.

Ritter

This Dortmund brewery is now part of the larger Dortmund giant DUB. The brewery produces a good range of fruity beers, including a strong, flavoursome export and a golden-coloured, hoppy First Pilsner (4.8%).

Below: Brass bands, national costume and beer are essential parts of the Oktoberfest.

St Pauli Girl

The sister brewery to Beck's in Bremen, St Pauli Girl produces a similar beer. The odd name is derived from its Girl brand featuring a popular German barmaid. The beer is very popular in the US.

Spezial

The oldest Rauchbier (smoked beer) brewer in Bamberg, dating back to 1536, Spezial produces a lightly smoky brew called Lagerbier (4.9%) plus a more intense Märzen and a Bock at its home-brew pub.

Thurn und Taxis

An aristocratic Bavarian family brewery in Regensburg, Thurn und Taxis dates back to 1834. It produces a Pilsner (4.9%), a pale export (5.5%) and hell hefe weissbier (5.5%). The family still lives in the ornate Schloss St Emmeram in Regensburg. The brewery, which owns a number of other Bavarian breweries, was sold to Paulaner in 1997.

.Uerige

The high altar of Alt. This rambling Düsseldorf tavern, Zum Uerige, has, since 1862, brewed the definitive version of this copper-coloured, top-fermenting beer, deep in flavour and bitterness. In the town it is known by the locals as "dat leckere Droppke" – that fine drop. The shining brewery can be seen from one of the many bars in the tavern.

Unertl

This tiny Bavarian brewery in Haag, east of Munich, has developed a big reputation for its delicious dark, organic wheat beers, notably its sourly fruity hefe weissbier (4.8%) and hefe weizenbock (6.2%).

Veltins

This specialist Rhineland Pilsner brewer led the fashion for premium brands with its sweetish Pilsner.

Weihenstephan

This brewery has long been a Bavarian institution. The former monastery brewery at Freising not only claims to be the oldest working brewery in the world, going back more than 950 years to 1040, it is also the home of Munich University's internationally famous Faculty of Brewing.

The modern hill-top brewery is now owned by the Bavarian Government, and sells its extensive range of excellent beers commercially. The brews include a malty hell, a dark, flavoursome dunkel, a hoppy, dry Edelpils and a range of deliciously fruity wheat beers.

Zum Schlüssel

The Schlüssel brewpub was the first Düsseldorf home of the Gatzweiler Alt brewery. Zum Schlüssel (the name means "The Key") still brews its own malty Schlüssel Alt.

Above: Serving beer in a hotel in Germany. The waitress appears to have four hands!

SMOKY SECRET

The Franconia region of Germany, in particular the small, beautiful medieval town of Bamberg, has maintained a smoky tradition. Here malt is produced for local brews over beech-wood fires, giving it and the final beer a lightly smoked taste.

Bamberg has nine breweries for only 70,000 people. The classic producer is probably the Brauerei Heller Trum, which makes Schlenkerla.

Right: The Schlenkerla Tavern is the main outlet for the Heller Trum brewery's smoked beers.

AUSTRIA

Pilsners may rule the world, but in the mountain fastness of Austria it is a different story. Most Austrian beer follows the style pioneered by Anton Dreher in 1841 – a darker, reddish-amber lager.

THE BULK OF AUSTRIAN BEER still draws on the original malty style, which was a halfway house between bottom-fermenting, brown beers of Munich and the golden Pilsners of the Czech Republic. This beer is known simply as lager or sometimes Märzen, indicating its darker origins in the old, dark lager styles, though it is now more like a deeper Bavarian Hell in colour. A fuller-bodied version is called Vollbier. Between them lager and Vollbier account for almost 80% of the Austrian beer market. The hoppier, drier Pilsner takes little more than 6%, while wheat beers, so popular in nearby Bavaria, manage just over 1%. Stronger lagers are referred to in ascending order of strength as Spezial, Bock and Starkbier. Weaker, low-alcohol styles are usually called Leichtbier or Radler.

Austrian beer is distinct from German brews. The country is not governed by a beer purity law, and allows the use of adjuncts (unmalted cereals) such as rice or corn in its brews, which tend to give Austrian beers a cleaner, less complex flavour. The structure of the Austrian brewing industry is much simpler than that of Germany. Although there are some 60 breweries, including a few new brewpubs and micro-breweries, two groups dominate: Brau AG in the west and north, and Steirische in the south. Schwechater, the brewery where Anton Dreher worked his magic, once controlled Vienna. Each of the two main groups courted this family firm with its aristocratic connections, and it was finally taken over by Brau AG in 1978. High society in the capital was shocked – the beer-brewing family of Mautner-Markhof had fallen.

Above: Austria is famed for its unique reddish-amber lagers, but Zipfer's pale lager appeals to more modern Austrian taste buds.

Since 1993, Brau AG and Steirische (made up of Gö sser and Reininghaus) have combined with other Austrian breweries in a new Brau Union to expand into Eastern Europe, buying up breweries in Hungary and the Czech Republic.

THE BEERS

Adam Spezial
See Adambräu.

Adambräu
A refreshing alpine lager (5.2%) that is now brewed in Brau AG's Bürgurbräu brewery in Innsbruck. There is also a stronger Adam Spezial (5.7%), and a brown, malty festbier.

Columbus
A rich, malty, well-hopped lager (5.3%) from the Stiegl brewery.

Edelweiss
Austria's most popular range of wheat beers is produced for the Brau AG group by Hofbräu Kaltenhausen of Hallein near Salzburg. The beers tend to be lighter in flavour than their Bavarian counterparts and there is a full range: cloudy-gold Edelweiss Hefetrüb with a spicy, malt taste; filtered (and therefore clear), bright Edelweiss Kristallklar; and darker-amber Edelweiss Dunkel (all 5.5%). There is also a stronger Edelweiss Bock (7.1%).

Gold Fassl Pils
This crisp, dry, pale-gold, hoppy Pilsner (4.6%) is one of the range of beers produced by the Ottakringer brewery of Vienna, a local independent brewery.

Gold Fassl Spezial
A full-bodied, meaty, malty Spezial (5.6%) produced by the Ottakringer brewery.

Gosser
This is probably Austria's best-known international brand name. It is produced by the Gosser brewery in Leoben-Goss. The range includes a light lager Gosser-Gold, the gold, malty Gosser Märzen, a fruity, malty Gosser Spezial and a deep-brown, full-bodied, sweet Gosser Export.

Hirter
This is a range of beers from the brewery of the same name. The golden Export Pils (5.8%) is probably the best-known, but there is also a Märzen (5%), an unfiltered Zwickl (5.2%) and a hefty, strong Festbock (7%).

Hopfenperle
A hoppy premium Pilsner (5.4%) from the Schwechater brewery near Vienna. It should not be confused with the Swiss brewery of the same name.

Kaiser
Kaiser is Austria's leading beer brand. Besides a standard Kaiser draught, the range also includes a malty Vollbier called Kaiser Märzen (5.2%), a Spezial Kaiser Goldquell (5.6%), and a hoppier Pilsner called Kaiser Premium (5.4%). Other Kaiser beers include the dark Doppelmalz (4.7%) and the strong Kaiser Piccolo Bock (7.1%). The Kaiser beers come from the Brau AG group which is the leading brewing group in Austria.

Keller Bräu
This is a range of seven quality beers from the private Kellerbrauerei of Ried. It includes a Märzen, a Pils, a Spezial, a Dunkel and a Festbock.

MacQueen's Nessie
This strong brew (7.5%) claims to be a whisky-malt beer. Nessie does not contain any of the Highland spirit, however, but uses imported peaty Scottish whisky-malt in the mash in order to produce a smooth, smoky, reddish-coloured beer with a biscuity, malt character and a smoky finish. It is one of the speciality brews produced by the Eggenberg brewery.

Morchl
An unpasteurized, malty, dark lager (5%), produced by the Hirter brewery.

Naturtrub
This is the unfiltered version of Keller Bräu's Annen-Bräu.

Nussdorf Doppel Hopfen Hell
A top-fermenting, dry, hoppy brew (3.8%). Hopfen Hell is one of a range of brews from the Nussdorf castle brewery.

Old Whisky
This strong, seasonal (5.5%), top-fermented beer uses whisky malt and is produced by Nussdorf.

Ottakringer Helles
This brew is a distinctive light-gold-coloured lager (5.1%) with a malty flavour, produced by Ottakringer, Vienna's local independent brewery.

Paracelsus
This unfiltered Vollbier (4.9%) comes from the Stiegl brewery of Salzburg.

Privat Pils
A strong, dry, golden Pilsner (5.2%) with a malty flavour, brewed by Hirter.

Ratsherrn Trunk
This tasty Vollbier (5.3%), which is produced by the Bräucommune Freistadt brewery, won a gold medal at the International Monde Sélection competition in Rome in 1995.

St Thomas Bräu
This is a dry, fruity top-fermented Altbier (4.6%) from the Nussdorf castle brewery.

Schlank & Rank

This dry, hoppy, golden Pilsner (4.9%) is produced at Brau AG's Bürgurbräu brewery in Innsbruck under the Adambrau label. The name means "Slim & Trim".

Sigl

A standard bottled lager (4.9%) from the Sigl brewery. It is known for its unusual "beer bop" characters on the labels.

Sir Henry's Stout

This distinctive, hearty, chocolatey stout (5.2%) was the first beer produced by the Nussdorf brewery.

Steffl

This is a gold, malty premium lager (5.4%) from the Schwechater brewery near Vienna.

Vienna brewpubs

The Austrian capital has a number of cellar bars brewing their own tasty, unfiltered lagers, notably Salmbräu which produces a Hell, a Pilsner and a dark malty Bock.

Stiegl Goldbräu

This amber, malty Vollbier (4.9%) is the best-known brew from the Stiegl brewery.

Stiftsbräu

This malty, softly sweet, deep-brown, dark Stiftsbräu (3.6%) is produced by the Gosser brewery.

Trumer Märzen

This classic Vollbier (4.8%) is produced by the Josef Sigl brewery of Obertrum.

Trumer Pils

An excellent extra-dry Pilsner (4.9%), produced by the Josef Sigl brewery. It is traditionally served in a tall, narrow glass.

Urbock 23

This strong, creamy, golden, slightly oaky Bock (9.9%) with a rich malt and hops flavour is allowed to mature for a full nine months in the Eggenberg brewery.

Weihnachtsbock

A deep-gold, rich, malty winter Bock (7%) from the Stiegl brewery in Salzburg. A darker version is brewed as Freistadter..

Weizen Gold

This range of wheat beers produced by the Josef Sigl brewery of Obertrum includes an unfiltered, hazy, gold, spicy Weizen Gold Hefe Hell, a dark-amber-coloured, malty Dunkel and a sparkling malty, Weizen Gold Champagner (all 5.5%).

Wieselburger Stammbräu

A traditional, pale-gold malty Austrian lager (5.4%). This beer emphasizes its history – the Wieselburg brewery dates back to 1770 – both on the label, which shows old lagering casks, and through its use of old-fashioned traditional swing-stoppered bottles.

Wieselburger Spezial

This strong Austrian lager (5.7%) is produced by the Wieselburger brewery.

Zipfer Märzen

A pale-gold, hoppy marzen (5.2%) with a pronounced sour, malt flavour, produced by the Zipfer brewery, part of the Brau AG group.

Zipfer Urtyp

This hoppy, pale-gold Vollbier (5.4%) is produced by the Zipfer brewery in the town of that name.

THE BREWERS

Augustiner

This Salzburg brewery dates back to 1621. It is still owned by the monks of Kloster Mullen, although it is now run by a secular company. The monastery has its own large beer hall where Augustiner Bräu is served in large, stone steins.

Brau AG

The full name of Austria's leading brewing group is Österreichische Brau-Aktiengesellschaft (the Austrian Brewing Corporation). This large company is a major player in the Austrian market and brews every third glass of beer that is sold in the country. The company is based in Linz and has breweries at Schwechat, Wieselburg, Zipf, Hallein (Kaltenhausen) and Innsbruck (Bürgerbräu), which produces regional beers. Its main brand is Austria's most popular draught lager, the sweetish Kaiser Draught. It also sells a wide range of other beers under the Kaiser brand name.

Eggenberg

This small brewery in the town of the same name which lies halfway between Linz and Salzburg produces some rare Austrian speciality beers, most notably the monstrously named MacQueen's Nessie. made with imported Scottish whisky malt in the mash. It also brews one of the strongest beers in the country, the creamy, golden Urbock 23, (9.9%) and a popular gold lager Hopfenkönig (5.3%).

Freistadter

The independent brewery, based in Freistadt since 1777, brews according to the stricter German beer purity law. Best known for its award-winning Vollbier Ratsherrn Trunk (5.2%), it also produces a Freistadter Märzen (4.9%), a dark Freistadter Spezial Dunkel (5.1%), a Freistadter Pils (4.5%) and a Freistadter Weihnachtsbock, which is a robust, full-flavoured, dark winter Bock (6.6%).

Hirter

The independent brewery in Hirt, Karnten, claims to date back as far as 1270. It is best known for its Hirter Export Pils.

Hubertus

The family brewery at Laa an der Thaya, close to the Czech border, is now run by the sixth generation of the Kuhtreiber family. Its well-matured beers, which are brewed to the German beer purity law, include Hubertus Märzen, the dark Hubertus Dunkel, two Pilsners and a strong Hubertus Festbock.

Keller Bräu

The private Kellerbrauerei of Ried, Hochfeld, dates back to 1446. The brewery has been run by the Mitterbucher family since 1926.

Nussdorfer

Baron Henrik Bachofen von Echt established this brewery in the wine cellars of his grand castle at Nussdorf in Vienna in 1984.

Ottakringer

Vienna's local independent brewery is a family firm that dates from 1837. It produces one of the more distinctive Austrian lagers in its Ottakringer Helles. It also brews a speciality Bräune, a Dunkel and a Bock.

Puntigamer

The brewery, based in Graz, produces a range of soft, mild beers, besides two stronger bocks.

Reininghaus

This Graz brewery produces a range of fruity beers.

Schlägl

Abbey in Upper Austria which brews its own beers including a top-fermenting rye beer Goldroggen (4.9%).

Schwechater

Anton Dreher's original brewery on the edge of Vienna betrays its old aristocratic links through grand pavilions and tree-lined courtyards in the brewery grounds. Besides a soft lager, Schwechater Bier (5.2%), it also brews a Schwechater Pils (5.2%), a premium Pilsner Hopfenperle and a Schwechater Festbock (7.1%).

Sigl

There has been an independent Josef Sigl brewery at Obertrum near Salzburg since 1601. It produces probably the best Pilsner in Austria, the deliciously dry Trumer Pils. It also brews a pioneering range of wheat beers under the Weizen Gold brand, a Sigl Bockbier (7.3%) and a bottled lager (4.9%), famous for its odd labels that feature different trendy characters in a "beer bop collection".

Stiegl

Austria's biggest private brewery dates back to 1492. As well as Goldbräu and Pils, it also produces a quality spezial and a winter Bock. Stiegl also has a brewing museum, along with a Bräu Welt (Beer World) experience for visitors, showing how beer is brewed.

Steirische Bräuindustrie

The second largest brewer in Austria is based in Graz. Many of its beers are brewed uner the Gösser label.

Zipfer

This brewery in Zipf, founded in 1858, produces probably the hoppiest beers in the Brau AG group. It produces a range of beers, including a Pilsner and two strong, malty bocks.

Anton Dreher

In the 19th century Anton Dreher, a brewer in Vienna, worked with Sedlmayr in Munich to develop lager brewing. He was the father of Vienna-style lager – an amber-coloured, subtly malty, sweetish, bottom-fermented lager, which is made using "Vienna malt". The pioneering brew was introduced in 1841 (just before the first Pilsner Urquell was brewed). The style proved a popular export, and Dreher went on to found breweries throughout the Austrian Empire – Italy, Hungary, Mexico and Bohemia – and the popular style reached out across the globe. The beer's prominence faded almost in parallel with the decline of the Austrian Empire, and Dreher's Vienna company closed in the 1930s, Vienna-style lager is still brewed in parts of South America and Scandinavia as well as in Europe.

POLAND

Poles enjoy a glass of beer, but for many years small, unmodernized breweries struggling to match demand. In addition to this handicap, the hoppy drop has always struggled to match the dominance of the national drink – vodka.

IN SHARP CONTRAST to its beer-loving neighbours to the west, Germany and the Czech Republic, Poland is a light imbiber, with Poles consuming less than 40 litres (70 pints) per head a year. This is partly because of a strong spirit-drinking tradition (especially in central and eastern areas), and partly because of the tax system that makes beer expensive compared to spirits.

At the turn of the century, Poland boasted more than 500 breweries. Lack of investment, however, meant that many closed. By the late 1980s a common sign in many shops and cafés was "Piwa Brak" – "no beer". Apart from a handful of larger companies like Okocim and the leading exporter Zywiec, most of the 80 or so breweries that remained were small and served a local area. Since the end of Communist rule, however, there have been fundamental changes in the Polish brewing industry. A growing number of breweries have been privatized, often linking up with western breweries to get funding for modernization. Most of the beer is still unpasteurized, although this is rapidly changing as modern processing techniques are introduced. By 1996, seven of the top 10 Polish breweries had some degree of foreign ownership, and the capital was bustling with many brands at higher prices. However, the government is trying to keep control of the industry in Polish hands by restricting foreign ownership of brewing companies to minority holdings.

A light, Pilsner-style of lager dominates, but there are also some fuller-bodied, export-style lagers and a few strong, bottom-fermenting dark brews called porters. These reflect the historical British influence throughout the Baltic. When the Napoleonic Wars stopped the export of British beers, local brewers responded to the existing demand by brewing their own dark beer.

Above: EB is one of the few Polish beers that is regularly exported. It is particularly popular in countries with large Polish communities.

THE BEERS

Dojlidy Porer

A strong, dark porter (9%) that is a typical example of the Polish porter style.

EB Specjal Pils

The mild, fresh, yellow-coloured lager (5.4%) from Elblag's brewery is triple-filtered. The liquor (water) with which it is made is drawn from the brewery's own deep wells.

Eurospecjal

This full-bodied, strong, golden lager (7.5%) is brewed by Zywiec in the city of Kraców.

Gdańskie

This is one of the leading lagers (5.6%) from the Hevelius brewery which is situated in the shipbuilding city of Gdańsk.

Grodzisk

This rare, top-fermenting beer is said by the brewers to have been brewed since the 14th century in the town of Grodzisk Wielkopolski, near Poznań. It uses a high proportion of smoked wheat and is spontaneously fermented before being bottle-conditioned. The result is a tart, refreshingly sour, hazy golden ale with a heavy, smoky aroma. It is sold in a variety of strengths, the weakest of which is 5%.

Herbowe

A deep-gold, Pilsner-style lager (5.6%) from the Dojlidy brewery.

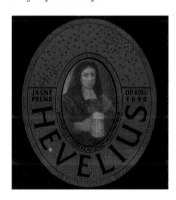

Hevelius

This super-premium, tasty lager (6.1%) is brewed by the firm of the same name in city of Gdańsk.

Kaper

A special, extra-powerful, malty, deep-gold lager (8.1%), which is brewed in Gdańsk by the Hevelius company.

Karmelowe

Adark, low-gravity beer (3.5%) from the Okocim brewery.

Krakus

The soft, malty lager (5.4%) from the Zywiec brewery is named after the old name for the city of Kraców.

Krolewskie

Krolewskie is brewed by the city of Warsaw's local Warszawski brewery. Before the end of Communist rule, this full-bodied lager (5.6%) was almost the only one that drinkers could find in the shops of Warsaw.

Lech Pils

A yellow-gold, hoppy, malty Pilsner (5.3%) from the Lech brewery.

Lech Porter

A strong, dark, cherry-coloured beer (7.4%) from the Lech brewery.

Lech Premium

This strong, malty, golden lager (5.4%) is one of Lech's leading brands.

Magnat

A full-bodied, strong golden lager (7.4%) from the Dojlidy brewery.

OK Jasne Pelne

Okocim's yellow-gold, malty "full light" lager has a strong, hoppy finish. It comes in various strengths.

Okocim Porter

A strong, dark, bottom-fermented porter (9%) from Okocim.

Warszawski Porter

A rich, dark, bottom-fermented porter (9%) from the Warsaw brewery.

Zywiec Full Light

This is a hoppy, fruity golden lager (5.6%), from Poland's famous Zywiec brewery, using fresh mountain water from Mount Skrzyczne.

Zywiec Porter

This rich, mahogany-coloured beer (9.2%) from Zywiec has heavy hints of roasted coffee and currants in the flavour.

THE BREWERS

Dojlidy

Located in Bialystok since 1891, this local brewery is typical of many of the smaller Polish breweries. It produced less than 200,000 litres (14,200 gallons) in 1992 while waiting to be privatized. Besides its main lagers, Zlote and Herbowe, it also produces Gotyckie, Magnat and Dojlidy Porter.

Hevelius

Founded in 1871 as the Danziger Aktien-Bierbrauerai-Kleinhammer in the port of Gdańsk, it was nationalized after the Second World War as Gdańskie Zaklady Piwowarskie. It was modernized in 1991 and renamed Hevelius that year, after the Polish astronomer. In 1996 the German brewers Binding took a 49% stake.

Above: The Old Town marketplace in Warsaw with open-air cafés and an old-fashioned horse and carriage designed for tourists.

Elbrewery

This is now the largest brewing company in Poland, and it controls nearly one fifth of the beer market. Elbrewery was founded in 1872 as the Brauerei Englisch Brunnen Elbing in the northern town of Elbing. The original name of the brewery demonstrates the early influence of English merchants in the Baltic beer trade.

The company, which also has a second modernized brewery in nearby Braniewo, really took off with the involvement of the Australian company Brewpole in 1991, followed by investment by the large Grolsch company of the Netherlands in 1995. Its flagship brew is the golden EB Specjal Pils.

Lech

Founded in 1951 in Poznań in west Poland, Lech also has a second brewery in Ostrow Wielkopolski and substantial maltings, making it the fifth largest brewer in the country. Following privatization in 1993, the firm is now owned by a Polish investor EAC, with a 15% share stake held by South African Breweries. It is best known for the golden lagers it produces – Lech Pils and Lech Premium – as well as the special, cherry-coloured Lech Porter.

Okocim

After Zywiec, this is the best-known Polish brewing company, with plants in Okocim, Krac ów and Jedrezejow. The brewery was founded by an Austrian, Jan Gotz, in 1845. Since privatization in 1992, when German giant Bräu und Brunnen gained a quarter share, Okocim has linked up with Danish brewer Carlsberg. Its OK Jasne Pelne (full light) lager appears in varying strengths. Dark beers include a low-gravity Karmelowe and a powerful Okocim Porter.

Warszawski

Founded in 1846, this is the leading brewer in the capital of Warsaw. Besides standard lagers under the names Krolewskie (5.6%) and Stoteczne (5.4%), it also brews Warszawski Porter. The bottles give a nod towards beer's Egyptian origins with a Sphinx on the label.

Zywiec

Poland's most famous brewery had noble origins. It was founded in 1856 in Zywiec near Kraców, by Archduke Charles Olbracht Habsburg, adopting a crown as its emblem. It was owned by the Habsburg family until the Second World War. Under state control, it became Poland's leading beer exporter. On privatization in 1991, the Zywiec plant was extensively modernized. The company also runs smaller breweries in Cieszyn and Bielsko. In 1994, Heineken took a 25% stake in the company. Its main beer is Zywiec Full Light. There is also a softer Krakus and much more full-bodied Eurospecjal. Zywiec also brews one of Poland's most distinctive porters.

EASTERN EUROPE

The common Communist heritage of Hungary, Bulgaria, Romania, Latvia, Lithuania and Estonia has now been shaken off. The nationalized industries, which for a long time struggled to meet even the modest demand from the region, have been thrown open to investment from the West.

THE FORMER COMMUNIST countries of Eastern Europe consume relatively little beer, in part due to a strong spirit-imbibing tradition, but also because of inadequate brewing capacity and a shortage of raw materials.

Although Hungary, Bulgaria and Romania are best known for their wine, they have a healthy appetite for light lagers. Hungarians drink about 80 litres (17½ gallons) of beer per head a year. Foreign companies have shown great interest in the region since the move away from Communism, and many countries have been welcoming foreign investment with open arms. Hungary's brewing industry is now almost entirely foreign-owned. In Bulgaria some 13 breweries were struggling to keep up with demand, but now foreign investors have poured in, and by 1996 western companies had an interest in more than a third of the industry. In Romania too, a wide range of companies from the West have obliged with investment. In 1996, South African Breweries took a major share of the Romanian market.

Since 1991, a joint company called Baltic Beverages Holding (BBH), established by Scandinavian brewers, has taken a major stake in the leading breweries of the three small Baltic states of Estonia, Latvia and Lithuania. The breweries have since been heavily modernized and the beer ranges revamped to a more international style of Pilsners, moving away from traditional beers.

In Russia and the Ukraine, at the start of the 20th century, there were about 1,000 home-owned breweries producing a range of German, Czech and even English-style beers. The beer industry was severely damaged during the Revolution and two world wars, and was slow to recover. It was then hit by Gorbachev's drive against alcohol when breweries were mothballed or turned into soft drinks factories, and the barley farming areas were badly hit by the Chernobyl nuclear disaster. But despite acute beer shortages, the former USSR has been wary of foreign involvement, and only 6% of production in 1995 was foreign-controlled, though imports, especially from the Czech Republic, are increasing and now account for about 10% of the market.

Above: One of the yeasty lagers, brewed by Aldaris, the biggest brewer in Latvia. The brewery was modernized in 1991 by the BBH group.

THE BEERS

Aldaris
This range of sweetish, yeasty lagers produced by Latvia's biggest brewery includes the light Aldaris Pilznes (4%), a hoppier Baltijas, a smoother Zelta (5%) and the more powerful Jubilejas and Latvijas (both 6%).

Amber Pilsner
This light, dry, unpasteurized Pilsner (4.5%) is brewed using rye and sugar in the mash as well as barley malt. It is produced by the Amber brewery in Nikolayev, in the Ukraine.

Astika Lager
This golden, soft, mild and refreshing lager (4.5%) is widely available in Bulgaria. It is produced by the country's best-known brewery, Astika of Haskovo.

Bak
Köbányai's Bak is Hungary's version of a German Bock. This beer is strong (7.5%), dark and sweet.

Baltijas
This hoppy, yeasty lager (4.5%) is produced by the Aldaris brewery in Latvia.

Bergenbier
This popular, standard, golden-coloured, Romanian lager has a refreshing alpine image, with a snowy mountain peak on the label. A deep-amber Bergenbier Bruna has also been added to Bergen's range.

Birziecie
This strong, malty, dark lager (6.1%) is brewed by Ragutu, Lithuania.

Burgasko Lager
This light lager comes from the Burgasko brewery at Burgas on the Black Sea coast of Bulgaria.

Dreher
The Austrian pioneer of Viennese red beers, Anton Dreher, bought the leading Budapest brewery Köbányai Serhaz in 1862 and so gave his name to Hungary's best-known beer brands.

After a gap of some 40 years during Communist rule from 1948, the Dreher name was revived for Köbányai's premium range of beers – including a refreshing, dry, hoppy Pilsner (5%), the fuller-bodied golden-coloured Export and a Bavarian-style bock called Bak.

Dvaro
This is a premium lager (5.2%) from Kalnapilis, Lithuania.

Ekstra
Like Dvaro, this is a premium lager (5.2%) produced by the Kalnapilis brewery, in Lithuania.

Gocseji Barna
This relatively dark lager, which is something like a German Dunkel, is produced by the Konizsai brewery in west Hungary.

Kamenitza Lager
Kamenitza is a regional lager brand produced by the Kamenitza brewery in Plovdiv, Bulgaria.

Kanizsai Korona
The Kanizsai brewery in Hungary brews this malty, export-style lager.

Lauku Tumsais
This hazy, amber brew (6%) has a warming, malty taste. It is produced by the Lacplesis brewery in Lielvarde, Latvia.

Moskovskoye
This fruity lager is the leading beer brand produced by the Moscow brewery.

Nikolaevskyi
An amber-coloured beer (5%) with a spicy hop character, brewed with rye and sugar as well as barley in the south Ukraine by the Amber brewery, built by the Czechs in 1973.

Palmse
A dark, malty lager brewed by Viru in Estonia.

Porteris
The ruby-black beer (7.4%), with a rich, liqueur-like texture from Aldaris, is reputedly the only porter brewed in Latvia.

Reval
A golden, all-malt, hoppy lager, produced by the Saku brewery of Estonia.

Ruutli Olu
A rich, dark, spicy bock (7.5%), which is lagered for 70 days. It is produced by the Estonian Tartu brewery. This strong, dark, cold-weather beer was introduced by the brewery in 1995. It is the strongest beer brewed in Estonia.

Below: A beer stall in Riga, Latvia, in summer.

Above and left: Pilsner-type lagers, typical of the Saku brewery in Estonia, which was founded in 1820.

Saku Originaal
Smooth-tasting Originaal is the premium, all-malt lager from Saku, Estonia.

Saku Pilsner
This fresh-tasting, golden, all-malt Pilsner is the main lager from Saku of Estonia.

Siraly (Seagull)
Siraly is a light, malty lager brewed by Kanizsai, Hungary.

Sirvenos
The leading lager (4.2%) from the Lithuanian brewer Ragutus, which, unusually, uses local peas in the mash to help with head retention and to give the beer a more rounded, full-bodied flavour.

Talleros
This is the local lager brewed by the Heineken-owned Komaromi, Hungary.

Tartu Olu
This rich lager (6%) is one of the beers brewed by Tartu in Estonia.

Tume
A reddish-coloured, malty lager, Tume is brewed by Saku, Estonia.

Zagorka Lager
The light, golden Zagorka lager is produced by the Zagorka brewery, Bulgaria.

Zhigulevskoe (Ziguli)
One of the main Soviet lager brands, which, under Communist rule, was brewed right across the USSR from Moscow to the Far East. A premium version (4.4%), produced by the Obolon brewery of Kiev, uses a proportion of rice in the mash. This lager has sometimes been exported to the West.

THE BREWERS

Aldaris
Latvia's biggest brewery has been based in the capital Riga since 1865. It brews a range of sweetish, yeasty lagers. Aldaris controls more than half the country's beer market and has been owned by Baltic Beverages Holdings since 1992. In 1995, BBH introduced a cleaner-tasting Pilsner, Aldara Luksusa.

Amber
Like many regional breweries in the former Soviet Union, this is a fairly new Czech-built brewery. It was constructed in 1973 in Nikolayev in the southern Ukraine. It produces two main beers, Amber Pilsner and spicy, amber-coloured Nikolaevskyi. Hops are grown locally around Zhitomir, but a shortage of barley malt means rye and sugar are also used. Roasted malt particularly is in short supply, which limits the chance to brew darker beers. All production is bottled and unpasteurized, with a shelf-life of seven days.

Baltika
Work only began on this St Petersburg brewery in 1990 and had still not been completed in 1993 when the unfinished plant was taken over by Baltic Beverages Holding, a joint venture by Scandinavian brewers Pripps of Sweden and Hartwall of Finland. Baltika has since grown rapidly to become one of the largest brewers in Russia, selling 120 million litres (26 million gallons) in 1995, the bulk of it around St Petersburg where it controls two-thirds of the market. It

produces a range of light lagers, including the premium Parnas and Baltika Export on draught.

Bergenbier
The Romanian Bergenbier brewery is owned by Belgian giant Interbrew, which completed a new brewery at Blaj in 1995.

Borsodi
Part of the Belgian Interbrew empire since 1991, the Borsodi brewery in Bocs is the second largest in Hungary, controlling around a quarter of the market. Its main local lagers are Borsodi Vilagos and Rakoczi.

New brewpubs

Hungary's rapidly advancing economy has embraced the western trend for micro-breweries. Since 1989, the pioneer brewer, Zsolt Gyenge, has set up around 50 pub plants. Most of the micros brew all-malt beers according to the German beer purity law.

FARMHOUSE BEER

The Baltic states still retain a local, farmhouse brewing tradition, producing rye and juniper beers similar to the Finnish sahti in the north, as well as other refreshing country brews. On a more commercial scale they produce a variety of lagers, some using unusual brewing materials such as peas, besides a few stronger porters.

Russia also has a tradition of producing its own country beer – a nourishing home-made rye brew called kvass, sometimes sweetened with local fruit juices, such as bilberries. Some breweries produce this relatively low-alcohol beer commercially.

Burgasko
This Bulgarian brewery was taken over by Belgian giant Interbrew in 1995.

Kalnapilis
This large brewery in Panevezys, Lithuania, complete with its own maltings, was founded in 1902 and was acquired by the huge Scandinavian conglomerate, BBH in 1994. Since then, the brewery has launched a new range of international-style lagers, led by the premium Dvaro and Ekstra brands.

Kamenitza
Interbrew's first grip on the Bulgarian market began when it took over this brewery early in 1995.

Kanizsai
The Kanizsai brewery in Nagykanizsa in western Hungary dates back to 1892. The German brewing giant Holsten of Hamburg has had an interest in the brewery since 1984. It is best known for its light Siraly (Seagull) lager and malty Korona (Crown), a common name for Hungarian beers. It also brews a darker lager, called Gocseji Barna.

Köbányai
First opened in 1855, this plant was bought by the Austrian brewer, Anton Dreher in 1862. Although he died the following year, his son made the Köbányai the largest brewery in Hungary. After merging with its main local rivals Reszveny and Haggenmacher in 1933, and Fovarosi in 1934, Dreher controlled three-quarters of the beer market. With nationalization in 1948, the Dreher name disappeared, but it was revived some 40 years later after privatization. South African Breweries gained control of the brewery in 1993. The Dreher range of beers, based on old recipes, uses a high proportion of malt. Some lagers from the Communist period are still produced.

Komaromi
Heineken bought this modern brewery at Komarom in 1991, primarily to brew Amstel for the Hungarian market. Nevertheless, it also continues to brew a number of local lagers, such as Talleros.

Lacplesis
This small country brewery in Lielvarde, Latvia, brews on a former collective farm, where it grows its own grain.

Magadan
This brewery is located in the east in the Stalinist city of Magadan on the Sea of Okhotsk. It still produces the four standard brands once widespread across the former Soviet Union. These are Zhigulevskoe (Ziguli), Moscovskoe (Moscow), Russkoe (Russian) and Ukrainskoe (Ukrainian). All are similar, light, pale lagers that vary in recipe depending on the brewing materials available. The main difference is in their lagering times. Ziguli is lagered for 21 days, and Moscow for double that time, giving it a drier more acidic taste than the fresher Ziguli. This acidic flavour is not due to production problems in the run-down plant, but because many Russians like a sour edge to their beer. All brews add sugar to beef up the limited malt mash. Magadan also produces several commercial brands of kvass, the cloudy, unhopped rye country-beer, which is indigenous to Russia – one kvass is flavoured with lemon. In summer, this refreshing brew is sold unfiltered direct from tanker trucks in the streets.

Above: Shady outdoor tables in a Budapest café are a pleasant place to enjoy a relaxing beer in the heat of the summer months.

Moscow

The Moscow City Brewery, next door to Tolstoy's House, has been brewing since 1863 and was once the main testing plant for beer in the Soviet Union. Its leading lager is the fruity Moskovskoye (4.6%). An all-malt August (4.5%), named after the month of the failed army coup in 1991 that led to Boris Yeltsin's revolution,is exported.

Proberco

This brewery at Baia Mare in Romania is owned by Interbrew.

Ragutus

Like some other Lithuanian breweries, the Ragutus company in the major city of Kaunas uses a proportion of local peas in the mash for its main lager, Sirvenos, to help head-retention. It also brews a dark, malty Birziecie.

Saku

Estonia's leading brewery was founded in 1820 on a former nobleman's estate outside the capital Tallinn. It was taken

Above: Gleaming copper vats at the modernized plant of the Saku brewery in Estonia.

over by BBH in 1991. A new brewhouse was completed in 1992, and Saku now controls more than half of the Estonian beer market. Its main all-malt lagers are Saku Pilsner, a hoppier Reval, the premium Saku Originaal, and the reddish, malty Tume. Saku also brews a coffee-like porter each Christmas.

Tartu

This brewery in Tartu, Estonia, dating back to 1826 has impressive castellated, tower maltings. It was once famous for its Imperial Extra Double Stout, sold to the Russian court when the company was owned by the Belgian merchant Le Coq, who exported the stout for Barclay Perkins of London. It produces a range of lagers including a Pilsner, Rae, a firm-bodied, export-style

Alexander and the richer Tartu Olu, as well as a dark bock called Ruutli Olu.

Viru

The Viru brewery was built on a former collective farm in Estonia in 1975. It is now owned by the large Danish brewer, Harboe.

Zagorka

Heineken has a large interest in this brewery in Stara Zagora, Bulgaria.

Fragmented market

Altogether, there are about 250 breweries in Russia and the Ukraine. They mainly produce light lagers containing adjuncts, such as corn and rice, that are matured for little more than two to three weeks. Breweries primarily serve a local market, but there are some more widely available brands – Ziguli is probably the best example.

Above: A modern brewery in Russia that was built using Austrian investment.

THE CZECH REPUBLIC AND SLOVAKIA

The Czechs have a long and proud brewing tradition and are the biggest beer drinkers in the world. They were among the first to use hops, and their pioneering golden lager has become the most popular beer style in the world.

SINCE THE BREAK-UP of the old Czechoslovakia into the wine-drinking Slovakia and the beer-loving Czech Republic, the Czechs now officially drink more beer per head of population than any other country.

Czech beer sprang to international fame when the citizens' brewery in Plzen developed the first golden lager in 1842. The town – Pilsen in German – gave its name to what was to become the world's leading beer style, Pilsner or just pils – an aromatic, hoppy, bottom-fermented pale beer.

In 1938 Czechoslovakia still boasted more than 300 breweries. But, some 60 years later, the brewing craft is at a crossroads. During the long period of Communist rule, little changed in what had become a nationalized industry. Ironically, the lack of investment in new technology meant that the traditional brewing methods were preserved almost intact. Since the "Velvet Revolution" of 1989 there has been a rush to modernize, with tried and trusted traditional methods often replaced by gleaming new plants. Plzen's dark cellars of wooden conditioning casks, for instance, have been replaced by stainless-steel conical vessels. Character and quality are declining. There are still 70 breweries in the Czech Republic, plus a few brewpubs, but as the larger groups expand and smaller plants are expected to close.

Most Czech beers today are divided into Pilsners of differing strengths, usually indicated by the old degree method of measurement, with 8 indicating a weak brew, 10 an everyday beer and 12 a premium. Before 1989, 12-degree beer was the most popular, but since then, as prices have risen, drinkers have switched dramatically to the weaker 10-degree brews.

Above: Budweiser Budvar is an internationally known, classic example of the Czech all-malt lager style.

THE BEERS

Alt Brunner Gold
This is the malty premium 12 Pilsner (5.1%) brewed by Starobrno.

Bernard Granat
A full-bodied, 11-degree, dark beer (4.9%), produced using two different types of malt, by the family-run Bernard brewery at Humpolec (founded in 1597), which also brews a golden, dry 12% beer (5.1%). The brewery has been one of the leaders of the movement to gain tax concessions for small-scale breweries.

Black Regent
A full-bodied, ruby-red dark beer (4%) with a dark-malt and coffee flavour, produced by the historic Regent brewery.

Bohemia Regent
This is a popular, fruity 12 (4.9%), produced by the Regent brewery.

Budweiser Budvar
This is the most famous of all Czech lagers internationally and perhaps now the classic example of its style. The all-malt Budvar (5%) still retains its soft fruitiness and heady aroma. The Budweiser brewery was founded in the town of Ceske Budejovice (Budweise in German) in 1895, using water from an underground lake. It rapidly became a major exporter, particularly to Germany and the US (where its beer was sold as Crystal). Since 1989 the company has doubled in size, with annual production rising from 450,000 to 900,000 hectolitres (10 million to 22.5 million gallons). Traditional horizontal lagering tanks are still used, and the export beer is matured for more than 60 days. This export beer accounts for 60% of the brewery's export sales. New conical fermenters are used for producing a weaker 10-degree version (4%) with a blue label for consumption in the domestic market.

THE BATTLE FOR BUDWEISER

Such is the fame of Budweiser Budvar that many of the leading breweries around the world have proposed mergers or other trading arrangements, but none have been as persistent as Anheuser-Busch of the United States, which sells its own leading beer under the Budweiser name. Over the last century, the two have frequently clashed in and out of court over the rights to the title. Anheuser-Busch argues that Budvar was not founded until 20 years after the American brewer launched his Bud, but the Czechs contend that, since the Samson brewery was operating in Budweis since 1795, this is irrelevant. Besides, any brewery in the town of Budweis should have the right to market its beers as Budweiser, as the word means "from Budweis". Nevertheless, Budweiser Budvar has been unable to market its beers under its own name in the United States (calling it Crystal instead), and Anheuser-Busch has to sell its flagship beer as Bud in countries like Spain, where the Czech company registered the Budweiser name first. The situation has intensified since the "Velvet Revolution", as exports were less of a priority under Communism. The American giant would like to resolve the long-running dispute by taking over the Czech brewery. However, the Czech Government, which owns the brewery, is wary of the overtures, not wanting to be accused of selling off the crown jewel of the nation's brewing industry.

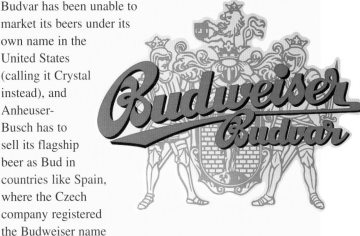

Cassovar
A rich, ruby-black, dark lager (5.5%) with a smooth cocoa and cream flavour, brewed in the Slovak town of Kosice.

Cernohorsky Granat
This dark, malty beer (3.5%) is brewed in Moravia by Cerna Hora.

Cernohorsky Lezak
An quality, golden Pilsner (3.5%) from Cerna Hora.

Chmelar

This pale, but relatively strong, hoppy beer (4.2%) is brewed by the small Zatec brewery. The name means hop-picker.

Crystal

Budweiser Budvar and Samson use this name for their premium beers when sold in the United States.

Drak

A rare, rich, dark, 14-degree Christmas brew (5.7%) from the Starobrono brewery. The name means dragon.

Dudak

A full-bodied premium pale 12 (5%) from the Stakonice brewery of South Bohemia.

Eggenberg

This is the name for a range of beers brewed at Cesky Crumlov in South Bohemia, which includes a pale and dark 10-degree (4%) and a full-bodied 12 (5%). The brewery, which dates back to 1560, is in an old armoury.

Gambrinus

The best-selling Czech beer is brewed by the brewery of the same name in Plzen. Gambrinus is restricted to domestic consumption, but still produces over 1.5 million hectolitres (33 million gallons) a year of a pale, aromatic 10-degree beer (4.1%) with a good,

hoppy character. A small amount of a stronger Gambrinus 12 (5.1%) is also brewed, mainly for export.

Granat

Granat is a popular name for a dark beer, which is used by a number of brewers including Olomouc, Cerna Hora and Hostan.

Herold Dark

A pitch-black, full-flavoured 13-degree brew (5.2%) which comes from the Herold brewery in Breznice. A pale 10-degree beer (3.8%) and stronger 12 (4.8%) are also available.

Holan 10

This hoppy, pale, unfiltered lager (3.5%) is brewed by Olomouc, for the local market.

Karamelové

The malty, dark, 10-degree lager (3.8%) comes from Starobrno of Brno.

Karel IV

A gold, fruity, pale 11-degree lager (4%) with a malty flavour. This is produced at the Karlovy Vary brewery in the famous spa town of that

name in western Bohemia, better known as Carlsbad. The beer is named after the king who founded the spa, .

Konik

This best-selling, hoppy, pale-gold Pilsner beer (3.8%) is produced by the Ostravar brewery.

Kozel

This range of beers from the Velke Popovice brewery near Prague gained notoriety in the mid-1990s with their raunchy advertising. The name means goat. Its popular beers include a hoppy, pale-golden Kozel 10 (4.3%) with a fruity, sweet, malt flavour, a deep-golden, hoppy 12 (5%) and a dark, deep-brown 10 (4.3%) with a rich, malt flavour.

Krusovice

These include a dark, malty 10 (3.7%) with a very bitter flavour and a pale, thirst-quenching 12 (5.1%) with an aromatic, hoppy, sweet-malt flavour.

Lobkowicz

The pale, hoppy 12 (5%), from this family-run brewery is exported as Lobkov. A malty, dark 12 (4.6%) and a weaker, pale 10 are also available, and a 14 (5.5%) is occasionally produced.

Lucan

This pale, hoppy beer (3.6%) is brewed by the small Zatec brewery.

Martin Porter

This richly roasted, bitter-sweet porter (8%) is the strongest beer brewed in Slovakia. It is produced in the town of Martin, by the brewery of the same name.

Martinsky Lager

A malty, amber lager from the small Martin brewery in Slovakia.

Mestan Dark

This is the dark-amber, award-winning, malty beer (4.6%) produced by the Mestan brewery in the Prague suburb of Holesovice.

Nectar

This range of three fruity beers (10, 11 and a dark 10) comes from the Strakonice brewery of South Bohemia.

Novomestsky

This unfiltered, fruity, pale 11 (4%) is brewed in a rambling brewpub in the heart of Prague, established in 1993 in a shopping arcade.

Ondras

This premium, hoppy, pale, Pilsner beer (5%) is produced by the Ostravar brewery.

Osma

This weak, pale, 8 Pilsner (3.2%) is brewed by Starobrno.

Pilsner Urquell

The original flagship Pilsner of the Czech brewing industry. Its development in Plzen launched golden lager on the world for the first time in 1842. Pilsner Urquell (4.4%) is still a quality beer by any standards, particularly when fresh, with its delicate hop aroma and deep soft fruitiness. Urquell means original source.

Pivo Herold Hefe-Weizen

This spicy, fruity, top-fermented wheat beer (5.2%) is brewed in the Bavarian style by the Herold brewery. The style, long dead in the Czech Republic, has been revived by this brewery in Breznice.

Platan

Three pale beers are produced under this title – 10 (3.9%), 11 (4.4%) and 12 (5%), besides a dark beer (3.6%). All these beers are pasteurized.

Ponik

This is the weakest of the hoppy, pale Pilsners (3%) produced by the Ostravar brewer in Moravia.

Pragovar

A hoppy, premium, golden lager (4.9%) from the Mestan brewery of Prague.

Primator

This range of distinctive dry beers is brewed by the Nachod brewery in north-east Bohemia, which is owned by the town of Nachod. The Primator beers include a pale 10 and 12 and a chocolatey, dark 12 (5.1%).

Primus

A pale-gold, cut-price brew (3.8%) from Gambrinus.

Prior

An unfiltered, yeasty wheat beer (5%), introduced by Pilsner Urquell in 1995.

Purkmistr

One of the best Czech dark lagers (4.8%) from the Pilsner Urquell group, Purkmistr has a bitter-chocolate flavour balancing the initial malty sweetness. It is brewed at Domazlice.

Radegast

The range of beers from the Radegast brewery includes a popular, pale-gold 10 (3.8%) with a dry, hop flavour. The 12 (5.1%), which is sold as Premium light, has a golden hue and a dry hops and malt taste. The brown Premium Dark (3.6%) has a light, malt flavour.

Rezak

This is a half-and-half pale and dark lager, (4.1%), produced to satisfy the demands of drinkers who often mix their pale and dark lagers. It is brewed by Starobrno.

Samson

A range of crisp, dry, pale beers, produced by the brewery of the same name. The 10 (4%) has a bright-gold colour and a clean, crisp hops flavour. The 11 (4.6%) is a tawny-gold-coloured beer, with a creamier, sweeter hop flavour. A hoppier version of the 11 is sold in England under the name Zamec, and the sweet, ripe 12 (5%) is sold as Crystal in the US.

Starobrno 10

This deep-golden, hoppy 10 (4.3%) with a rich, bold flavour is a popular beer from the Starobrno brewery's range.

Staropramen 10

Besides a fresh and hoppy pale 10 (4.2%), this major Prague brewery produces a full-bodied 12 (5%) and a mellow dark (4.6%). The quality of the beers reflect the fact that the brewery has retained traditional methods of brewing.

Tas

A light, golden, tasty Pilsner (2.8%) brewed by the Cerna Hora brewery in Moravia.

Tatran

A range of lagers from the Vega brewery of Poprad in the Tatran mountains, Slovakia. It includes a Tatran export (8%) and a lighter Kamzik (4.1%).

Urpin Pils

The deep-gold, hoppy, Pilsner with a light, malt flavour from the Urpin brewery in Slovakia.

Vaclav 12

A hoppy, pale lager (5.6%), brewed by Olomouc.

Velke Popovice

See Kozel.

Vranik

A delicate, malty, dry, dark 10 (3.8%) from Ostravar.

Zamek

Export name for Samson 11.

Zatecka Desitka

A pale, hoppy beer (3.1%) from the Zatec brewery.

Zlaty Bazant

This gold-coloured, firm, dry Pilsner (4.4%) with a sweet, creamy, malt flavour is one of the popular lagers produced by the Slovakian Zlaty Bazant brewery.

THE BREWERS

Bernard

This family-owned brewery at Humpolec on the main road between Prague and Brno was founded in 1597.

Branik

Originally established by a group of innkeepers in 1900, Branik is now part of the Bass-owned Prague Breweries group led by Staropramen. The dramatic brewhouse and maltings lie among trees in the south of the city. Unfortunately, much of the traditional equipment inside was replaced with conical fermenters and a pasteurization plant in 1992 before Bass took over. Once famous for a strong 14-degree dark lager, it now brews a sweetish pale 10 and 12, and a dark 10.

Budweiser Budvar

The world-famous Budweiser brewery was founded in the town of Ceské Budejovice in 1895, using water from an underground lake. It rapidly became a major exporter, particularly to Germany and the US. Since 1989 the company has doubled in size, with annual production rising from 450,000 to 900,000 hectolitres ((10 million to 22.5 million gallons).

Cerna Hora

The small Moravian country brewery at Cerna Hora, north of Brno, built in 1896, produces a range of light but tasty Pilsners.

Chodovar

This small brewery with a long history dates back to 1573. It is located close to the Bavarian border at Chodova Plana, and brews three pale and one dark, nutty 10-degree beer.

Gambrinus

This brewery, in Plzen, was once restricted to domestic production, but now produces over 1.5 million hectolitres (33 million gallons) a year of the best-selling Czech beer – a pale, 10-degree lager. It is part of the Pilsner Urquell group.

HOPPING WITH HISTORY

The Czech Republic hop-growing tradition dates back to the 9th century, making it one of the longest-standing hop producers in the world. The area around the town of Zatec – better known under its German name of Saaz – became world-famous for the quality of its hops. One Bohemian king, Vaclav IV, even forbade growers from selling cuttings abroad on penalty of death to try to protect the green crop which was worth its weight in gold.

For much of the 19th century, Bohemian hops ruled the world, dictating quality, standards and prices. The town of Zatec was at the heart of a global business, only losing its dominant position after the First World War and the break-up of the Austro-Hungarian Empire.

Even today, major brewers like Anheuser-Busch of the United States still import large amounts of Czech hops. Their quality is so widely respected that the vast bulk of the crop is exported.

Herold

This ancient brewery in Breznice, south of Prague, came back from the dead and is now going strong. It was closed down by the Communist authorities in 1988, but brewer Stanislav Janostik rescued the baroque buildings that date back to 1720, and started up brewing operations there again in 1990. The traditional plant now produces a dark 13-degree, a pale 10-degree and a 12-degree, as well as a wheat beer.

Jihlava

The south-Moravian brewery in Jihlava dates back to 1860. In 1995 it was bought by the Austrian brewer Zwettl and it is now being modernized. However, it is uncertain whether its Jezek (hedgehog) beer brand will survive this restructuring.

Above: This promotional postcard from Ceske Budejovice acknowledges beer's Egyptian origins.

Krusovice

This historic brewery to the west of Prague in the Zatec hop-growing region was taken over by the German brewing group, Binding of Frankfurt, in 1994. The German giant has since invested heavily in modernizing the plant – and in the brewery's ancient heritage, calling its products the beers of King Rudolf II. Krusovice, dating back to 1581, was once part of the royal estate.

Lobkowicz

A family brewery south of Prague near Sedlcany.

Mestan

Part of the Bass-owned Prague Breweries group led by Staropramen, this plant in the suburb of Holesovice is best known for its award-winning, malty, dark 11.

Olomouc

The Moravian brewery, north-east of Brno, typifies the present contradictions in the Czech brewing industry. On the one hand it offers a tasty, unfiltered lager for Czech locals; on the other it now brews American beers under licence.

Ostravar

This substantial brewery in the mining town of Ostrava in northern Moravia was bought by Bass in 1995. The brewery, which dates back to 1897, received the last new brewhouse installed by the Communists in 1987. It produces a wide range of local beers, including three hoppy pale Pilsners called Ponik, Konik and the premium Ondras. It also brews Staropramen 10.

Pilsner Urquell

For 150 years Pilsner Urquell in Plzen has managed to maintain its traditional brewing methods, using huge wooden casks to mature each batch of its revered beer for three months. Watching these massive barrels being rolled out of the underground tunnels and into the brewery for repitching and repair was once one of the famous sights of the old brewing town, along with the grand gates to the brewery. Now only the triumphal arches remain, but behind, everything else has changed. Stacks of conical fermenters have replaced the old casks in a bid to increase the brewery's production and efficiency – and with them has gone a little of the complexity of the famous brew. Pilsner Urquell is the largest brewing group in the Czech Republic by far, producing 72.5 million gallons in 1994, almost double the output of its nearest rival. Pilsner Urquell accounts for about a fifth of the total Czech beer market and a large part of the country's exports. Besides the Urquell brewery itself, the brewing group also includes the neighbouring, larger plant of Gambrinus in Plzen, Domazlice and Karlovy Vary.

Platan

The Platan brewery is part of the South Bohemia breweries group along with Regent and Samson. Platan was originally developed by aristocratic landowners in Protivín, with records dating back to 1598. It takes its name from the local plane (platan) trees in its parkland home.

Radegast

Radegast has risen from being a distant local brewery in north-eastern Moravia, at Nosovice, to become the third largest national concern in the Czech Republic. Built in 1971, mainly to supply the Slovak and Polish markets, the privatized company markets its beers under the symbol of Nordic the god of hospitality, Radegast.

Regent

One of the oldest and most historic Czech breweries, Regent dates back to the 14th century in Trebon. Behind its fine facade, however, it is switching to conical fermenters.

Samson

This is probably the brewery in Ceské Budejovice (Budweis in German) that inspired Adolphus Busch to call his American beer Budweiser. Samson dates from 1795. Its heavily modernized brewery produces a wide range of crisp, dry, pale beers.

Starobrno

This is the major brewery in the Moravian city of Brno. It was founded in 1872 and brews a wide range of beers.

Staropramen

Staropramen – the name means "old spring" – has been brewing in the Smichov district of Prague since 1869. Taken over the the English brewers Bass in 1993, it has retained its open fermenting vessels and traditional lagering tanks.

U Fleku

Probably the most famous home-brew pub in the world, U Fleku also claims to be the oldest. U Fleku has been brewing in Prague since 1499 and its softly spicy, dark brew (5.5%) and wood-panelled rooms and courtyard are one of the taste-and-see attractions of the grand city.

Zlaty Bazant

This is Slovakia's best-known brewery. It produces the popular Golden Pheasant brand of lagers, in the southern town of Hurbanovo. The company is now controlled by the Dutch giant Heineken.

ITALY

The Mediterranean countries of Europe have traditionally been lands flowing with wine. At best, beer is viewed as a summer thirst-quencher. Italian consumption of beer might still be one of the lowest in Europe, but unlike most other markets it is expanding.

Above: Italian beer may not have the cachet of the country's wine, but it is an increasingly popular drink. Peroni, the leading brewer, is making the most of the expanding market.

BREWING, IMPORTED FROM OVER THE ALPS, did not appear in Italy on any significant scale until the 19th century, and then it was limited mainly to the northern region. The Wuhrer brewery of Brescia, founded in 1828 by an Austrian, claims to be the first large commercial concern in the country. The number of breweries grew to about 100 by the end of the century, but then it rapidly declined as production was concentrated in the hands of a few leading companies such as Peroni and Moretti. Brewing – nearly all in a light Pilsner style – was still very small beer until the 1960s. Annual consumption in 1950 was no more than three litres (five pints) a head. However, in the next few decades demand surged, reaching 26 litres (46 pints) by 1995. Most of this (nearly 80%) is sold in bottles. Younger people began to regard beer as a fashionable drink; wine was for their parents or peasants. English-style pubs opened and imports from countries such as Germany and England rocketed, accounting for about one-fifth of all beer sales.

Altogether there are about 20 breweries in Italy today, and many of the major brewers of northern Europe have stepped into this land of expanding opportunity, exporting enthusiastically and buying into the native breweries. Heineken, for example, now controls 40% of production since its purchase of Moretti and the Dreher Group. The French giant BSN (which produces Kronenbourg) has a stake in the country's top brewer Peroni, and through this accounts for 36% of the market. Carlsberg of Denmark also has an interest in the Poretti company.

THE BEERS

Birra Moretti

A light, crisp, yellow-gold lager (4.6%) from Moretti.

Birra Peroni

A pale-gold lager with a malt and hop aroma and a hoppy taste, from Peroni.

Bruna

A reddish, all-malt, strong Munich-style lager (6.25%), with a smooth, spicy, roasted flavour. Brewed by Moretti.

Crystal

Peroni's range of draught premium lagers includes a Speciale and a darker, Viennese-style, malty Crystal Red (both 5.6%), plus an even stronger Crystal Gold (6.6%). Crystal Speciale is a clear, yellow-gold lager (5.6%) with a smooth, rich barley and malt flavour.

Forst Sixtus

This unusual, dark, abbey-style beer (6.5%) is brewed by the Forst family brewery in Lagundo.

Gran Riserva

Strong beers in Italy are known as double malts, and in 1996, to mark its 150th anniversary, Peroni introduced one in distinctive, tall, embossed bottles. Gran Riserva is a deep-gold, full-bodied lager (6.6%).

Italia Pilsner

This yellow-gold, light Italian Pilsner (4.7%) has a dry, bitter flavour. It is a leading brand in the north-west of the country. Itala Pilsen of Padua was taken over by Peroni in 1960.

Kronen

This bright-gold, export-style lager (5%) with a malty taste, from Forst, shows a Viennese influence.

McFarland

Despite its Irish image, this bottom-fermented red beer (5.5%) from Dreher is more a Viennese-style lager.

Nastro Azzuro

Peroni's pale-gold, clean, sweetish premium Pilsner (5.2%) was introduced in 1964. The name means "Blue Ribbon".

Raffo

A light, golden-yellow, dry, mildly bitter Pilsner (4.7%) from Peroni. Raffo is sold mainly around its home city of Taranto in southern Italy.

Right: A Roman relief of a tavern scene. The Romans preferred wine to beer.

Rossa

This is probably the most characterful of Italy's red beers. The rosy-amber-coloured, richly flavoured, all-malt La Rossa (7.5%) from Moretti of Udine gives a robust reminder of northern Italy's former connections with Vienna and its Märzen-style brews.

Sans Souci

A pale-gold, malty export-style lager (5.6%) brewed by Moretti of Udine. It has a good hop balance.

Splügen

The brand name for this range of speciality lagers produced by the Poretti Brewery of Varese is taken from the name of a high mountain pass. The most celebrated of the beers is the deep-copper-coloured, faintly smoky Splügen Fumée, which is made with Franconian malt. There is also a coppery-red, robust, fruity Splügen Rossa (7%) and a German-style, black beer Scura (6%).

Werner Brau

A light Pilsner (4.5%) brewed by Poretti.

Wuhrer Pilsner

This pale Pilsner (4.7%) with a light, hoppy taste, is produced by the Wuhrer brewery in Brescia.

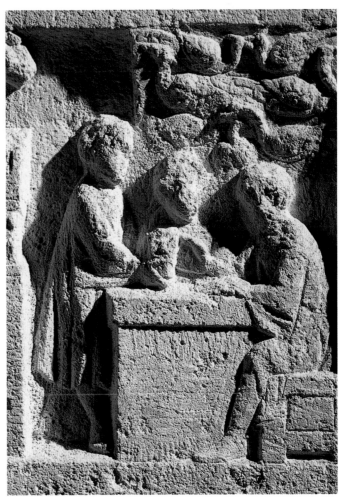

THE BREWERS

Dreher

Italy was once part of a vast Austrian empire, and the celebrated brewer Anton Dreher of Vienna crossed the Alps to establish a brewery in Trieste in the 1860s. Today, the Dreher name lives on in a Milan-based group owned by Heineken. Besides a range of light lagers, its beers include a Vienna-style red lager called McFarland.

Forst

The medium-sized brewery in the mountains at Lagundo is owned by the Fuchs family. It brews beers that show an Austrian influence, notably in the export-style lager Kronen. Forst means "forest" in German.

Moretti

Founded in Udine in 1859, the Moretti brewery became well known on the international markets despite its relatively small size. This is helped by its appealing labels showing a moustachioed man blowing the froth off his glass of beer. Besides a light, crisp Birra Moretti there is also a more malty export Sans Souci and two more characterful, darker brews – an all-malt Moretti Bruna and the richly flavoured red Moretti Rossa. In recent years, the company has changed hands at a dizzy rate and is now owned by Dutch giant Heineken.

Peroni

Until Heineken combined Dreher with Moretti in 1996, Peroni was the leading Italian brewer. Founded in Vigevano in 1846, it soon concentrated its activities in Rome then spread out, taking over breweries throughout the peninsula. Since merging with Wuhrer in 1988, it has concentrated production at five plants. Its leading blue-ribbon brand is Nastro Azzurro, but it also brews a lighter Peroni Birra. Other similar regional brands include Itala Pilsen, Raffo and Wuhrer. There is also a "Crystal" range. In 1996, Peroni added a more full-bodied bottled Gran Riserva.

Poretti

The Poretti company was founded in 1877 in Varese, north of Milan. It now has a second brewery in Ceccano, south of Rome. Besides a light Pilsner – Werner Brau – it also produces a number of distinctive specialities under the Splügen brand name. Carlsberg has now bought the brewery.

Wunster

Wunster is another Italian brewery that has Germanic origins. The brewery was founded by the Bavarian Heinrich von Wunster and is based in Bergamo. For many years it was a family concern, but it is now part of the large Belgian Interbrew group.

MALTA AND THE ENGLISH CONNECTION

The tiny island country of Malta off the coast of Sicily has a distinctive brewing tradition and is something of an anomaly in the Mediterranean region.

The legacy of the British Empire still lingers over this independent Mediterranean island. Its one brewery, Simonds, Farsons, Cisk (which is now commonly known as Farsons) started up to brew beers for the sailors at the British naval base there, in the top-fermenting ale styles that they enjoyed back home. Simonds of Reading, England exported ale and stout to Malta in the 19th century, then helped to set up a brewery in cooperation with a local company Farrugian and Sons. Although the British are long gone, the brewery remains, still producing these English-style, top-fermenting ales and a range of lagers under the Cisk brand name.

The Farsons brewery now produces a darkish, soft, mild ale (3.6%) called Blue Label and a stronger ale (5%) called Brewer's Choice. It also brews a hoppy pale ale (4%), Hop Leaf and a creamy, milk stout (3.4%) with a dry finish,, Lacto, which is brewed using lactose (milk sugar) and claims to be "Milk Stout with Vitamin B for Extra Energy". The brewery at Mriehel also produces lagers under the Cisk label. As well as alcoholic drinks, Farsons is the island's main soft drink producer.

Water is a scarce resource on the rocky island of Malta so Farsons collects every spare drop of rainwater in huge rooftop reservoirs, to be stored in underground tanks.

GREECE AND TURKEY

Civilized chat over a drink is a key part of both Turkish and Greek social customs. But on these occasions beer has always come a rather ragged second to wine, or strong coffee and potent aniseed ouzo or raki.

CONTROL BY breweries from northern Europe has reached saturation point in Greece, virtually wiping out the local industry. The only large, Greek-owned brewery – Fix – closed in 1983, and foreign companies and brands now dominate the market. The country's Bavarian-influenced beer purity law (which insisted that beers were made using all-malt) has gone, under pressure from foreign brewers. However, the island of Cyprus has managed to maintain a popular local lager – Keo.

Turkey, in contrast, has a thriving local producer in the shape of Efes, which worked hard to develop the market for international-style light lager after the state brewing monopoly, Tekel, was relaxed in 1955. The Danish-owned Turk Tuborg and state-run breweries in Istanbul, Ankara and Yozgat compete, but Efes dominates the Turkish market.

Above: Keo, from Cyprus, won a Gold Medal for Excellence at the 1987 World Bottled Lager Competition.

THE BEERS AND BREWERS

Aegean
This sweetish, malty Pilsner (5%) is produced in the north of Greece by Athenian Breweries, which is wholly owned by the Dutch giant Heineken. It has a hint of toffee and a slightly bittersweet edge.

Efes Pilsener
This golden, sweetish, full-bodied premium lager (5%), produced by Efes in Turkey, is widely exported. The company takes its name from the ancient Roman city of Ephesus, and its full title, Efes Pilsen Bira Fabrikasi, indicates an intention to brew a dry, hoppy Pilsner. The company also brews Efes Light, an Extra and an alcohol-free Alkolsuz Efes.

The Efes brewery has branched out in recent years and as well as running four breweries in its home country, it now also runs two malting plants and a brewery in Romania.

Keo
This sweetish, full-bodied, Pilsner-type lager (4.5%) is brewed in Lemesos, southern Cyprus, by the Keo brewery. It is bottled fresh and unpasteurized. Keo is one of the few remaining local brewers.

FRANCE

France is mainly associated with some of the great wines of the world, and French beer is rarely given a second thought. Beer in France is treated as a refreshment, not as a serious drink in its own right, and the industry is dominated by a few large companies.

DROP INTO MOST FRENCH cafés and ask for *une bière* and you will be served a *pression* (draught) of light, refreshing but undemanding lager. Most of this beer is brewed in the Alsace region, close to the German border in the east of the country. The German influence is obvious in the place-names and the cuisine of the area, but most of the beer is a pale shadow of the better-quality brews across the border. The French do not have a beer purity law but use a variety of adjuncts, and have been the most vigorous campaigners against the German Rheinheitsgebot, claiming that it restrains trade. In addition, they allow their lagers much less time to mature than German brewers and they tend to use a relatively small quantity of hops.

The centre of the French lager brewing industry is Strasbourg and the major names are Kronenbourg and Kanterbräu, both owned by the same BSN conglomerate, which dominates about half the domestic beer market. The Dutch giant Heineken also has a major stake in the French market, owning the "33", Mutzig and Pelforth brands and controlling almost a quarter of the trade. In 1996, they added to this by taking over the sizeable Fischer group.

One region of France, the Nord-Pas de Calais in the north-east close to Belgium, does boast its own distinctive traditional beer style. A number of small breweries in this region, especially around Lille, brew "bières de garde" (keeping beers), which are strong, top-fermenting, bottle-conditioned ales. These were traditionally made in farmhouses in the winter and spring before the heat of summer made brewing too unpredictable. More commercial versions are now produced, some of which are bottom-fermented and filtered, but still retain an ale-like fruitiness through warm fermentation. They are often sold in champagne-style wired and corked bottles. The brewers who use barley and hops from the region are entitled to use the appellation "Pas de Calais/Région du Nord".

Above: Bière de garde from the rural north of France is still sold in large corked bottles. Jenlain is probably the most famous example of the type.

THE BEERS

Abbaye de Vaucelles

Not so much a Belgian abbey-style beer as a French bière de garde (7.5%), this amber-coloured, honey-like drink is brewed with herbs by the Choulette brewery for an abbey near Cambrai.

Ackerland

Two strong, malty lagers – the rich, malty, amber-coloured Ackerland Blonde (5.9%) and the dark Ackerland Brune (6.3%), which has a sweeter flavour – are sold under this brand name. Both are produced by the independent Meteor brewery of Hochfelden in Alsace. The name is taken from the agricultural area which lies around the village.

Adelscott

Labelled a "Bière au Malt à Whisky", this faintly smoky, amber-red, pale lager (6.4%) from the Adelschoffen brewery, is made using peaty Scottish malt. It created a niche market when it was launched in the early 1980s.

Adelscott Noir

This is another (6.6%) Bière au Malt à Whisky from Adelschoffen. It is almost black, with red highlights, and has an intense, peaty, slightly smoky flavour.

Amberley

Pelforth brewery of Lille introduced this whisky malt beer (7.3%) in 1993 as a rival to the popular brews produced by Adelscott.

Ambre de Flandres

A mellow, oaky, bottom-fermented bière de garde (6.4%) from the Jeanne d'Arc brewery at Ronchin, near Lille, sold under the Orpal brand name.

Ancre

A popular Alsace lager (4.8%), Ancre is brewed by Heineken at Schiltigheim.

Bière des Templiers

A dark, fruity, sedimented bière de garde (8.5%) from the Saint Sylvestre brewery..

Bière du Désert

This strong, pale-yellow-gold, fruity beer (7%) is brewed by Gayant.

Breug

See Terken.

Brune Spéciale

A deep, amber-brown dark lager (6.7%) with a roasted malt flavour, produced by the Terken brewery.

Certa

This alcohol-free beer was the first of its kind to be produced in France. Unusually, it is available on draught. Certa is brewed by Les Brasseurs de Gayant, a firm normally famous for its strong beers.

Ch'ti

The name is local Picardy patois for a French north-easterner and is the brand name for the bières de garde produced by the Castelain brewery of Bénifontaine, near Lens. The richly fruity beers from this coal-scarred region, featuring a rugged miner on the label, include a deep-gold, malty-fruity blonde and a darker brune version (both 6.5%) as well as a deep-amber-coloured Ch'ti Amber (5.9%).

Choulette Framboise

A seasonal, speciality, top-fermented, unpasteurized bière de garde (6%). It is flavoured with natural raspberry extract to produce a tart, fruity flavour and is brewed by La Choulette farmhouse brewery.

Cuivrée

Cuivrée is a powerfully smooth, Vienna-style reddish lager (8%) with a strong, fruity, malty flavour brewed by the independent Schutzenberger brewery of Schiltigheim.

Cuvée de Jonquilles

This is a golden-coloured, flowery, fruity, top-fermented, bottle-conditioned spring brew (7%) produced by the Bailleux family brewery in the Café Restaurant au Baron in Gussignies.

Démon

La Bière du Démon from Les Brasseurs de Gayant of Douai claims to be the strongest blonde beer in the world, with 12% alcohol. Brewed with extra malt and a special lager yeast, it has a fiery but rather heavy, honeyish character with a small head.

Fischer Gold

A strong lager (6.5%) with a perfumy aroma and a hoppy flavour from Fischer. It is sold in a distinctive swing-stoppered bottle.

Goldenberg

A strong, malty, golden beer (6.4%) from Gayant of Douai.

Goudale

Goudale is a pale top-fermented traditional bière de garde (7.2%) with a full, fruity flavour, from Les Brasseurs de Gayant. The beer is bottle-conditioned and wire-corked in the traditional manner.

Jade

This is a *bière biologique* or organic beer. Jade is a refreshing, pale-yellow, fruity lager (4.6%) that is produced using only organically grown malt and hops by the Castelain brewery of Bénifontaine, near Lens. The unpasteurized, fresh, hoppy brew can be sold in a large, champagne-style bottle.

Jenlain

This strong, reddish-amber, all-malt bière de garde (6.5%) is the best-known of its type. It is a top-fermented brew, packed with spicy, fruity flavours. The Duyck brewery of Jenlain, near Valenciennes, still sells Jenlain in classic corked and wired bottles, but it is also available in smaller, capped bottles.

Jubilator

Jubilator is a golden, aromatic, full-bodied, pale doppelbock (7%) in the German style, from the Schutzenberger brewery of Schiltigheim.

Killian

George Killian's Bière Rousse (6.5%), an Irish-style, strong, malty red ale, is brewed by Pelforth of Lille. The beer is sold in the Netherlands as Kylian.

Kronenbourg

The main Kronenbourg beer (5.2%) is a light-tasting lager and the stronger 1664 (5.9%), popularly known as "soixante-quatre", is smoother but a little more full-bodied. There is also a weaker Kronenbourg Légère (3.1%). A hoppier variant of the standard lager is called Kronenbourg Tradition Allemande, while Kronenbourg Tradition Anglaise is softer and deeper amber in colour. There is also a maltier, dark version of 1664 called Brune, and two seasonal brews, a rosy La Bière de Noël and a golden Kronenbourg Bière de Mars.

L'Angélus

The label for Annoeullin's hazy golden-bronze wheat bière de garde (7%) features J. F. Millet's painting of pious peasants at prayer in the fields. The beer has a very fresh, fruity, creamy flavour.

La Bière Amoureuse

This is a distinctly un-beerlike lager (4.9%). It is flavoured with ginseng and herbs. According to the brewers Fischer these "natural plant extracts" produce an aphrodisiac effect on the lucky drinker.

La Choulette

This is an amber-coloured, soft, fruity bière de garde (7.5%), produced by La Choulette farmhouse brewery using a blend of top and bottom-fermenting yeasts at warm temperatures. Local malts and Flemish and Hallertau hops are used in the brew, and the beers are roughly filtered in order to leave some yeast in the bottle. A blonde version is also available. Both are bottle-conditioned. The name comes from a traditional local game similar to golf.

Lutèce

This powerful, malty sourish bière de garde (6.4%) is produced by the Enfants de Gayant brewery in Douai.

Meteor

This light, hoppy, unpasteurized, Pilsner-style lager (4.6%) is produced by the Alsace brewery, Meteor.

Mortimer

Meteor's fruity, all-malt, copper-coloured, Vienna-style strong lager (8%) was first brewed in Hochfelden in 1993. It is bottled and packaged to look like a malt whisky.

Mutzig Old Lager

A strong, characterful, amber lager (7.3%), with a rich malt-and-hops flavour, produced by the Mutzig brewery in Alsace near the French-German border.

Mutzig Pilsner

A standard, golden, hoppy Pilsner (4.8%) brewed by the Mutzig brewery, Schiltingheim, Alsace.

Noordheim

A creamy, pale lager (4.7%) brewed by Terken of Roubaix for sale in supermarkets. It is sold in small 25 cl bottles.

Pastor Ale

Subtitled "C'est une symphonie", this all-malt, amber-coloured bière de garde (6.5%) hits all the right tart, fruity, hoppy notes. It is brewed using bottom-fermenting yeasts and Saaz and Flemish hops by one of the classic bière de garde producers, the Annoeullin farm brewery near Lille. It can be bought either unfiltered in tall, wire-corked bottles or in more conventional small capped bottles in packs. The name is a pun on Beethoven's *Pastorale Symphony*.

Patriator

Darker and fruitier than its sister beer Jubilator, Patriator (7%) is a doppelbock which is produced by the Schutzenberger brewery of Schiltigheim.

Pêcheur

See Fischer.

Pelforth Brune

A strong, sweetish, dark lager (6.5%) with a warm, rich, chocolatey-malt flavour, produced by the Pelforth brewery.

Pelforth Blonde

A light, fruity lager (5.8%) from the Pelforth brewery near Lille.

Pelican Lager

A standard, golden lager (4.8%) with a malty flavour, from the Pelforth brewery near Lille.

Porter 39

A rich, strong, roasted porter (6.9%), produced by the Pelforth brewery.

Saaz

A hoppy lager (5.2%) brewed by Gayant of Douai.

Saint Arnoldus

A fruity, abbey-style sediment beer (7.5%) from the Castelain brewery of Bénifontaine, near Lens. The beer is filtered, then yeast is added again before bottling.

Saint Landelin

A range of French top-fermenting abbey-style beers from Les Brasseurs de Gayant of Douai named after the founder of L'Abbaye de Crespin. The range includes: a sweet, creamy Blonde (5.9%), which has a rich-gold hue and a fruity flavour; a reddish-brown Saint Landelin Ambrée (6.1%), with a full, biscuity-malt

flavour; and a richer, dark Brune (6.2%), with a coffee-chocolatey flavour. All the beers are matured for two months before bottling.

Sans Culottes

There is nothing missing from this classic, golden bière de garde (6.5%) produced by La Choulette brewery of north-eastern France. Top-fermented and bottle-conditioned, it is full of yeasty character. The name, usually interpreted as meaning "without trousers", refers to the French revolutionary soldiers.

Schutz Deux Milles

This richly fruity, bottle-conditioned brew (6.5%) from Schutzenberger was originally brewed to mark the 2,000th anniversary of Strasbourg.

Sebourg

The blonde sister to Jenlain from the Duyck brewery of Valenciennes, this full-flavoured, aromatic bière de garde (6%) also comes in tall

corked and wired bottles. It is not brewed in Jenlain, but in the neighbouring village of Sebourg.

Septante Cinq

This powerful, reddish-amber-coloured lager (7.5%) is described as a bière de garde. It is the flagship brand of the Terken brewery.

Tourtel

This low-alcohol lager (1%) from Kanterbräu comes in blonde, amber or brown versions.

Trois Monts

This classic, harvest-gold, top-fermenting bière de garde (8%) is produced by the Saint Sylvestre brewery near the Belgian border. This complex, dry and winey brew is named after three local hills which stand out in the flat Flanders landscape.

Upstaal

A mild, pale lager (3%) with a sweet, appley taste, from Terken.

Wel Scotch

This dark-amber-coloured lager (6.2%) is produced by Kronenbourg, using Scottish whisky malt.

Willfort

A malty, dark lager (6.6%) from the Kronenbourg group.

"33"

Trente-trois is a popular number in France, south-east Asia and Africa, where this light export Pilsner (4.8%) with a malted cereal flavour has developed a large market in the old French empire. Originally brewed near Paris, it is now comes from Marseilles.

THE BREWERS

Adelschoffen

The Alsatian brewery in Schiltigheim, near Strasbourg, founded in 1864, has been described as a brewing laboratory. Its most famous creation is the Adelscott whisky malt beer.

Castelain

Specialist brewer of the Ch'ti bières de garde based at Bénifontaine near Lens.

La Choulette

La Choulette farmhouse brewery began to market the traditional, fruity La Choulette bière de garde in 1981. They are top-fermented and bottle-conditioned, and there are also seasonal specials. The brewery in Hordain, near Valenciennes, dates back to 1885.

Deux Rivières

Two Bretons set up this micro-brewery in 1985 in Morlaix in Brittany, inspired by tasting traditional Welsh ales. Its two main bitters are Coreff Red Label (4.6%) and Black Label (6%).

Duyck

The family farmhouse brewery near Valenciennes, near the Belgian border, has brewed the best-known bière de garde, Jenlain, since 1922. Duyck kept the style alive when most other brewers in the region were abandoning these traditional beers. It also markets another golden country beer called Sebourg and two seasonal specialities, Duyck Bière de Noël (6.8%) and a refreshing pale Duyck Bière de Printemps.

Above: Bière du Démon.

Fischer

Founded in 1821, the brewery in Schiltigheim, near Strasbourg, also sells its beers under a French version of its name, Pêcheur. It brews a variety of lagers, such as Poussez, the cherry-flavoured Fischer Kriek and the so-called aphrodisiac lager – La Bière Amoureuse.

Gayant

Les Brasseurs de Gayant at Douai was formed in 1919 from a merger of four family breweries. Named after the two giants who traditionally protected this French Flanders town near Lille, the firm is famous for its strong beers. It produces a bière de garde, the top-fermented speciality of the region, called La Goudale (7.2%) but is better known for its devilishly powerful Bière du Démon (12%), which claims to be the strongest blonde beer in the world. It also brews a less strong, but far from arid, fruity Bière du Désert, and a rare abbey-style range of beers, Saint Landelin, and some more standard lagers which are marketed under the Saaz and Goldenberg brands.

Above: The handsome Duyck brewery in the hamlet of Jenlain.

Kanterbräu

Now seen as Kronenbourg's second-string brand, at one time Kanterbräu was the largest brewing group in France. Its main brewery at Champigneulles, near Nancy in Lorraine, dates back to 1887 and it also has a second smaller plant at Rennes in Brittany. Besides a light lager Kanterbrau (4.5%), it also brews a stronger Kanterbräu Gold and a low-alcohol lager called Tourtel. The brewery is named after a German brewmaster, Maître Kanter. In 1994 Kanterbräu formally combined with Kronenbourg under the name Les Brasseries Kronenbourg.

Kronenbourg

France's dominant beer brand takes its name from the Cronenbourg quarter of Strasbourg (the use of the K was felt to be more beerily Germanic). The company grew after the Second World War by selling its premium Bière d'Alsace across France in small bottles, at a time when most take-home lagers were low in strength and sold in litre bottles. In 1952 a "super premium" Kronenbourg 1664, named after the firm's founding date, was added. In 1969 a vast brewery was opened at Obernai, and shortly afterwards the company became part of BSN.

Meteor

Probably the best of the Alsace lager brewers, this family company in Hochfelden, dating back to 1640, asked the Czechs if they could use the term Pilsner in 1927 and received a written agreement from Pilsner Urquell. Météor sells more than half its beers on draught in bars where it is unpasteurized. It also sells two strong lagers, Ackerland Blonde and Brune.

Mutzig

An Alsace brewery, that brews its beers at Schiltigheim.

Pelforth

This brewery near Lille, with its pelican trademark, has become famous for its strong speciality beers, notably its Pelforth Brune which was introduced in 1937. There's also a Pelforth Blonde and a standard Pelican lager. The name Pelforth is an anglicized abbreviation of "pelican" and "forte" (strong), which was adopted in 1972. It also brews George Killian's Bière Rousse, a porter, a whisky malt brew called Amberley, a rich bière de Noël (both 7.3%) and a seasonal spring bière de Mars (5.3%).

Saint Sylvestre

One of the classic country brewers of French Flanders, it has been brewing in the village of Saint Sylvestre Cappel near Hazebrouck for over a century. It produces a traditional bière de garde, Bock du Moulin, and the seasonal brews Bière de Mars and de Noël.

Schutzenberger

The only independent brewery left in the famous brewing town of Schiltigheim, near Strasbourg, was founded in 1740. It brews some of the most distinctive beers in Alsace, notably two French bockbiers, a pale Jubilator and the darker Patriator and a stronger-still Cuivrée (8%). Other beers include the bottle-conditioned Schutz Deux Milles and two seasonal brews for Christmas and spring.

Terken

Roubaix's independent brewery produces a wide range of beers under various brand names. It is best known for its flagship Septante Cinq, but it also brews Brune Spéciale, a blonde lager called Orland (5.9%), the festive Terken Bière de Noël (7%) and a low-alcohol brew called Elsoner. Its supermarket brands include Breug, Noordheim, Ubald, Überland and Upstaal.

BREWPUBS

Brasseurs

Les Brasseurs is a chain of home-brew pubs in northern France, which started with a palatial pub by the main railway station in Lille. The colourful, unpasteurized, all-malt beers include a Brasseurs ambre – blonde and brune – and a cloudy, fruity wheat beer, blanche.

Frog & Rosbif

The Paris home-brew pub in the Rue St Denis has been brewing English-style ales with Anglo-French punning names since 1993. The beers include a bitter Inseine, a stronger ale Parislytic and a stout Dark de Triomphe. In 1996 it opened a second brewpub, the Frog & Princess, across the Seine in St-Germain-des-Prés.

SWITZERLAND

Despite having one of the earliest-known, large-scale breweries in Europe – the Abbey of St Gallen, which dates back to the 9th century – the Swiss were predominantly wine drinkers until well into the 19th century.

Above: The Swiss beer market is dominated by two big names – Feldschlösschen and Hürlimann. Feldschlösschen's hoppy lager is a best-selling brew.

SWISS BEERS tend to be as clean as the mountain air, but less breathtaking than the scenery. Little malting barley and few hops are grown in the rugged country. Led by the German-speaking areas of the north, however, in the mid-1800s the Swiss began to adopt the new bottom-fermenting lager beers from Bavaria. Some enterprising brewers in Zurich even chipped away their ice supplies from the Grindelwald glacier. Between 1850 and 1885 the number of breweries snowballed from 150 to 530. Since that date, much of the choice has melted away, leaving little more than 30 breweries remaining today. Once sales agreements helped to keep local breweries alive but now, like its alpine neighbour Austria, the country is dominated by two main groups – Feldschlösschen (which also controls Cardinal, Gurten, Valaisanne and Warteck) and the more internationally known Hürlimann (which includes Löwenbräu of Zurich). Heineken of the Netherlands also owns Haldengut and Calanda.

Like Austria, the main beer in Switzerland is a fresh, clean-tasting, malty lager. Although there is no complete beer purity law, most beers are all-malt and most brands are fairly similar in taste. Pilsners are barely mentioned. The Swiss prefer to ask for blonde lagers. Dark beers account for little more than 1% of sales. Most of the so-called specialities are just stronger, golden lagers, and only a few wheat beers are produced.

On international markets, Switzerland is probably best known for two distinctly different products. On the light side are low or no-alcohol brews, such as Birell, while at the heavyweight end of the market there is Samichlaus from Hürlimann , one of the strongest beers in the world. A recent innovation is the establishment of a chain of home-brew pubs, Back und Brau (Bake and Brew) which, as the name suggests, bakes baguettes and quiches while brewing fresh, unfiltered Huus (house) lagers and other beers, such as an Altbier.

THE BEERS

Anker

A rare, dark, top-fermenting Altbier (5.8%) that was launched by the Cardinal brewery of Fribourg in 1980 in a bid to develop the limited speciality beer trade. It was marketed as a move back to tradition – "the way beer used to be".

Barbara

The patron saint of the artillery has given her name to this deep-golden-coloured "de luxe" strong lager (5.9%), produced by the Eichhof brewery in Luzern . It is a smooth, slightly sweet beer with a hint of malt.

Birell

Hürlimann of Zurich's golden, low-alcohol lager is now brewed around the world. Unlike many other near beers, the alcohol is not removed by distillation after fermentation, or by osmosis. Instead it uses a special yeast strain, which produces just 0.8% alcohol.

Braugold

This light, clear-gold premium lager beer (5.2%) is brewed to a special recipe using only the best ingredients. Eichhof claims that it is the best-selling premium brand beer in Switzerland.

Calanda Weizen

One of the few Swiss wheat beers, Calanda Weizen is a lightly fruity brew in the Bavarian style. It comes from the Calanda brewery, based in Chur in the eastern side of the country, and it was founded in 1780.

Cardinal Lager

A light, tawny-gold lager (4.9%), with a smooth, malt and hops flavour, produced at the Fribourg brewery.

Cardinal Rheingold

An amber, malty, strong lager (6.3%) with a gentle perfumed aroma, from the Fribourg brewery.

Castello

This strong, full-bodied, sweetish lager, has a malty flavour. It is brewed by Feldschlösschen.

Dreikönigs

Hürlimann's stark (strong), sweetish pale lager (6.5%) is brewed in Zurich. The name of this rich, malty beer means "Three Kings", from the coat of arms of a Zurich district.

Dunkle Perle

A dark, malty lager (5.2%) brewed by Feldschlösschen.

Eichhof Lager

This standard, refreshing, clear-gold lager (4.8%) is the flagship brew of the Eichhof brewery in Luzern . It is available on tap and in bottles and cans.

Hexen Bräu

A creamy, amber-brown Dunkel (5.4%) with a chocolatey flavour produced by Hürlimann. Its name means "witches' brew" and brewing coincides with the full moon. (See Swiss Moonshine panel.)

Hopfenperle

Feldschlösschen's hoppy lager (5.2%) from Rheinfelden is probably the most widely distributed beer in Switzerland.

Hubertus

This is a dark, strong, deep-amber-coloured, premium lager (5.7%) brewed by

Eichhof in Luzern . The unusual colour comes from the roasted malts used in the mash. Its smooth, malty, slightly sweet flavour goes well with cold meats, especially game.

Hürlimann Lager Bier

This malty, golden, standard lager (4.8%) is the main brew from the Hürlimann brewery.

Löwenbräu

A malty, golden Pilsner-style lager (4.7%) with a light, hoppy flavour, from the Löwenbräu subsidiary of Hürlimann (no connection to the famous German, international brewing giant).

Moussy

A deep, bright-gold, alcohol-free beer with an intense malt flavour, from the Cardinal brewery, Fribourg.

Pony

This clear, sparkling deep-golden Pilsner-type of beer (5.7%) with a strong, but well-balanced, bitter, hoppy flavour, is produced by the Eichhof brewery, Luzern .

Rheingold

This is a strong, full-bodied golden-coloured lager (6.3%). Rheingold is produced by the Cardinal brewery of Fribourg.

highly alcoholic cognac and cough-mixture character, it is a smooth beer to sip and savour before going to sleep.

Samichlaus

Classed as the world's strongest lager at a staggering 14%, Samichlaus (Santa Claus) is brewed just once a year at the beginning of December by Hürlimann of Zurich and then left to mature for 12 months before being ready to redden Father Christmas's nose the following festive season. This reddish-brown brew, first introduced in 1980, is testimony to the gutsy fighting qualities of Hürlimann's quality yeast strain, and a constant contender for the *Guinness Book of Records*. With its

Spiess Edelhell

This pale-gold lager (4.8%) is brewed to the original recipe of the Eichhof brewery's founder in 1834, and the label has changed little since then. The beer's smooth, well-rounded flavour is not too bitter, and the Eichhof brewery attributes this to the "secret" mix of cereals in the mash.

Sternbräu

A golden-amber, full-bodied Spezial (5.2%) with a malt and hops flavour, brewed by Hürlimann. The name means "star beer" and is inspired by the brewery's five-pointed star emblem.

Tambour

A strong, golden Starkbier (Starkbier means "strong beer") produced by the Wartek brewery.

Vollmond

See panel.

Wartek Lager

A hazy, golden lager, with a good malty flavour, produced by the Wartek brewery, Basel. There is also a malty Wartek Brune, and a fruity, copper-coloured, top-fermenting Wartek Alt.

THE BREWERS

Cardinal

The Fribourg brewery, founded in 1788, originally developed its Cardinal beers to celebrate the election of the bishop of Fribourg to the Papacy. It is one of the few national brands.

Eichhof

This is Switzerland's largest independent brewery, commanding a market share of 7%. The name Eichhof was born in 1937, but the company's origins can be traced back to a brewery set up by Traugott Spiess in Luzern in 1834.

Feldschlösschen

Switzerland's largest brewer, based at Rheinfelden, near Basel since 1874, merged with Cardinal of Fribourg, in 1992 and Hurlimann in 1996 to become Feldschlösschen-Hurlimann, the biggest brewer in the land by far.

The Feldschlösschen castle-like plant at Rheinfelden, set in grand grounds, looks a fitting home for the country's ruling beer dynasty. Its polished brewhouse even comes complete with stained-glass windows and marble pillars.

Feldschlösschen's main lager is the hoppy Hopfenperle. There is also a darker Dunkle Perle, a stronger, sweeter Castello and an alcohol-free Ex-Bier.

Hürlimann

Hürlimann was founded in 1836 in Zurich, where it now dominates the market. It is Switzerland's best-known brewery abroad.

Löwenbräu

No relation to the Munich giant, this lion brewery is a subsidiary of Hürlimann, producing a range of similar lagers, as well as a Celtic Whisky Brew.

Ueli

This small brewery, established behind the Fischerstube café in Basle in 1974 was Switzerland's first micro-brewery. It brews a fruity Ueli Weizenbier, a malty Ueli Dunkel and a light Ueli Lager.

Wartek

This is the leading brewery in Basel, established in 1856.

SWISS MOONSHINE

The Swiss may have a rather conservative image, but one beer casts them in a totally different light. In 1992, the family-run Locher brewery of Appenzell, near St Gallen, revived an old tradition when it started brewing beers at the full moon, reflecting local beliefs about the effect of the moon's pull on earthly, particularly biological, events. Brewer Karl Locher claims that beer brewed at this time ferments more quickly. His golden Vollmond (full moon) lager, produced in two strengths (4.8% and 5.2%), caught the public's imagination – so much so that Hürlimann of Zurich began to brew its chocolatey, dark lager Hexen Bräu (5.4%) on the same monthly night shift when the full moon was peering through the clouds. The name means "witches' brew".

SPAIN

Recently, chilled, thirst-quenching, pale lager has taken a firm hold on the wine-drinking Spanish. Few other beers are now brewed or drunk there, and consumption has been rising rapidly over the last 20 years.

THE SPANIARDS HAVE a brewing tradition going back centuries. The Romans were impressed by the grain-based brews of the Iberian peninsula. The 16th-century King of Spain, Charles I, was a great lover of beer, and under his influence the first commercial Spanish breweries were set up by Flemish and German members of his court. However, it is only in the last few decades that beer has become a truly popular drink. Spain has witnessed a remarkable revolution. In 1948, drinkers in this country of robust wines drank less than three litres (five pints) of beer per head, per annum. Now, however, the Spaniards are the keenest imbibers in the Mediterranean region, consuming about 70 litres (125 pints) per person each year – considerably more than either France or Italy. Most of the beer that is drunk is a light, thirst-quenching lager – cerveza Pilsner that is brewed with a mix of malt and corn grits and matured for a short period, with a strength of about 4.5%. The bulk of this is sold in bottles, with a substantial amount on draught in bars and cafés. In recent years, influenced by the demands of northern European tourists and the growing amounts of imported beers, there has been a switch to a stronger, more malty, full-bodied "especial" beer (around 5.5%) approximately in the Dortmunder style, or a stronger-still "especial extra". A few dark lagers and some low or no ("sin") alcohol brews can also be found.

The country is dominated by five major breweries – Cruzcampo, Aguila, San Miguel, Damm and Mahou – and there is a strong international presence. Guinness owns the largest brewer, Cruzcampo, while Heineken controls its main rival, Aguila. Since Franco's demise in 1975 opened the door to foreign investors, international companies have been active in Spain, making the most of the boom in beer consumption.

Above: The best-known brand outside Spain, San Miguel, was originally brewed by a Filippino company.

THE BEERS

Adlerbräu

The copper-coloured, sweetish, fruity, malty cerveza especial (5.5%) with the German-sounding name is influenced by the style of Munich dunkels. It is brewed by Aguila (the Eagle).

Aguila Pilsner

Aguila's standard golden lager (4.5%) with a full-bodied, corn-sweet taste. It is allowed to mature for three weeks during its production.

Aguila Reserva Extra

At 6.5%, this is a powerful, malty "extra" from Aguila.

Alhambra

The refreshing Alhambra Pilsen (4.6%), which is also sold as "Star", the more malty Especial (5.4%), and dark Alhambra Negra (5.4%) all come from the brewery of the same name based in Granada.

Ambar

A refreshing, golden lager (4.2%) and stronger deep-amber-coloured especial (5.2%) with a malty flavour, from La Zaragozana.

Bock-Damm

This is a deep, black-brown, malty, German-style bock beer (5.4%) with a thick, pale-cream head, produced by Damm. It is a specialist beer in Spanish terms, as well as a reminder of the Damm brewery's Germanic origins.

Cinco Estrellas

The name means "five stars" and this is the strong, darker, malty especial (5.5%) produced by the Mahou brewery of Madrid.

Cruzcampo

The Cruzcampo brewery is breaking out of its traditional market in Andalucía in the south of Spain, to launch national brands, including this pale-gold lager (4.7%) with a dry, sourish, citrus flavour.

Edel

This light-golden, all-malt, refreshing Pilsner (4.8%) is produced by Spain's pioneering lager producer, Damm. It is a premium product and is aimed at the quality end of the beer market.

Estrella Damm

This bright-gold, honeyish, premium-quality Pilsner (5.4%) is one of Damm's best-known beers. This "star" lager is a thirst-quencher, intended to be served cold on a hot day. A "light", low-calorie version is also available (3.2%).

Mahou Classic

This sweet, malty beer with a hoppy finish is the standard lager (4.8%) produced by Madrid's main brewery of the same name.

Marlen

A malty, Dortmunder-style lager (5.8%), Marlen is brewed by Zaragoza's La Zaragozana brewery.

Nostrum de San Miguel

This lager is smoother and richer than its stablemate San Miguel. It is an amber-gold-coloured, full-bodied, strong especial lager (6.2%).

San Miguel Premium

The malty, hoppy flagship lager of the San Miguel company is a relatively strong lager (5.4%) with light, citrus notes and good body. Like much of the company's output, it is aimed at the quality end of the market.

Estrella

Estrella, meaning "star", is a popular name for lagers, including Estrella del Sur from Cruzcampo, especials from Damm and Mahou (Cinco Estrellas) and an extra-powerful Estrella Extra from Coruna.

Voll-Damm

This tawny golden, full-bodied, robust, strong lager (7.2%) with a creamy, hop flavour is produced by Damm. It is much more similar to a Dortmunder Export lager than to the dark, Franconian Vollbier it is named after.

Xibeca

This popular, refreshing light-golden Pilsner (4.6%) is brewed by Damm of Barcelona. It is mainly produced and sold for home consumption in large 1-litre bottles as well as cans.

Zaragozana Export

This rich, reddish, extra-strong export lager (7%) is brewed by La Zaragozana brewery in the town of Zaragoza.

THE BREWERS

Aguila

A famous Spanish brewery dating back to 1900, Aguila (the Eagle) for many years flew high above the rest of the industry. Aguila had its roots in Madrid, but by 1980 the company was running eight breweries across the country and was half as big again as any of its rivals. By 1987, however, the rival Cruzcampo group was threatening to ease the eagle off the top perch, and Aguila came under the control of international giant Heineken. The number of plants was reduced from seven to four – in Madrid, Valencia, Córdoba and Zaragoza. Aguila, always well-known for its draught beer, brews a light Pilsner, a sweeter especial called Adlerbräu and more full-bodied Reserva Extra. Like many Spanish lagers, the beers are brewed with corn grits as well as barley malt and lagered for three weeks. Production is now concentrated in two large, modern breweries in Madrid and Valencia.

Alhambra

This is one of Spain's smaller breweries. It was founded in 1925 in the far south of the country in Granada. It has links with Damm in Barcelona.

Cruzcampo

Spain's largest brewing group was formed through the merger of a number of regional breweries in 1987. Since 1990, it has been owned by Irish stout brewers Guinness, who added Union Cervecera in 1991. The combine now controls about

Above: Cruzcampo is now owned by Guinness of Ireland.

a quarter of the market, with its traditional heartland in Andalucía in the south. It has five breweries in Seville, Jaen, Madrid, Valencia and Navarra. The group is building national brands, notably its main beer Cruzcampo. More local lagers include Keler, Alcázar, Victoria, Calatrava and Estrella del Sur.

Damm

The firm that pioneered lager-brewing in Spain was introduced by an Alsatian brewer Auguste Damm in 1876. The company later absorbed other breweries such as La Bohemia. Damm dominates Catalonia in north-eastern Spain and has breweries in Barcelona and nearby Llobregat, besides

plants in Murcia and at Palma on the island of Majorca. As well as a popular Pilsner Xibeca and especial Estrella, it brews a number of speciality beers, which reflect its Germanic roots, including an all-malt Edel, a dark Bock-Damm and a robust Voll-Damm. There is also a golden Estrella Light (3.2%) and a non-alcoholic Damm-Bier.

Mahou

The dominant brewer in the Spanish capital Madrid dates back to 1890. It has two breweries, one in Madrid and the other in Abrera.

San Miguel

The Asian brewing giant of the Philippines entered the Spanish market in 1956, building a plant in Lerida in Catalonia. From the start it concentrated on the premium end of the market and led the move to stronger especial beers. The company

also developed barley growing in Spain and the brewing of near all-malt beers. Its two main brews are the malty San Miguel and smoother, richer Nostrum de San Miguel. The Spanish San Miguel, with additional breweries in Burgos and Málaga, is now linked to Kronenbourg of France.

La Zaragozana

This small brewery has been operating in Zaragoza since 1900. Besides an Ambar lager (4.2%) and especial (5.2%), it also brews a German-style Dortmunder called Marlen (5.8%) and an extra-strong Export (7%).

Above: La Zaragozana uses horse-drawn drays to promote its beers.

PORTUGAL

Beer drinking has only become popular in Portugal in recent years, though breweries were founded on the Iberian peninsula in the 19th century. Golden lagers predominate, but there is an occasional native dark beer to be found.

Above: Portuguese brewers concentrate on stronger lagers, such as Sagres.

THE PORTUGUESE DICTATOR Salazar kept the country in isolation for many years, shutting the local brewing industry off from foreign influence and investment. In 1889, seven small companies in Oporto combined, followed by another merger in 1934 based in Lisbon. These two groups dominated the country and survived nationalization (1977–1990) to form the basis of the modern industry.

Sociedad Central de Cervejas (Centralcer) and Uniao Cervejeira (Unicer) both run three breweries apiece and control about half the market each. Both concentrate on malty mild lagers.

Portugal's beers tend to be good-quality interpretations of German styles and there are also a few dark lagers. Most beer is bottled. There are separate breweries on the islands of Madeira (Empresa) and the Azores (Melo Abreu).

THE BEERS

Cergal
A mildly bitter, Pilsner-style lager (4.6%) with a light dry taste from Centralcer.

Coral
The main brand from Madeira's Empresa brewery is a light, golden lager with a light malt and hops flavour and a dry aftertaste.

Cristal
Unicer's deep-yellow-coloured, hoppy, sweetish lager (5.2%) also comes in a dark version, Cristal Brown.

Melo Abreu Especial
This orangey-coloured lager (5%) has a sweet, malt flavour. It is the main brand from the small Melo Abreu brewery in the Azores.

Onix
A mild, dark, Vienna-style lager (4.3%) with a medium body and pleasant caramel and hoppy flavour which comes from Centralcer.

Sagres
Central's best-selling fruity lager (5.1%) is sold in both popular, pale-yellow blonde (Sagres Pale) and rarer brown versions. The smoother, dark-brown-coloured, chocolatey, molasses-flavoured, dark beer is in the style of a Munich Dunkel. There is also a premium Sagres Golden.

Super Bock
Unicer's pale, robust, malty, fruity lager (5.8%) is one of the most popular brands drunk in Portugal.

Topazio
A deep-gold, malty lager with a sweet aftertaste. It is a regional brand from Sociedad Central de Cervejas.

Sagres

The Sagres brew from Central de Cervejas is named after the old, beautiful cape on the south-western tip of Portugal, where Prince Henry, the Navigator started his naval school in the 15th century.

AFRICA

The Egyptians were the earliest recorded beer makers, and the tradition of brewing is widespread across the African continent. Local beers, made from fermented maize or millet, are still commonly brewed and enjoyed.

DRINKING POTENT, cloudy home-brew has been a communal occasion for centuries across Africa. Thanksgivings, initiations, marriages and births have all long been celebrated around a pot or two of home-brewed beer. The enduring popularity of these native, top-fermented brews has meant that Africa is one of the areas of the world where the increasing dominance of bottom-fermented lagers has been kept partially at bay.

European settlers in Africa brought their own beer and brewing tradition to the continent. Africa's first commercial brewery was set up by a sailor from Antwerp, Pieter Visagie, in Rondebosch in the Cape of Good Hope as early as 1655. It took more than a century after that before local commercial production in southern Africa posed a challenge to imported beer but leading breweries, such as the Cape brewery and the Mariedahl brewery in Newlands, South Africa, were established in the early 1820s. European brews made their mark across the continent, and stouts from England remain an enduring favourite. However, once lager brewing arrived in the 1890s, pioneered by Castle Lager from South African Breweries, it rapidly replaced the earlier top-fermenting ales in the commercial market.

In the north of the continent, breweries tended to arrive later. More recent ventures have been set up by international groups such as Heineken and Interbrew, often as joint ventures with local companies. Carlsberg, for example, established Carlsberg Malawi Ltd in partnership with the Malawi Government in 1968. Virtually all these breweries produce local versions of international Pilsners, often made by mixing in local cereals such as maize, since little barley is grown in Africa.

Above: Tusker is a well-known, malty lager beer from Kenya, one of the few African countries where barley and hops are grown.

THE BEERS

Allsopp's White Cap

A sweetish, fruity, aromatic lager (4%) from Kenya Breweries. White Cap is named after the snowy peak of Mount Kenya. This lager was originally brewed by Allsopp, East Africa, but the company merged with Kenya Breweries in 1962.

Asmara Lager

The golden Asmara Lager, which is matured for more than four weeks, has a firm, malty flavour and excellent body. It is the only beer produced by the Asmara brewery in Eritrea.

Bière Bénin

This light, French-style lager comes from the Bénin brewery in Togo.

Bohlinger's

Bohlinger's is a dry, golden lager brewed by National Breweries of Zimbabwe, which was founded in 1911, and for many years was known as Rhodesian Breweries.

Bosun's

This light, fruity, golden bitter (4.5%) is brewed by the first European-style micro-brewery to be established in Africa – Mitchell's of Knysna in South Africa.

Camel Beer

This is the Blue Nile brewery's famous Sudanese lager brand. It was first launched in 1955. The recipe was originally based on an early English lager, brewed by the Barclay Perkins company, and was widely exported to Africa from London at the time.

Castle Golden Pilsner

This light lager from South African Breweries is brewed using barley malt and maize.

Castle Lager

This pale, lemony-tasting lager (5%) with a dry, hoppy finish is the leading beer brand from South African Breweries. It is brewed using barley malt, maize and sucrose. The name comes from the Castle brewery founded by Charles Glass in Johannesburg in 1884.

Castle Lager was the first bottom-fermenting beer produced in Africa, using plant bought by the South African Breweries pioneer, Frederick Mead, from the

Pfaudler Vacuum Company of the US. Once introduced in 1898, the lager proved to be such a popular refreshing drink in the hot African climate that South African Breweries decided to adopt the Castle name for all of its beers and breweries. Rival breweries, impressed by the success of the golden brew, rushed to imitate the trend and brew lager as well.

Castle Milk Stout

South African Breweries' full-bodied, dark, smooth milk stout (8%) is brewed using milk sugar (lactose), The range of Castle beers are also produced by National Breweries of Zimbabwe in which SAB has a stake.

Chibuku

A fast-fermenting, cloudy, traditional beer (3.5%) from Zimbabwe, with a chewy, cereal consistency. Chibuku has a refreshing, sour taste and a shelf-life of 3–4 days. It is sold as a value-for-money, low-cost product, particularly on draught in large, communal beer halls. In 1991 a premium version was introduced in a plastic bottle and because of its shape it was nicknamed "the Scud" after the missiles used in the Gulf War.

Club Pilsner

This light, refreshing Pilsner (4.5%) is lagered for an average of three weeks and uses cane sugar in the mash. It comes from Nile Breweries of Uganda.

ESB

One of the strongest beers in the whole of Africa. This smooth, golden, chill-filtered lager (7%) is produced by Nile Breweries of Uganda. It is made using cane sugar as well as barley malt in the mash. The beer's full name is Chairman's Extra Strong Brew.

Flag

This range of popular local light lagers is produced by Brasseries du Maroc (of Morocco). It includes Flag Pilsner, Flag Spéciale and a golden, hoppy, malty Flag Export.

Forester's

Following the world trend for real beers, this unfiltered and unpasteurized, full-bodied lager (5%) is brewed by the Mitchell's micro-brewery in Knysna, South Africa.

Gulder

A refreshing, slightly hoppy, dry lager (5%) that is the flagship brand of Nigerian Breweries. Gulder is also brewed in the company's plant in Ghana.

Hansa Urbock

The rich, reddish Urbock (6%) is brewed by the German-founded Hansa brewery in Swakopmund. Like all Namibian beers, it is brewed according to the German beer purity law. The warming winter brew provides Africa with a rare, German-style, dark lager.

Hunter's

A pale-gold, refreshing lager that is nevertheless full of flavour. Hunter's is brewed by a Czech brewmaster in accordance with the German beer purity law, using only malt, hops, barley and yeast. It is produced by the private Nesbitt brewery of Zimbabwe.

Legend Stout

A strong, rich stout (7%), with a roasted-chocolate flavour, produced by Nigerian Breweries. It is a rival to Guinness in the country that is the third largest market for stout in the world.

Lion Lager

Another leading lager (5%) from South African Breweries. It is slightly sweeter than SAB's other major brand, Castle. The Lion brand has been roaring since a Norwegian merchant Anders Ohlsson, who had

been involved in beer brewing in Africa since 1862, established the Annaberg brewery in Cape Town in 1883.

Mamba Lager

This bright-gold, malty lager is probably the best-known beer from French West Africa. It has been brewed by Solibra in Abidjan in the Ivory Coast since 1960. The Solibra brewery also produces a Mamba Bock and a rich, tawny Mamba Brune.

Ngoma

A range of beers from Brasseries du Bénin of Lome, Togo. It includes a light, hazy-gold Pilsner with a well-balanced, hoppy flavour, and a darker, more malty, amber-coloured Special with a sourish malt flavour. The brand name Ngoma means "a drum".

Nile Special

This full-bodied lager (5.6%) is brewed by Nile Breweries, using cane sugar as well as barley malt. It is lagered for an average of three weeks.

Ohlsson's Lager

A golden lager (5%) named after the Ohlsson's brewery that is now owned by SAB.

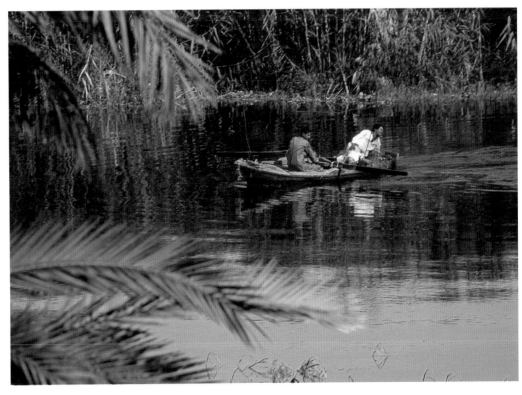

Above: The Nile snakes through the African continent for over 4,000 miles (6,500 km). At its source in Uganda, Nile Breweries is now flourishing thanks to help from overseas. The great river slows as it nears the end of its course in Egypt, the country where the world's earliest brewers once produced their beer.

Raven Stout

This dark, rich, heavy stout (6%) is brewed by the Mitchell's micro-brewery of Knysna in South Africa.

Rex

A dry, golden lager produced by Nigerian Breweries.

Simba Lager

A popular golden lager in Zaire (formerly the Belgian Congo) Simba has been produced by the Brasimba brewery (in which the Belgian giant Interbrew has a stake) since 1923.

Tafel Lager

A refreshing, standard lager (4%) with a slightly bitter flavour, brewed according to the German beer purity law. Tafel is produced by the Hansa brewery in Swakopmund on the Namibian coast.

Windhoek

The Windhoek beers include a low-alcohol light (1.9%), a refreshing Windhoek lager (4%), a more hoppy export (4.5%) and a fuller-bodied, malty special (5.3%). The range of lagers, all brewed according to the German beer purity law, comes from Namibia Breweries' modern plant in Windhoek. The brewery opened in the outskirts of the town in 1986 when the old Garten Street premises were closed.

Zambezi

A pale-gold, light, refreshing lager (4.5%) with a sweet-sour flavour, from National Breweries, Zimbabwe.

Star

A sweetish, hazy, golden, hoppy lager (5%). Star lager beer was first produced in 1949 in a Lagos brewery that is now owned by Nigerian Breweries. This most popular lager brand is now brewed and sold all the way across West Africa – from Sierra Leone to Ghana.

Tusker

Kenya Breweries' creamy, dry, golden lager appears in a variety of strengths. Tusker Premium, a strong, all-malt beer (5%), is brewed for international export. According to legend, it was named after the angry elephant which trampled to death one of the two brothers who founded the brewery.

DARKEST AFRICA

Some areas of Africa have a strong stout-drinking tradition. Nowhere is this more true than in Nigeria, the third-largest stout market in the world. Guinness Nigeria alone boasts four breweries in this heavily populated country. Local rivals to Guinness in Nigeria include Legend Stout by Nigerian Breweries, Power Stout by North brewery of Kano, Eagle Stout by Golden Guinea brewery of Umuahia, and Lion Stout by the Mopa brewery. The stouts produced by these breweries are much more than faint shadows left over from the British Empire. The Guinness sold here, for instance, is not the standard Guinness brewed in Ireland or even the more substantial Foreign Extra Stout sold elsewhere in Africa, but a stronger version still, weighing in at 8% alcohol by volume. This rich, bitter-sweet brew is a blend of a strong local pale beer and concentrated dark wort supplied from Dublin. It is sold as an energy-giving stimulant, "Guinness for Power", with potent properties. Advertising campaigns, free from the restrictions of Europe or America, once even suggested the possibility of "a baby in every bottle".

THE BREWERS

Asmara

An Italian, Luigi Melotti, originally set up this company in Asmara, Eritrea, in 1939 to produce pure alcohol and spirits. It began to produce lager three years later. In 1984, it changed its name from Melotti to Asmara.

Blue Nile

This was the first brewery in the Sudan. It was built in the early 1950s and was established by the English brewing company Barclay Perkins. It brewed a little stout and brown ale (known as dark) when it opened in 1955. Today, however, production is mainly devoted to its main beer – a bottom-fermenting lager, Camel.

Brasseries du Bénin

Brasseries du Bénin of Togo in the former French West Africa produces a light, French-style, Bière Bénin lager and also markets beers under the Ngoma (Drum) brand name.

Brasseries du Maroc

Breweries of Morocco in north-western Africa is one of the few thriving brewing groups in a Muslim country. It runs three modern breweries in Casablanca, Tangier and Fès, alongside an extensive soft drinks operation. Brasseries du Maroc produces its own popular range of light lagers in bottles and cans, mainly

under the Flag brand name. These account for four-fifths of production and also include the Bock 49 and Stork brands, besides the non-alcoholic Crown.

Chibuku

Chibuku is the leading commercial producer of traditional native beer in Zimbabwe. It has 16 breweries scattered around the country in order to ensure fresh, live beer in each local market. It is sold mainly on draught in large, communal beer halls.

By 1995, a newly introduced take-home bottle accounted for 40% of the brewery's production.

East African Breweries

See Kenya Breweries.

Hansa

The Hansa brewery was founded in 1929 in the picturesque Namibian coastal town of Swakopmund. In 1968, it was taken over by South West (later Namibian) Breweries. As well as a refreshing Tafel Lager, it also produces a rich, reddish urbock and a refreshing golden Pilsner. Like all Namibian beers, these beers are brewed according to the German beer purity law Rheinheitsgetbot.

Kenya Breweries

Kenya Breweries was founded by two brothers in Nairobi in the early 1920s, using equipment from England. It was for many years known as East African Breweries. Some English-style ales and stouts were produced initially, using locally grown barley, but the company soon concentrated on a golden lager called Tusker. In 1952, the company opened a second brewery on the coast at Mombasa. It was bad timing, though, as the country exploded in the Mau Mau rebellion against British rule, and the African population boycotted European beers. As independence approached, the company merged in 1962 with its local rival, Allsopp, East Africa. Seven years later, the combine added another Nairobi brewery, City. In 1982, the group opened a new brewery in Kisumu near Lake Victoria. Today, the main lagers are Tusker and the more fruity White Cap (both around 4.2%), and a slightly more hoppy Pilsner. Unmalted barley is added as an adjunct to all three. Less full-bodied "export" versions are also produced using cane sugar, and a stronger, nearly all-malt, Tusker Premium (5%) for international sales.

Mitchell's

Africa's first micro-brewery was set up in 1984 by a former SAB brewer Lex Mitchell in Knysna on the southern coast of Cape Province, South Africa. His unfiltered and unpasteurized malty beers include a lightly fruity Bosun's Bitter (4.5%) and fuller-bodied Forester's.

Namibia

The Namibia Company was founded in 1920 as South West Breweries, when four German colonial breweries in the area amalgamated. In 1968, the Windhoek-based group absorbed its rival, Hansa of Swakopmund. When Namibia gained independence in 1990, the group was renamed Namibia Breweries. The company brews quality lagers such as Windhoek Export Lager following the beer purity law.

National

Founded in 1911 and known for many years as Rhodesian Breweries, National Breweries of Zimbabwe has two plants in Harare and Bulawayo.

Nesbitt

Zimbabwe's first independent brewery was founded at Chiredzi in 1990 and employs a Czech brewmaster, F. Mrazek, to brew its all-malt beers. Its main beer is the crisp Hunter's Lager.

Nigerian Breweries

The largest brewing company in Africa's leading brewing nation is Nigerian Breweries, with plants in Iganmu, Ibadan, Aba and Kaduna. Nigerian opened its first brewery in 1949 with the support of Heineken. It began by brewing a sweetish Star lager. Other lager brands have now been developed, notably the drier Gulder and Rex beers. The Nigerian Breweries group also produces a rich rival to Guinness – Legend Stout.

Nile Breweries

This Ugandan brewery was built with German investment and assistance in the town of Jinja in 1954, close to the source of the Nile. The brewery flourished until 1972, but it struggled in the years that followed. For 20 years, during and after Idi Amin's regime, the brewery was allowed to disintegrate.

The Nile brewery was revived in 1992 with help from the international giant Carlsberg. Three main lagers are produced: a light Club Pilsner, the fuller-bodied Nile Special and the extra-strong ESB. All of the brews use cane sugar as well as barley malt and are lagered for an average of three weeks. Nile Breweries controls more than 60% of the Ugandan beer market.

Solibra

This brewery was set up in the Ivory Coast in 1960. Its beers include the rich, the golden, malty Mamba, a bock and a brune. Mamba beer is now exported.

South African Breweries

This was the first brewing giant of the African continent. The company's roots lie in the Natal brewery of Pietermaritzburg, which was set up by Frederick Mead in 1891. In 1892 Natal took over Glass's Castle Brewery in Johannesburg to form South African United Breweries, which then became South African Breweries (SAB) in 1895.

SAB was not to dominate the country, however, until 1956 when it merged with its two main rivals, Ohlsson's (Lion), which controlled the Cape, and Union Breweries (Chandler's).

Today the main lagers that it produces – Castle and Lion – reflect this history. SAB also offers a wide range of other lager brands which includes Ohlsson's, Chandler's, Rogue and Old Dutch.

The company now holds substantial share stakes in many other African breweries and and has expanded into breweries in Eastern Europe.

Above: Even in bygone days, the need to supply beer to a thirsty nation meant that Namibia Breweries had to expand its brewery.

SOUTH AFRICAN SORGHUM BEERS

Beer brewing using sorghum and relying on spontaneous fermentation has long been a domestic industry in Africa, and it is not unusual to find women still selling home-brewed beers in the marketplaces. These thick, tawny brews or "porridge beers" are cheap and must be consumed within two or three days. They are generally regarded by African drinkers as more nutritious than pale European lagers.

Commercially brewed sorghum (millet) beers have been produced in South Africa from the early 20th century to meet the demands for beer from the black, urban population. They originated in Natal.

Their popularity, however, is partly due to the fact that until 1962 the majority of the black population was not allowed to buy European-style beers. Sorghum beers, which were called "Kaffir beers" by white South Africans, were sold in special bars reserved only for blacks, in open-air "beer gardens" or at roadside stalls.

Since the collapse of the apartheid regime, although the consumption of golden lagers has certainly soared, there has been no mass switch. In the late 1970s there were 32 commercial sorghum beer breweries in South Africa, and new ones are still being opened.

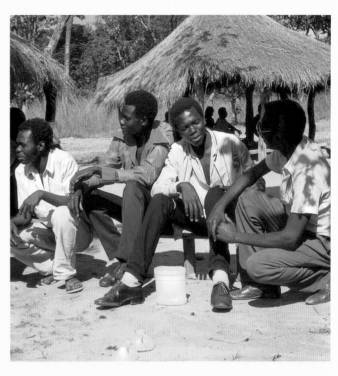

Above: Enjoying a sorghum beer in an open-air bar.

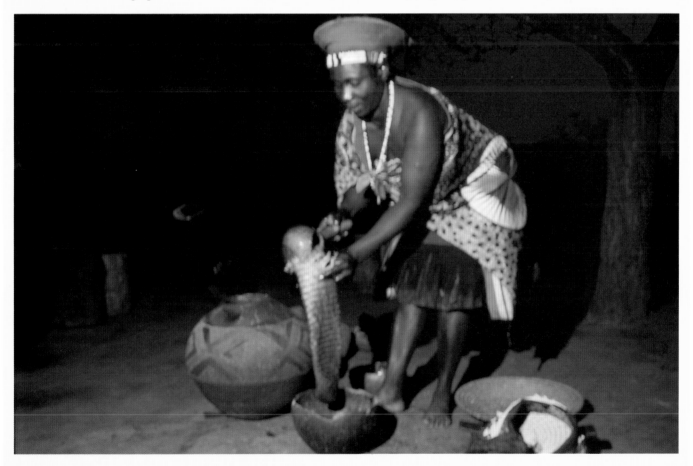

Above: A Zulu woman in South Africa prepares the mash for a sorghum brew. The thick, porridge-like mixture will be left open to the air and the action of wild yeasts for a few days in order to ferment, and will then be drunk within two or three days.

CHINA

Although the Chinese have been making alcoholic drinks for centuries, they have no real beer-brewing tradition. However, this is not going to stop China becoming the largest beer-brewing nation in the world by the year 2000.

FOREIGN EXPERTISE played a great part in the initial development of the beer-brewing industry in China. The trend started at the beginning of this century – the Russians brewed in Harbin and the Germans in Tsingtao. Today, joint venture partners are bringing in new technology and capital to modernize the creaking Chinese industry. Some sources estimate that by the year 2000 China will be the world's largest beer producer in terms of volume.

Official estimates of the number of breweries in China put it at approximately 850, though there are probably hundreds more "unregistered" breweries. No single brewer has a market share larger than 4%. The breweries fall into three main categories – joint-owned Chinese and foreign ventures, large national breweries and local breweries. They are owned and run in a bewildering diversity of ways – publicly quoted companies (such as Tsingtao), town breweries run by local entrepreneurs and state-owned concerns run by government agencies.

Although the current consumption of beer is relatively low, this seems set to change. Personal disposable income is rising steeply among some of the population, and at least some of this money seems to be being spent on beer.

Most beer is sold in the form of "value for money" brands. Large, returnable bottles of local brews make up the majority of sales. Most consumers are fiercely loyal to their local beer – seemingly no matter what the quality. Regional markets are often protected by official and unofficial restrictions – such as fines levied on "substandard" beers imported from other areas and charges to retailers for each crate of beer brought in from outside the region. In their protected markets, substandard local brewers have little incentive to improve.

Above: Germany leased the port of Tsingtao (now called Quingdao) and built a brewery there which still survives today, though it is now Chinese-owned.

THE BEERS

Baiyun Beer

A hazy-yellow lager beer from the Guangzhou brewery, Guangzhou City.

Canton Lager Beer

A gold-coloured, malty lager, from the Guangzhou brewery, Guangzhou City.

Chinese Ginseng Beer

A thin, pale lager (4.1%) brewed under licence in Britain using only natural ingredients and some Ginseng herbal seasoning.

Chu Sing

A pale-gold, malty lager from the Chu Jiang brewery, Guangzhou City.

Double Happiness Guangzhou Beer

A pale-gold, highly carbonated lager with a light, malt flavour. It is produced by Guangzhou brewery, Guangzhou City.

Emperor's Gold Beer

A gold lager with a slightly molasses aftertaste, produced by the Hangzhou brewery, Hangzhou City, using Zhejiang barley.

Five Star Beer

This golden lager has a mild, malty flavour. It is produced by the Shen Ho Shing brewery, Beijing.

Guangminpai

An unusual dark lager produced by the Shanghai brewery.

Hua Nan Beer

A pleasant, refreshing, yellow-gold lager beer, from the Guangzhou brewery, Guangzhou City.

Mon-Lei Beer

A reddish-coloured lager, brewed by the Beijing Wuxing and Shen Ho Shing breweries.

Nine Star Premium

This gold lager beer has a good malt and hop flavour. It is brewed by the Five Star brewery, Beijing.

Peking Beer

A pale-golden lager from the Feng Shon brewery, Beijing.

Shanghai (Swan) Lager

The popular name for lager which in this case comes from the emblem on the label of this malty, lightly hopped lager. It is brewed by the Shanghai brewery and is said to have once been the official drink served at Communist Party conferences.

Song Hay Double Happiness Beer

Gold, well-flavoured lager beer from the Guangzhou brewery, Guangzhou City.

Sun Lik

A traditional Chinese dragon decorates the label of this golden, malty lager (5%), brewed by the Hong Kong brewery.

Sweet China

A pineapple-flavoured, yellow-gold lager which comes from the Guangzhou brewery, Guangzhou City.

Tientan Beer

A hazy, yellow-gold lager from the Beijing brewery. The name means "Temple of Heaven".

Tsingtao Beer

A pale-gold, Pilsner-style lager (5%), with a malt and hops, vanilla flavour, brewed by the Tsingtao brewery in Quingdao, Shandong province. Tsingtao is widely exported around the world in both bottles and cans, partly to fuel the thirst of Chinese populations in other countries. It is also popular among Westerners as an accompaniment to Chinese food. It is something of a cult beer in the US.

There is also a deep-amber Tsingtao Dark Beer.

West Lake Beer

A dark-gold-coloured, light lager beer (3.8%) which has a sweet, fruity flavour, and claims to contain no artificial ingredients – only hops, malt, rice and spring water from the West Lake region. It is brewed by the Hangzhou Zhongce Beer Co Ltd.

JAPAN

The first commercial brewery in Japan, Spring Valley in Yokohama, was started by an American, William Copeland, in 1869, when Japan opened up to trade with the West. At that time the beer was mainly for foreign traders and seamen.

B EER IS A RELATIVELY recent arrival in Japan. Gradually, the Japanese tried out the new drink and then embraced it with a passion, so that today the country is one of the leading beer-drinking nations in the world. As has been their way with many outside inventions they have adopted, the Japanese have refined and developed the product. Most of the lagers are ultra-clean, hi-tech versions of golden international Pilsners, using rice in the mash. The Japanese were pioneers in developing new styles, such as dry beers. There is a constant conveyor-belt of ingenious variations on a light lager, along with novelty presentations such as Sapporo's can that turns into a cup. Some dark beers are produced – a legacy from the early German influence.

Today, the brewing industry is dominated by four main groups: Kirin, Asahi, Sapporo and Suntory (with Orion on the island of Okinawa). A ruling that allowed only breweries producing a minimum of 450,000 gallons (two million litres) a year to operate froze small-scale, independent brewers out of the market. This ruling was repealed in 1994. The result was a flood of new micro-breweries and brewpubs producing fresh ji-biru (local beer). A number of these new ventures have been set up by established saké makers. The major brewers have responded to the rising popularity of more unusual brews by producing regional beers and opening their own brewpubs. At the same time, there has been growing demand for imported beers, which has encouraged the large groups to try out new beer styles, such as an alt-style beer produced by Kirin.

Most beer in Japan is sold in bottles or cans, with only a small amount available on draught. Bottled and canned beers marked "draft" are fine-filtered (in a process known as micro-filtration) but the majority are usually sold unpasteurized for the the home market.

Above: Japanese brewers have long been in the vanguard of technological innovation, producing high-tech beer styles such as dry beer.

The Beers

Asahi Black Beer

Many Japanese like to blend this sweetish, red-brown, beer (5%) with a light lager.

Asahi Stout

This richly roasted, top-fermented stout is a potent brew (8%). It also has a hint of lactic sourness, like early English porters and stouts.

Kirin Beer

Japan's best-selling beer (4.9%) is a crisp, full-bodied, fresh-flavoured Pilsner brewed using Saaz and Hallertau hops. It is matured for up to two months before being sold unpasteurized.

Kirin Black Beer

This smoky, traditional, dark beer (5%) has a hint of roasted coffee and hops.

Kirin Ichiban Shibori

Kirin's second-best-selling beer was introduced in 1990. Brewed using just the first liquid run-off from the mash tun, Ichiban Shibori ("first wort") gives a smoother malt taste. It is sold in distinctive, tall bottles. This soft golden

lager (5.5%) has proved a major marketing success.

Kirin Stout

This marvellously rich, complex, bottom-fermenting stout (8%) has a hint of toffee.

Kuro-nama

This light, golden lager is marketed by Asahi as a late-night drink.

Kyoto Alt

See Kirin.

Malt's

Suntory's appropriately named malty, flagship lager is, unusually for a Japanese beer, brewed with 100% malt

Sapporo Black Beer

Sapporo was the first Japanese brewery to brew a German-style, dark lager in 1892 and this classic, full-flavoured black beer (5%) is still brewed today, using crystal, chocolate and Munich malts as well as rice.

Sapporo Original Draft Black Label

The fourth-best-selling beer in Japan, this lively, light Pilsner (4.7%) was the first to use the micro-filtration technique instead of pasteurization to produce what is called a "draft" beer. It is sold abroad in stylish silver cans as Sapporo Draft.

Shirayuki

Two Belgian-style ales, a soft Shirayuki Blonde and a creamy Shirayuki Dark, are produced in the saké town of Itami, near Osaka, in a brewery restaurant run by the Shirayuki (White Snow) saké firm.

Shokusai Bakushu

Asahi launched this lager in 1996. It was designed to accompany meals and is sold under two different labels, pink and green. The pink version has a milder flavour.

Spring Valley

This hoppy, golden lager takes its name from Japan's first brewery, which was founded in Yokohama in 1869. It is brewed at a pub brewery in a tourist beer village close to Kirin's modern brewery in the port of Yokohama, near Tokyo.

Below: An old beer poster advertising Yebisu and Sapporo beer in the museum at the Sapporo brewery, Hokkaido.

Suntory Daichi

A smooth golden lager (4.8%) from Suntory which emphasizes its natural ingredients. It is brewed with 100% barley malts.

Super Dry

The original pioneer of the dry beer style, Super Dry became fashionable around the world for a brief time in the late 1980s and early 1990s. In the mid-1980s the Asahi brewery was in trouble, with falling sales and a reduced market share. A taste test on 5,000 consumers in 1985 found that people wanted a smooth, light-tasting beer. The resulting Asahi Super Dry was launched in 1987. This is a pale Pilsner, fermented for longer than normal. This reduces the body of the beer while increasing the alcohol content (to 5% from the then more usual 4.5%). The beer is less bitter than usual Pilsners, with virtually no aftertaste and a characteristic, dry, parching effect in the mouth. The intention was to create a thin, clean beer with little flavour, which would leave consumers in need of another drink. In both aims it succeeded beyond Asahi's most extravagant dreams. Since the early 1990s, while dry beers have fallen out of favour elsewhere, Super Dry has remained popular in Japan. In 1995, it was the country's second-best-selling beer after Kirin Lager, selling more than 121 million cases.

Right: The Asahi brewery in Tokyo, designed by Philippe Stark.

Yebisu

Sapporo's premium all-malt Dortmunder-style lager (5%) uses German aroma hops in order to produce one of the most fully flavoured mainstream beers brewed in Japan. It is named after a Tokyo brewery that was built at the turn of the century.

Z

Asahi brews this faintly fruity, top-fermenting light ale. The company claims that this unpasteurized brew is one of the "most technologically advanced beers" in Japan. In keeping with the Asahi company's policy of linking beers to different occasions, Z beer is marketed specifically as a holiday drink.

THE BREWERS

Asahi

Founded as the Osaka brewery in 1889, Asahi became part of the Dai Nippon brewing company in 1906. This was Japan's first beer giant. After the Second World War, Dai Nippon was split up into Nippon (later renamed Sapporo) and Asahi. The latter was the smaller of the two parts, but this changed dramatically in 1987 when Asahi launched Super Dry. The huge success of this brand rocketed Asahi's share of the market from 10% to 28% in 1995, making it Japan's second-largest brewing group. Other Asahi beers include Z, Double Yeasts and two more traditional brews, a sweetish red-brown, Asahi, Black Beer (5%), and a richly roasted, top-fermented Asahi Stout (8%). In 1996, Asahi launched a new marketing strategy linking such beers as Shokusai Bakushu and Kuro-nama to different occasions.

Kirin

Japan's largest brewer accounts for about half of the country's production, with 14 breweries. The company can trace its history back to Japan's first brewery, Spring Valley of Yokohama of 1869, and was foreign-owned until it was bought by Japanese interests, led by Mitsubishi, in 1970. It brews Japan's best-selling beer, Kirin Lager. Its other main beer is the more malty Ichiban. In 1995, Kirin Lager sold more than 151 million cases; Ichiban 76 million. In the search for a new sales success to equal Ichiban, the company has launched a wide range of local and speciality beers including a copper-coloured alt brewed from crystal malt in a micro-brewery in Kyoto. It also brews a slightly smoky Kirin Black Beer and a richer, more chewy bottom-fermenting Kirin Stout.

Sapporo

The oldest continuously operating brewery in Japan was founded in the town of Sapporo in 1876. It became part of Dai Nippon in 1906, before being split up again in 1949 and regaining its original name in 1964. This leading exporter of Japanese beer, has pioneered a number of beer styles and brewing techniques. It was the first Japanese brewery to brew a German-style dark lager in 1892. In 1971, it launched Japan's original all-malt premium beer, Yebisu, and was the first to introduce seasonal and regional beers.

It also pioneered the use of micro-filtration to produce unpasteurized "draft" beers. Today its best-selling beer is its Original Draft Black

Label, a lively dryish Pilsner, which is sold abroad as Sapporo Draft. There is also a low-priced, low-malt lager called Drafty.

The company runs a brewpub in Kawaguchi and popular German-style beer gardens alongside its breweries in Sapporo, Nagoya, Sendai and Shizuoka.

Suntory

The smallest of Japan's four main breweries, Suntory is primarily a wine-maker and distiller dating from 1899. It began brewing in 1963. Its flagship beer, the softly sweetish all-malt Malt's. A lighter brew named Super Hop's is also available. In addition there is a North American-style lager, Dynamic (brewed with Canadian yeast).

Above: The beautiful stained-glass window in the Sapporo brewery.

MICRO-BREWERIES AND BREWPUBS

Since 1994, Japan has seen a boom in micro-breweries and brewpubs. The result is more variety of beer styles.

Akasaka

A soft-drinks company set up this micro-brewery in a suburb of Tokyo. It brews a Pilsner and a dark Kuro Half.

Doppo

This micro was set up by the Miyashita saké company in Okayama. It brews German-style beers – Doppo Pilsner and a reddish Doppo Dunkel.

Gotenba Kohgen

The hot springs tourist town of Gotenba is home to a beer hall and brewery. It offers a light Pilsner, a malty Gotenba Dunkel and a fruity Weizen.

KIRIN

The Kirin is a legendary animal of ancient China – half dragon, half horse – which appeared to the mother of Confucius just before his birth 2,500 years ago. The sight of this benevolent creature was supposed to herald the arrival of great men, and it is regarded as a symbol of good luck, a harbinger of happy events to come. The name was first adopted by the Spring Valley Brewery for its beer in 1888, and the fabled animal still appears on Kirin's main brands today.

Kizakura Kappa

The Kappa saké company set up this brewpub in Kyoto. Its German-style ales include a Kappa Alt, a fruity kölsch and a sweeter Kölsch Mild, all brewed using saké yeast.

Kyoto
See Kirin.

Moku Moku

This rural micro-brewery in Nishiyubune, near Ueno, was set up by a farming co-operative. It brews a variety of country beers, including a Pilsner, a fruity amber ale, a peaty smoked ale and a tart Biscuit Weizen.

Okhotsk

This brewpub in Kitami on the island of Hokkaido is named after the nearby Sea of Okhotsk. Its wide range of beers includes a finely balanced Okhotsk Bitter.

Otaru

This brewpub in the port of Otaru, near Sapporo, produces German-style lagers, including a hoppy Otaru Helles and a malty, dark dunkel.

Sandaya

This brewpub near Osaka is run by a smoked meat company. The unfiltered beers include a yeasty Pilsner, a malty Festbier, a black beer and a well-roasted Sandaya Smoked Beer, which is served to accompany the smoked meat produced by the parent company.

Sankt Gallen

This small Tokyo brewpub was one of the first to open. It brews a range of seasonal, spiced ales including a hoppy Sankt Gallen Spring Ale and the sweeter St Valentine's.

Sumida River

Asahi's brewpub in its Tokyo office complex makes three German-style draught beers: a mild Altbier, a Kölsch called River Beer and a full-bodied, unfiltered Zwickelbier.

Uehara

One of Japan's first micro-breweries was set up in the Echigo pub in Makimachi. Its wide range of beers includes a fruity Uehara Pale Ale, a cloudy Uehara Weizen and a very powerful Old Ale.

THE REST OF ASIA

In the booming economies of the Far East, the beer market is expanding. There is a strong European influence on the industry in the shape of machinery and investment, and in the predominance of lagers.

ASIA'S BREWERIES are spread far and wide – from the far north of India, through Sri Lanka, Thailand, Malaysia and Vietnam, to Singapore and Indonesia. As a result, the influences are wide-ranging, and the brewers have to contend with a diversity of laws, even within some country boundaries. Some states of India, for example, are strictly prohibitionist, while others are very relaxed in their attitude to alcohol.

The colonial heritage has had a profound influence on beer drinking and brewing. Adventurers from Europe brought their technical brewing knowledge and their own particular tastes with them, and these in turn were adopted by the local drinkers. British ales have made their mark on the Indian subcontinent, particularly in the form of India Pale Ale and rich, dark stouts. Despite its distance, the Pilsner revolution in Europe, which has transformed the beer-drinking landscape into one of pale lagers, has taken a grip on Asia too.

Beer consumption per head is relatively low in the region. Singaporeans for example, who are believed to be among the highest consumers of beer in Asia, drink a meagre 25 litres (5½ gallons) per head per annum, compared to 130 litres (28½ gallons) in England. Nevertheless, the large population of the region means that there is still scope for the marketing muscle of international companies such as Heineken to be flexed, and for the development of large "local" brewers. San Miguel of the Philippines has been brewing for over 100 years and is one of the major players in the Asian market, with joint ventures throughout the region. Asian Pacific Breweries from Singapore is also a large-scale producer, with hundreds of breweries throughout Asia. The strong, golden lagers that the region's brewers tend to produce are now bouncing back across the globe on the coat-tails of Asian cuisine to become household names in the West.

Above: Indonesia's most famous brew is the award-winning Bintang. The Dutch influence is apparent both in its taste and in the squat bottle design.

THE BEERS

ABC Stout
This powerful, creamy bottom-fermenting stout (8.1%) is produced by Asia Pacific Breweries.

Amarit
A malty, sweet, pale-gold lager from Thailand, brewed by Thai Amarit Bangkok.

Anchor Beer
This dry, hoppy Pilsner was introduced by Asia Pacific Breweries in 1941.

BGI
A golden lager brewed in My Tho, Vietnam, by a joint venture between the French BGI group and the Vietnamese Government.

Bintang
A light, malty lager (5%) from Bintang in Indonesia.

Cerveza Negra
A black beer (5.2%) with a roasted malty taste, from San Miguel in the Philippines.

Cobra
One of the best-known lagers from India and a successful export to the West.

Flying Horse
A premium, golden lager beer (5%) from the Vinedale Breweries, Hyderabad, India.

Hite
A pale-gold, dry, hoppy Korean lager (4.5%).

Jubilee
A premium, amber-gold lager (5%) from the Vinedale Breweries, Hyderabad, India.

Kingfisher
This sweetish, malty draught lager (5%) from the Vinedale Breweries, Hyderabad, India, is brewed under licence in England. There is also a pleasant Kingfisher stout.

Lion Stout
A top-fermenting stout (7.5%) produced using Czech, British and Danish malt, Styrian hops and an English yeast strain. The ingredients are transported to the Ceylon brewery in Nuwara Eliya high in the tea-planting area of Sri Lanka. It is served by handpump in the Beer Shop in the town, and in UKD Silva in the holy city of Kandy.

Red Horse
A bock-style, pale-gold lager (6.8%) with a full-bodied flavour, from San Miguel in the Philippines.

Sando Stout
A rich, fruity, bottom-fermented stout (6%) from the Three Coins Brewery in Colombo, Sri Lanka. It is named after a Hungarian circus strongman.

San Miguel
This golden, Pilsner-style beer, made with 80% malt, is lagered for a month by the Filipino giant San Miguel.

Singha
A bright-gold lager (6%) with a hoppy flavour, brewed by the Boon Rawd Brewery in Thailand. It is named after the mythical half-lion creature shown on the label.

Tiger
This refreshing, gold-coloured lager (5.1%) is one of the best-known Asian beers. It is brewed in Singapore and Kuala Lumpur by Asia Pacific Breweries. Its marketing slogan, "Time for a Tiger", was even the title of a novel by the British writer Anthony Burgess.

Tiger Classic
A mellow, golden, seasonal beer, brewed by APB using crystal malt, in time for each New Year's festivities.

THE BREWERS

Asia Pacific Breweries
APB is a regional giant based in Singapore. It was formed in 1931 as a joint venture between Fraser & Neame and Heineken, and was originally called Malayan Breweries. It is involved in many joint ventures in the region.

Boon Rawd Brewery
This Thai brewery was set up in Bangkok in the 19th century using German technology.

Mohan Meakin
Edward Dyer established a brewery at Kasauli in 1855. In 1935 this company merged with the Meakin brewery, set up by Mr H.G. Meakin, to become Dyer Meakin Breweries Limited. The Mohan Meakin company's main brewery is the Solan Brewery in the Simla Hills.

San Miguel
This Filipino giant producer was the first brewery in South-east Asia. It was established as La Fabrica de Cerveza de San Miguel in a small brewery next to the colonial mansion of the Spanish governor-general in the heart of Manila in 1890. It is now responsible for 85% of the Filipino beer market and has many breweries in other countries in the region, including ventures in Guangzhou and Guangdong, China, and a brewery in Hong Kong. It has also set up joint ventures in Vietnam, Indonesia, Nepal and Cambodia. In total, San Miguel has over 250,000 retail outlets in Asia.

AUSTRALIA

The image of beer drinking in Australia has often been ice-cold lager firmly clenched in the fists of macho men. But, like the legendary six o'clock swill that forced drinkers to knock back their beers in double-quick time, this hard-drinking reputation is now gradually draining away.

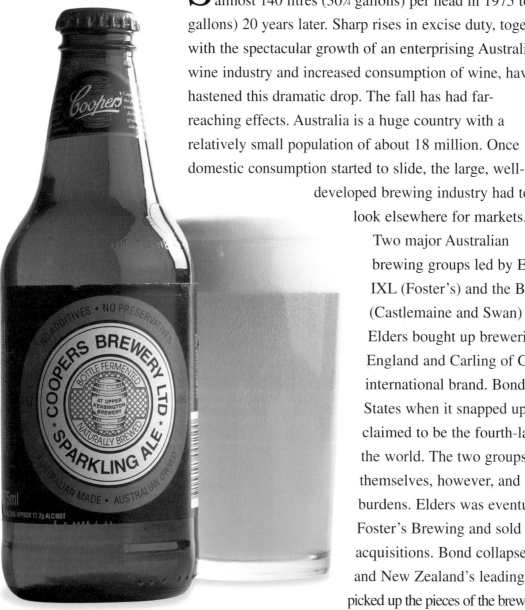

SINCE 1975, BEER DRINKING in Australia has remorselessly declined from almost 140 litres (30¾ gallons) per head in 1975 to less than 100 litres (22 gallons) 20 years later. Sharp rises in excise duty, together with the spectacular growth of an enterprising Australian wine industry and increased consumption of wine, have hastened this dramatic drop. The fall has had far-reaching effects. Australia is a huge country with a relatively small population of about 18 million. Once domestic consumption started to slide, the large, well-developed brewing industry had to look elsewhere for markets.

Two major Australian brewing groups led by Elders IXL (Foster's) and the Bond Corporation (Castlemaine and Swan) began to scour the globe. Elders bought up breweries such as Courage of England and Carling of Canada, making Foster's an international brand. Bond moved into the United States when it snapped up Heileman and eventually claimed to be the fourth-largest brewing company in the world. The two groups had overreached themselves, however, and struggled under heavy debt burdens. Elders was eventually reconstructed as Foster's Brewing and sold off some of its earlier acquisitions. Bond collapsed in a spectacular fashion, and New Zealand's leading brewer, Lion Nathan, then picked up the pieces of the brewing business in Australia.

These two combines still completely dominate the country. Foster's, which trades in Australia through its subsidiary, Carlton and United Breweries (CUB), controls 54% of the beer market, while Lion Nathan now controls almost 44%. This leaves little more than 2% for the two remaining independent breweries, Boag of Tasmania and Coopers of Adelaide, plus a handful of new micro-breweries and brewpubs.

Above: Most people equate Australian beer with Foster's or Castlemaine mass-market lagers, but there are a number of independent breweries, notably Coopers of Adelaide.

THE BEERS

Abbots Invalid Stout

CUB's strong stout (5.6%) is a rare reminder of Australia's early brewing links with England. Although now bottom-fermented, it still has a creamy, coffee character. Only found in Victoria, it is named after the co-operative Abbotsford brewery of Melbourne, which was taken over by CUB in 1925. The site now houses one of CUB's largest and most modern plants.

Black Crow

A fruity, all-malt dark ale (3.6%) from Coopers of Adelaide. Unlike the company's more celebrated brews, it is filtered before being bottled.

Blue Label

See Tooheys.

Broken Hill Draught

A dry, malty lager (4.9%) from the South Australian brewery of Adelaide, this beer is named after the famous mining town. It is one of Australia's truly regional brews and has been produced for the "Silver City" and surrounding areas for nearly 80 years. It is only available in kegs in the Broken Hill area.

Carbine Stout

Castlemaine's full-bodied dark beer (5.1%) from Brisbane was introduced in 1925. Despite the name, it is a bottom-fermented lager with a roasted-malt flavour.

Cascade

The Cascade range of bottom-fermented beers, produced at the Cascade brewery, includes a full-bodied Cascade Pale Ale (5.2%), a lighter Cascade Bitter (4.8%) and a pleasantly roasted Cascade Stout (5.8%). They also produce a crisp Cascade Lager (4.8%), a darker, Cascade Draught (4.7%) and the fuller-flavoured Cascade Premium (5.2%).

Castlemaine XXXX

Still described in Australia as a bitter ale, Castlemaine XXXX is a malty golden lager (4.8%), which uses whole hops rather than pellets or hop extracts. The brewery also brews an all-malt Castlemaine Malt 75 (4.8%), a Castlemaine Special Dry (5%), a low-carbohydrate Castlemaine DL (4.1%), XXXX Gold (3.5%), a low-alcohol Light (2.7%) and XL (2.3%).

Coopers Sparkling Ale

Coopers' best-known, yeasty, cloudy brew (5.8%) is a full-flavoured, bottle-conditioned strong pale ale. Coopers also brews two other bottle-conditioned beers – a richly roasted, robust Coopers Best Extra Stout (6.8%) and a fruity middle-strength Coopers Original Pale Ale (4.5%). The company also produces the filtered ale, Coopers Premium Clear (4.9%). All the beers are free of additives and preservatives.

Crown

This sweetish brew (4.9%) comes from Carlton.

D-Ale

See Diamond Draught.

Diamond Draught

A more fully fermented, low-carbohydrate beer (4.6%) than others from Carlton, this is also known as D-Ale.

Dogbolter

A powerful ale (7%), Dogbolter was initially brewed at the Sail and Anchor brewpub in Fremantle in 1983, but is now a bottom-fermenting, creamy, dark lager from the CUB-owned Matilda Bay Brewing Co. of Perth. The beer is cask-matured before bottling and takes twice as long to brew and ferment as most Australian beers.

Eagle Blue

This deep-amber-coloured low-alcohol beer (2.7%) is refreshingly bitter. The ice-brewing process has also been used to produce another low-alcohol alternative in the light-amber lager, Eagle Blue Ice (2.7%). Both are produced by the South Australian Brewing Company.

Eagle Super

This golden-amber, full-strength lager (5%) produced by the South Australian brewery, is available in bottles and cans.

Emu

Swan's Emu beers take their name from a Perth brewery taken over by Swan in 1928. The range includes four lagers, Emu Pilsner, Emu Export (4.9%), a hoppier Emu Bitter (4.6%) and the darker, more malty Emu Draft (3.5%).

Export Mongrel

This bronze-coloured wheat beer (5.1%), produced by the Traditional Brewing Company, is a variation on Yellow Mongrel, using a light crystal malt as well as wheat and barley malts.

Foster's Beer

This light, fruity lager (4%) has a worldwide reputation and is the beer most drinkers abroad associate with the Foster's name.

Foster's Light

A low-alcohol brew (2.5%) from Foster's.

Foster's Special
A bright-gold low-alcohol lager (2.8%) from Foster's.

Fremantle Bitter
This full-bodied, amber-coloured, bottom-fermenting beer (4.9%) is brewed by Matilda Bay.

Hahn Gold
A mid-strength lager (3.5%) with a smooth, hop and malt flavour and sweetish finish, from the Hahn Brewery.

Hahn Premium
A full-strength, straw-coloured, European-style lager (5%) with a balanced character and bitter taste, created by late-hopping with Tasmanian hops.

James Boag's Premium
The pale, full-flavoured premium lager, with a fresh, hayfield aroma, is lagered for more than 60 days. Like all Boag lagers, it is batch-brewed and made from Tasmanian malt and Pride of Ringwood hops. It was voted Australia's best beer in 1995.

Kent Old Brown
One of Australia's rare, top-fermented beers, this dark, fruity ale (4.9%) is one of the Tooth brewery's KB range.

Loaded Dog Steam Beer
A deep-copper, lager-style beer (4%) with a smooth, wheaty flavour and biscuity overtones. The "steam" style comes from the burst of gas released when the cask is tapped. The logo of a snarling dog comes from a short story, in which a mongrel wanders into a pub carrying a stick of dynamite. Brewed by the Traditional Brewing Company.

Longbrew
A speciality lager produced by Lion under the Hahn name, this is a more fully fermented beer (4.5%) than most Australian brews.

Matilda Bay Bitter
An amber, all-malt, bottom-fermenting, Australian-style bitter (3.5%) from the Matilda Bay brewery in Western Australia.

Melbourne Bitter
This dryish lager (4.9%) comes from CUB. It is quite similar to Victoria Bitter (Victoria's best-selling beer), also brewed by CUB.

Moonshine
The strong, spirited barley wine called Moonshine (8%) is produced by the small Grand Ridge brewery in rural Victoria.

O'Flanagan's
The Swan brewery of Perth sells this draught stout (4.8%) as a rival to Guinness.

Old Southwark Stout
See Southwark Old Stout.

Original Chilli Beer
The Traditional Brewing Company in Melbourne brews this fiery chilli beer (4%). It is a smooth lager, but chilli is added at the second fermentation in the bottle to give an unmistakable bite.

Power's Bitter
A light-amber bitter (4.8%) with a dense, creamy head and a hoppy flavour.

Power's Gold
This light-gold, full-bodied, mid-strength lager (3.4%) from the Power brewery, has a hoppy aroma.

Power's Light
A pale-amber, low-alcohol lager (2.8%) with a full-bodied flavour and a clean, crisp aroma.

Razor Back
A creamy, roasted stout, named after a local pig, brewed by Traditional Brewing Company of Melbourne.

COOPERS ORIGINAL

Thomas Cooper, a shoemaker, emigrated to Australia from Yorkshire in England in 1852 with his wife Alice. She was the daughter of a publican and when she fell ill, asked her husband to make her some beer as a tonic, giving him the recipe from her sickbed. According to family legend, this brew was so successful that Thomas Cooper went into brewing full-time in 1862. However, as a devout Wesleyan, he regarded pubs (but not beer) as evil, and so restricted his trade to direct deliveries to private houses. The brewery moved to its present site in Upper Kensington in 1880.

Red Ant
A hearty, robust red lager (4.5%) in the Australian style, produced by the Jerningham Street brewery.

Redback
Australia's first wheat beer (4.8%) was introduced by the pioneering Matilda Bay Brewing Co. of Perth. Named after a local spider, it is brewed using 65% wheat. Since being taken over by CUB, this filtered, fruity, golden brew is less spicy than before. Besides Redback Original, there is also now a lower-alcohol Redback Light. An associated brewpub in Melbourne, also called Redback, produces a more distinctive, unfiltered Redback Hefe-Weizen.

Red Bitter
Sometimes called Tooheys Red, this is a light-gold, dry lager (5%) that uses a high proportion of malt and hops in the brewing process.

Reschs DA
Dinner Ale is a deep-amber, full-strength lager (4.9%) with a robust, aromatic flavour and a sweet aftertaste, produced by the NSW brewery.

Reschs Draught
This fruity, golden lager (4.7%) is one of the distinctive range of lagers produced by the Resch brewery. There is also a lighter lager called Reschs Real Bitter.

Reschs Pilsner
A light, golden Pilsner (4.6%) with a distinct bitterness, from the Resch brewery in NSW.

Sheaf Stout
This dry, bitter, top-fermented stout (5.7%) from Tooth's brewery in Sydney is one of Australia's most distinctive beers.

Southwark Old Stout
This reminder of the English origins of many people in South Australia is a heavy, chocolatey brew (7.4%), reminiscent of a 19th-century London-style stout.

Southwark Premium
The South Australian brewery produces its sweeter beers under the Southwark label. These include Southwark Bitter (4.5%), the full-bodied, fruity Premium lager (5.2%) and Southwark Old Black Ale (4.4%).

Swan Draught
This crisp, gold, malty lager (4.9%) is the best-known beer produced by the Swan plant at Canning Vale. Others include Swan Export lager and Swan Gold (3.5%), for the low-calorie market.

Swan Lite
An ultra-low-alcohol, golden, lightly malted brew (0.9%) where the alcohol is removed by vacuum distillation.

Sydney Bitter
Despite its name, this is a pale, golden lager (4.9%) with a lightly hopped flavour and a light, bitter finish. It was one of the first speciality brews from Hahn.

Tooheys Draught
This pale, sweetish lager (4.6%) is one of Tooheys most popular brews.

Tooheys Old Black
A dark, fruity ale (4.4%) from Tooheys brewery. It is one of the few surviving "Old" top-fermenting beers produced by this concern.

Victoria Bitter
Despite the international reputation of Foster's Lager, this is the best-selling beer in Australia (4.9%). It accounts for a quarter of the total beer market and 60% of CUB's output. A similar brew is sold as Melbourne Bitter.

EARLY BREWS

Brewing arrived in Australia with the first European settlers. John Boston, who landed in Sydney in 1794, manufactured the first recorded beer. It would have been an interesting drink, as it was made from maize and flavoured with the leaves and stalks of the Cape Gooseberry. In 1804, the government set up the colony's first commercial brewery in Parramatta.

The early brews had a poor reputation. Good-quality ingredients were difficult to obtain, and fermentation of English-style, top-fermenting ales was difficult to control in the hot, harsh climate. Yeast deteriorated rapidly, and even if the brewing process could be controlled, the beer itself quickly went off once it was hauled away by bullock cart. The laxative effects of this warm, sour soup earned it the unsavoury nickname "swipes". Most drinkers preferred rum or strong imported beer.

The quality of the beer improved in the 1860s, with the founding of the Swan brewery in 1857 and Coopers brewery in 1862, but the real breakthrough came with the introduction of refrigeration in the 1880s. This allowed the controlled use of yeast, as well as bottom-fermentation, and meant that more reliable beers could be produced. In 1885, two German immigrants, Friedrich and Renne, set up the first lager brewery in Melbourne. Foster's was established nearby by the American Foster brothers in 1888. Although now famous throughout the world, the two brothers only stayed in Australia for 18 months, selling their Collingwood brewery within a year before returning to New York.

West End
South Australia's drier, slightly more hoppy lagers include West End Draught (4.5%), Export Bitter (4.9%) and West End Light (2.6%).

Yellow Mongrel
The rare, golden-straw-coloured, refreshingly fruity Australian wheat beer (3.5%) comes from Traditional

Brewing Company of Sydney. Green Bullet hops are used to offset the natural sweetness of the wheat, and give a characteristic bitter finish.

1857
These two lagers, the crisp 1857 Pilsner (4.8%) and more malty 1857 Bitter (3.5%) from Swan are named after the founding date of the brewery on the Swan River in Western Australia.

THE BREWERS

Boag's

Scottish immigrant James Boag and his son bought the Esk brewery on the island of Tasmania at Launceston in 1881. From 1922 until 1993, Boag's was linked with rival island brewers, Cascade of Hobart. This partnership was broken when CUB took over Cascade. Since then, Boag's has taken on new life as one of the few remaining independent breweries, and has revamped its range of beers with a Boag's Original Bitter (4.7%) and a cold-filtered Boag's Classic Bitter (4.9%). All use local Tasmanian malt and Pride of Ringwood hops. Unlike many Australian beers, the beers are batch-brewed in the traditional way. The company's lagers are also matured for 30 days instead of the more usual ten.

Carlton United Brewers

Victoria's leading brewery was founded in Melbourne in 1864 as Carlton and merged with five local rivals including Victoria and Foster's to form Carlton and United Breweries in 1907. In 1990, the combine was renamed the Foster's Brewing Group, but the CUB subsidiary remained in charge of brewing in Australia. Today, it brews in five of the country's seven states, producing 950 million litres (209 million gallons) a year.

Many of CUB's national brands are sold under the Carlton name, including the dryish Carlton Draught, Crown, the more fully fermented Diamond Draught or D-Ale, the extremely clean-tasting Carlton Cold Filtered Bitter (4.9%) and Carlton Light (3.3%).

Cascade

Founded by a Frenchman in 1824, Cascade is the oldest continuously operating brewery in Australia. It also has the grandest location. The fine front of the stone brewhouse in Hobart, Tasmania, is set against the soaring cliffs of the Cascade Mountains. Cascade was badly damaged by bush fires in 1967, but within 12 weeks was brewing again. In 1993, Cascade, then part of Tasmanian Breweries, was bought by CUB. It still produces Cascade beers.

Castlemaine

This Brisbane brewery began life many miles away in the town of Castlemaine in Victoria, where the Fitzgerald brothers had established a brewery in 1859. They set up another Castlemaine brewery in Melbourne in 1871 and then expanded across the country to Brisbane, converting a distillery in Milton into a brewery in 1878. The Victoria interests were later sold to become part of CUB, but the Castlemaine brewery in Brisbane remained part of the rival group, merging with local brewers, Perkins, in 1928 to form Castlemaine Perkins. The main beer, Castlemaine XXXX, introduced in 1924, became Queensland's favourite beer and an international rival to Foster's. Castlemaine's other famous beer is the heavy, dark Carbine Stout. Castlemaine controls 65% of the Queensland market, but is now part of Lion Nathan.

Cooper's

When most other Australian brewers were switching wholesale to producing pasteurized, continuously brewed, pale mass-market lagers (even if some were called bitters), Coopers of

Above: Boag's advertising plays on the Australian image of hard drinking macho beer drinkers.

Adelaide stuck to its guns and continued to brew traditional, top-fermenting ales, which are still sold unfiltered, allowing the beer to mature in the bottle. The Cooper's brews remain the classics of the continent.

Founded in 1862 and still run by the Coopers family, the Upper Kensington brewery in the suburb of Leabrook still ferments its ales in open vats made of native jarrah wood using a distinctive yeast strain that is at least 85 years old. Extra wort is added to the beer on bottling in order to ensure a secondary fermentation of the beer in the bottle. Given the sediment that this process leaves in the bottle, it is surprising that Cooper's best-known yeasty, cloudy brew is called Sparkling Ale.

Coopers introduced their own lagers in 1969 and now use stainless-steel conical fermenters to produce a Draught Lager, a Dry Lager (both 4.5%), Coopers Light (2.9%) and the malty, dark Black Crow (3.6%).

The firm began exporting its ales in 1963 and now they are famous around the world. As a result, today less than a third of total production is sold in South Australia.

Foster's Brewing Group
The international name for Australian beer is also now the overall title of the country's leading combine. The Foster's Brewing Group includes Australia's leading brewer CUB as well as its international arms including Foster's Asia. Originally founded in Melbourne in 1888, Foster's was a lager pioneer, importing ice-making equipment from America. It was also a bottled-beer specialist and leader in the export field.

Grand Ridge
A small brewery in rural Victora at Mirboo North. It brews an Australian-style bitter ale (4.9%) – Gippsland Gold; a hoppy Pilsner (4.9%) – Brewer's Pilsner; an Irish-style stout (4.9%) – Hatlifter Stout; and a powerful extra-strong, pure-malt barley wine (8.5%) – Moonshine.

Hahn
Dr Charles Hahn founded a new brewery in Camperdown, Sydney, in 1988. Hahn had worked in New Zealand where he helped to develop Steinlager. His new brewery produced an all-malt Hahn Premium lager and a Sydney Bitter. It gained such a reputation it was bought by Lion Nathan

in 1993. Its name is still used for speciality lagers, including Hahn Dark Ice (5.2%) and a cold-filtered Hahn Gold (3.5%).

Lion Nathan
In 1992, New Zealand's leading brewery group bought up Bond Brewing in Australia (Castlemaine, Swan and Tooheys) and has since added South Australian and Hahn. It now dominates the Australian industry alongside Foster's CUB.

Matilda Bay
This pioneer of the new brewery and speciality beer movement was founded at Nedlands in Western Australia in the mid-1980s by Philip Sexton, a former brewer with Swan in Perth. Matilda Bay launched the country's first wheat beer called Redback and also a strong ale, Dogbolter. The company accepted substantial investment in 1988 from CUB, which acquired a controlling interest, to expand and build a new brewery in Perth. Matilda Bay still brews Redback and Dogbolter, Matilda Bay Bitter and a Fremantle Bitter.

Power
Hotel owner Bernard Power decided to challenge the might of the two big groups and set up his own large brewery at Yatala, near Brisbane, in 1988. However, after early success, his Power Brewing venture was taken over by CUB in 1992. The Queensland plant still brews Power's creamy, full-bodied Bitter, the weaker Power's Gold, and Light, and Brisbane Bitter and Pilsner.

Reschs

Edmund Resch bought the New South Wales Lager Company in Waverley, Sydney, in 1900 and soon established a sound reputation for his beers. The company merged with Sydney rivals Tooth's in 1920. Today, Resch beers are still brewed at Tooth's Kent brewery, now part of CUB.

South Australian

This major Adelaide brewery was founded in 1888 by the amalgamation of the city's Kent Town and West End breweries. In 1938 it bought the Southwark brewery and all production is now concentrated there in a modern brewery. The company controls almost 70% of the state market. The beers are sold under three main brands, Southwark, West End and Eagle.

Swan

Beer in Western Australia has traditionally been all about the birds. The Swan brewery was built in Perth by the Swan River in 1857 and in 1928 took over the rival Emu brewery. Now part of Lion Nathan, it controls almost three-quarters of the state market. In addition to the well-known Swan lagers, the company also markets a strong, top-fermenting dark Swan Stout (6.8%) and a smooth O'Flanagan's Cream Stout. Other lagers include 1857 Pilsner and 1857 Bitter, and a range of Emu lagers.

Tooheys

Sydney's Catholic Irish brewery was founded in 1869 when John Thomas and his brother James bought the Darling brewery. They moved to a new site to build the Standard brewery, used

until 1978 when production was moved to a modern site at Lidcombe in Sydney. It is now part of Lion Nathan. Tooheys' first beers were top-fermenting darkish ales. When the company started producing bottom-fermenting, golden lagers in the 1930s, it called these "new" beers as opposed to the "old" style ales. Lagers now dominate, notably Tooheys Draught (4.6%). Since 1985 Tooheys has pioneered the development of full-bodied, low-alcohol beers using crystal malt, through its Blue Label.

Below: Brisbane, home of Castlemaine brewery, showing the modern skyline and Brisbane River.

Tooth's

Merchant John Tooth founded the Sydney brewery in 1835. He called it the Kent brewery, after the English hop-growing county he came from. Its beers were sold under the KB brand. Tooth's absorbed its local rival, Reschs of Waverley, in 1929 but was taken over by CUB in 1983. Its beers are still brewed in NSW, including a soft malty KB Lager (4.7%) and two top-fermenting beers – a dark, rich Kent Old Brown and a full-bodied Sheaf Stout.

Traditional Brewing Company

This small brewery at the Geebung Polo Club pub in Hawthorn, Melbourne, has developed a reputation for brewing tasty, stylishly bottled ales. It started in 1985 and claims to be Melbourne's oldest established "boutique brewer".

ICE BEER

As the alcohol content rises in a brew, fermentation becomes more difficult because the action of the yeast is subdued by the alcohol it produces. One way around this difficulty is to freeze the brew. The water freezes before the alcohol and can then be removed to produce a concentrated, purified beer. However it is the effect of the freezing process on the flavour of the beer that has become popular, and few of the fashionable, ultra-smooth lagers weigh in at more than 5.5%. The ice beer craze has certainly arrived in Australia, with most of the main brewers introducing their own brands over the last couple of years.

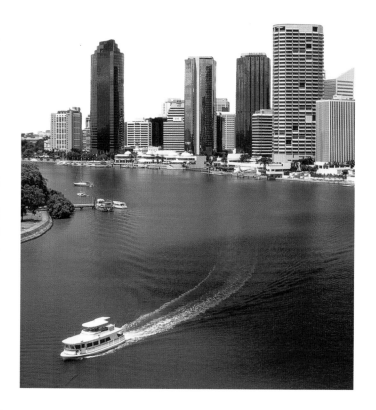

BREWPUBS

Lion

This small brewery in North Adelaide was built in a pub complex in the mid 1980s. Its Old Lion beers include a hoppy Pilsner, a Sparkling Ale and a Porter.

Lord Nelson

Sydney's oldest hotel is home to a brewery which produces English-style ales, including Trafalgar Pale (4%), Victory Bitter (4.8%) and a rich, dark, malty Old Admiral (6.5%).

Port Dock

The Port Dock Hotel, a brewpub in Port Adelaide, was built in 1855. It uses malt extract to produce golden Lighthouse Ale (3.9%), creamy Black Diamond Bitter (4.9%) and strong Old Preacher (6%).

Pumphouse

A waterside brewpub in Sydney, Pumphouse's beers include the hoppy, English-style Bull's Head Bitter and the darker, more malty Federation.

Redback

This Melbourne brewpub is associated with the Matilda Bay Brewing Company and produces its own distinctive, unfiltered Redback Hefe-Weizen. It also offers Redback Original wheat beer (4.8%) and a lower-alcohol Redback Light.

Rifle Brigade

One of Australia's smallest breweries was installed in the Rifle Brigade pub in the central Victoria mining town of Bendigo in 1986. Its malt extract plant produces seven

different beers, including the full-bodied Old Fashioned Bitter (5.3%), the richly roasted Iron Bark Dark (5.3%) and a wheat beer called Platman's (5%).

Sail and Anchor

Australia's first modern brewpub was set up in 1983 by Philip Sexton, a former brewer with the Swan brewery in Perth, when he bought the Freemason's Hotel in Fremantle, renamed it the Sail and Anchor, and installed a brewery on the premises. Later he went on to found the Matilda Bay

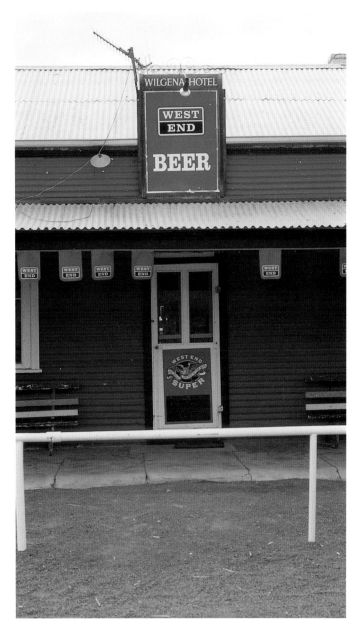

Above: An outback pub in Toncoola, South Australia. The rail was originally used for tethering horses.

Brewing Company in nearby Perth. The Sail and Anchor brews several top-fermenting ales served on a handpump, including a fruity English-style bitter called Seven Seas Real Ale (4.6%), a Brass Monkey Stout (6%) with a coffee character and a warming, rich, dark ale, Ironbrew (7%).

Scharer's

The small New South Wales brewery based at the George IV pub in Picton has been

brewing German-style lagers since the mid-1980s, most notably a creamy, malty Burragarang Bock (6.4%), an amber Scharer's Lager (5%) and D'lite (3%).

The Inn, which is said to have been built in 1819, originally catered for "Officers and Gentlemen" passing through the town. Convicts, road gangs and future inmates of Berrima and Goulburn jails were often held in what are now the lagering cellars.

NEW ZEALAND

New Zealand has had a long love-hate relationship with beer. Although it is one of the world's top beer-drinking nations, the country has also been the home of a powerful temperance movement.

IN 1885, THE SCATTERED POPULATION of New Zealand boasted one brewery for every 6,000 people. These early breweries brewed British-style ales in a climate not far removed from that of northern Europe. Lager was not introduced until 1900, and then only in Auckland in the warmer north. This industry served hotels, which were more like American wild-west saloons than English pubs. Heavy drinking provoked a powerful temperance movement, which closed down hotels and introduced six o'clock closing during the First World War. This lasted for 50 years, and total Prohibition was narrowly avoided in a referendum in 1919.

Under pressure and struggling to survive, the New Zealand brewing industry concentrated at a much earlier stage than in most countries. The first national brewing company, New Zealand Breweries (later Lion Breweries), was formed in 1923 when ten of the largest breweries joined forces, thus controlling 40% of the trade. Seven years later, the rival Dominion Breweries group was formed. Today, the two combines, known as Lion Nathan and DB, dominate the beer market.

The early concentration of the brewing industry meant it invested heavily in research, influenced by the high standards of cleanliness in New Zealand's dairy industry. In the 1950s, Morton Coutts of Dominion developed continuous fermentation whereby beer is produced from a never-ending flow of wort and yeast through four aligned vessels. Rival New Zealand Breweries soon also adopted this cost-efficient system, replacing the traditional batch method. The result was that all beers were chilled, filtered and bottom-fermented. Most draught beers also abandoned the barrel in favour of large tankers that deliver beer direct to hotel cellar tanks. These mild, full-coloured lagers – often referred to as "brown" beers or ales – are sweet, most being primed with sugar and served very cold and highly carbonated.

With the removal of strict licensing restrictions in 1967, New Zealand has gradually adopted a more relaxed attitude to beer drinking. Since the 1980s, a few brewpubs and micro-breweries have appeared.

Above: New Zealand brewing is dominated by two groups. Many of the beers have their origins in Britain, and ale and stout are brewed as well as lager.

THE BEERS

Canterbury

A regional, amber-coloured "brown" beer (4%) with a malty, smooth flavour, barley overtones and a dry finish. It comes from Lion's Christchurch brewery on the South Island.

Coromandel Draught

A full-flavoured bitter beer (4%) is brewed by the Coromandel Brewing Company.

DB Export Dry

A pale-gold, hoppy, crisp beer (5%) from Dominion Breweries with a smooth, light, malt taste. It is lagered for longer than most New Zealand brews.

DB Natural

A fresh, unpasteurized, amber-coloured ale (4%) with a sweetish, roast-malt taste and a hoppy finish. It is bottom-fermented and micro-filtered by Dominion Breweries (DB).

Double Brown

A full-flavoured, amber-gold, bottom-fermented speciality beer (4%) with a fruity-malt flavour, brewed by Dominion.

Flame

This amber-gold lager with a smooth finish (5.2%) is produced by the Black Dog brewery in Auckland using the extreme brewing process. This first heats the malt and hops to 106°C (223°F) and then crash-cools the beer to emphasize the flavours.

Hawkes Bay Draught

This amber-coloured ale (4%) with a dry, malt taste, is a regional beer, brewed by Leopard in Hastings. Leopard, now part of Lion, was once New Zealand's third brewing force, behind Lion and Dominion.

Leopard Black Label

A golden-amber lager (4%) with a crisp, fruity flavour. It is brewed by Lion, using the traditional Leopard Brewery's batch-brewing process and a combination of New Zealand hops and a new, recently developed "black label" yeast.

Lion Brown

This amber-gold, sweet and fruity, malt-flavoured ale (4%) is one of Lion's best-selling brews.

Lion Ice

This light-golden-amber modern lager (4.7%) is a smooth, easy-drinking beer from Lion Breweries.

Lion Red

A deep-gold, malty, hoppy, sweetish beer (4%) with a good body. It is one of the leading brands in New Zealand produced by Lion Breweries.

Mainland Dark

Described as a dark ale, this is a richer lager (4%) than others from Dominion, brewed using a blend of roasted malts and barleys by DB's South Island brewery at Timaru.

Mako

This low-alcohol, light beer (2.5%) is brewed by Dominion. It is an authentic, bitter-style beer, brewed with extra hops.

Monteith's Black Beer

This black-coloured beer (5.2%) is stronger than an ale, yet it is lighter than a stout. It is produced by Monteith's using the traditional batch-brewing method and combining five crystal and chocolate malts in a special mash.

Monteith's Original Ale

The Monteith label is used for Dominion Breweries' new "boutique" range of beers, including the malty Monteith's Original Ale (4%), which is brewed from an original 1860s recipe.

Nugget Golden Lager

A crisp speciality lager (5%) from Monteith's.

Rheineck Lager

Relatively light, this golden lager (3.8%) is drier than most New Zealand brews.

Cook's special

Captain Cook, the English explorer who literally put New Zealand on the map, is credited with being the country's first beer brewer. Concerned about scurvy on his second visit in 1773, he brewed "beer" for the ship's crew by boiling up spruce and tea shrub leaves and twigs, mixed with molasses. The concoction was served to the sailors with a shot of rum and brown sugar stirred in, perhaps to help disguise the flavour!

Speight's Gold Medal Ale

A deep-gold, fruity, malt-and-hop-tasting ale (4%). It is still a major malty "brown" beer brand on the South Island. Speight's, established in Dunedin in 1876, was New Zealand's largest brewery before the First World War and the leading company in the merger that formed New Zealand Breweries (Lion) in 1923. The Lion group still brews in Dunedin.

Steinlager

Lion's premium, pale-gold, international lager (5%), much drier and more aromatic than its other beers, is mainly sold abroad. This sweetish, hoppy brew was originally introduced as Steinecker in 1958, named after the new, German-made, Steinecker continuous-fermentation brewing plant that had been installed in its Auckland brewery. After a legal challenge in the US from Dutch giant Heineken, the name was changed to Steinlager in 1962.

Steinlager Blue

Lion introduced this variant on its premium lager in 1993. It is a golden, medium-dry, malty lager with a light hop aroma.

Taranaki Draught

A dark, full-bodied, malty regional lager (4%) with a bitter flavour. It carries the name of the Taranaki brewery of New Plymouth, which was taken over and closed in the 1960s by Dominion Breweries (DB).

Trapper's Red Beer

Monteith's of Greymouth on the South Island produces this deep-red, speciality beer (4.4%), brewed with roasted crystal malt, using a batch-brewing method.

Tui

Although described as an East India Pale Ale, this is a sweet, golden-reddish lager (4%) with a clear, hoppy flavour and malty aftertaste from DB's Tui Brewery at Mangatainoka. The brewery itself dates back to 1889. It is most closely associated with the Hawke's Bay region on the North Island.

Vita Stout

The name of Dominion's smooth, sweet, dark-brown beer (4%) with a chocolate-malt and roasted-barley flavour hints at health-giving properties. Faced with a strong temperance movement in the early part of the 20th century, Kiwi breweries regularly claimed that their beer was full of health-giving properties and should be drunk regularly. Dominion's early Waitemata beer was sold as "The Secret of Good Health and Long Life" and "As Nourishing as Bread or Milk".

THE BREWERS

Dominion Breweries (DB)

Formed in 1930 in Auckland, Dominion Breweries has prided itself on its technological advances, notably the introduction of continuous fermentation in the 1950s. Besides its modern Waitemata brewery in Auckland, it also runs the Tui brewery at Mangatainoka, Monteith's at Greymouth and the Mainland brewery at Timaru. The main beers are the best-selling, sweetish DB Draught, which uses the company's famous Clydesdale horses in its promotion, and the drier DB Bitter. Regional brands include Tui and Taranaki.

Although described as brown beers and ales, these are mid-strength, reddish-tinted and softly sweet lagers (all 4%). Paler lagers are led by DB Export Gold (4%) and the crisper Export Dry (5%). The company also produces a low-alcohol light beer, Mako (2.5%). Speciality brews, all bottom-fermented, include a fresher-flavoured, unpasteurized DB Natural, a fuller-flavoured Double Brown, a smoothly sweet Vita Stout and richer, more roasted Mainland Dark. DB have recently promoted a range of "boutique" beers, which are sold under the Monteith label in the speciality beer market.

Harrington

The Christchurch micro-brewery produces a rare New Zealand wheat beer and a tasty Dark Beer, besides more conventional lagers.

Lion

New Zealand's largest brewing company controls almost 60% of the domestic market. The overall group, which also owns substantial brewing interests in Australia, is called Lion Nathan. In New Zealand the company trades as Lion Breweries in the North Island and under its older name of New Zealand Breweries in the South Island. The group runs two breweries in the North Island, in Auckland and Hastings, and two in the South Island, in Dunedin and Christchurch. Its main brand is the best-selling, malty Lion Red and the sweeter, fruity

Salvation

The birth of New Zealand's second-largest brewing group sums up the country's love-hate relationship with beer. When the Coutts family opened the Waitemata brewery in Auckland in 1929, the Women's Christian Temperance Movement marched to the site and prayed that the new brewery be turned into a food factory. In part their prayers were answered, for the new venture struggled to find a market and only survived by merging with a drinks wholesaler in 1930 to form Dominion.

Lion Brown. There are also regional bottom-fermenting "brown" beers, including Hawkes Bay and Waikato Draught and, in the South Island, Speight's and Canterbury Draught. More golden, drier brews include a light Rheineck Lager and the company's international flagship brand, the crisp Steinlager (5%). In the 1980s, Lion abandoned the continuous fermentation system and reverted to more traditional batch methods to meet the demand for a wider variety of beers.

Mac's

When the Prime Minister Sir Robert Muldoon opened New Zealand's first micro-brewery in Stoke, in 1981, he described it as a David in an industry of two Goliaths. Nevertheless, the venture launched by former All-Black rugby player Terry McCashin has survived, and has even set up its own maltings to ensure supplies. The marketing for the all-malt beers, brewed to the German beer purity law using a bottom-fermenting lager yeast, emphasizes that no chemicals or preservatives are added. The main brews are a malty Mac's Ale, a hoppy Gold, a darker, fuller-bodied Black Mac (all 4%), a more powerful lager Extra (7%) and a Mac Special Light (1%).

Monteith

Dominion took over the Westland brewery in Greymouth in 1969, renamed it Monteith's Brewing Co. in 1995 and began to brew beers for the speciality market. These include the malty Monteith's Original Ale, a deeper-coloured Trapper's Red Beer and a crisp Nugget Golden Lager. The Westland brewery, established in 1858, retains open fermenting vessels, coal-fired boilers and traditional batch brewing. Greymouth, a mining area of the west coast of the South Island, has a large Irish population and prides itself on its pubs and beer.

Newbegin

Established in Onehunga near Auckland in 1987, this micro-brewery produces an all-malt lager, Silver Fern (4%) and a dark more robust Old Thumper.

New Zealand Breweries (NZB)

New Zealand's largest beer company, Lion, trades under its older name of New Zealand Breweries in the South Island. NZB was formed in 1923 when ten of the country's largest breweries merged, including Speight's of Dunedin, Staples in Wellington, Ward's of Christchurch and the Great Northern brewery (Lion) of Auckland.

Petone

Two former Lion employees set up this "boutique" brewery in Petone, near Wellington. They imported yeast from Britain to start fermenting the malty Strongcroft's Bitter.

Shakespeare

The country's first brewpub was founded in Auckland in 1986. Its beers include the soft, malty Macbeth's Red Ale, bitter Falstaff Real Ale, Barraclough Lager, pale gold with a light hop finish, and lightly bittered Willpower Stout, as well as the dramatically rich, hoppy King Lear Old Ale (7.5%).

Stockan

Henderson, near Auckland, is home to this brewery, which was partly financed by a vineyard. Set up in the mid-1980s on a larger scale than most micro-breweries, its beers include a spicy Stockan Ale and the chocolatey Dark Ale.

BREWING IN THE PACIFIC

The vast Pacific Ocean is peppered with hundreds of tiny islands, and on some of these there are brewers gallantly turning out brews for their small populations.

The South Pacific brewery in Papua New Guinea was set up in the 1940s by Australians who travelled to Papua New Guinea to work in the gold fields. They were frustrated by the lack of good quality beer, all of which was imported, so they built their own brewery in Port Moresby and used rain water collected in tanks to produce their own beers. Production started in 1952. Sales soared in the 1960s when Prohibition was ended for the islanders. The brewery is still going strong. It produces a malty, dry, golden lager (4.5%) called SP Lager and South Pacific Export Lager –a delicate malt lager (5.5%) that won the Brewex international gold medal award in 1980. There is also a deep-brown-black stout (8%) called Niugini Gold Extra Stout.

Western Samoa Breweries boasts Vailima, a smooth, refreshing lager (4.9%), which is actually brewed in Auckland, New Zealand, and the small Pacific islands of Tahiti and Fiji also have their own breweries. On Tahiti the Brasserie de Tahiti produces a prestigious, pale-gold Hinano Tahiti lager (4.9%), which won a World Gold Medal for quality in 1990, as well as two local beers, Hei Lager Gold, a premium lager (5%), and Vaita, a virtually non-alcoholic lager (0.8%). The Calton brewery in Fiji makes a tawny brew with a malty flavour called Fiji Bitter Beer.

The Kona Brewing Company on Hawaii, the 52nd State of the US, brews Fire Rock Ale, a dark amber beer (4.1%), using pale and Munich malts and Cascade, Galena and Mount Hood hops, while the same company's Pacific Golden Ale (3.5%) is a golden-amber pale ale, created with a blend of pale and honey malts, hopped with Bullion and Willamette varieties.

CANADA

Prohibition hit Canada hard, and as a result the industry is dominated by the few big names that survived. The Canadians are not big beer drinkers, but the picture is now changing slowly and more small breweries are appearing.

REWING IN CANADA has run parallel with its big neighbour south of the border, although technically Canada has often led the way. The first commercial brewery in Canada was set up in Montreal in 1786, by English immigrant John Molson, making it the oldest brewery in North America. He was followed by two other familiar names, Thomas Carling who started his brewery in London, Ontario, in 1840, and John Labatt who founded his brewery in the same town seven years later. Canada has had a love-hate relationship with alcohol, and, following the passing of the Scott Local Option Law in 1878, a nightmare cobweb of regulations ensnared the production and sale of beer. There was also the dry period of national Prohibition, which lasted from 1918 until 1932. When that ended, each province developed its own set of rigid rules – many of them are still in existence. In Ontario, for example, the Liquor Control Board is one of the biggest purchasers of alcohol in the world, and it has a monopoly on selling beer throughout its 585 stores. Also, taxes on alcohol in Canada are the highest of any nation, with tariffs making up 53% of the price in 1995. As a result of all this, beer in Canada is relatively expensive.

Local laws in Canada require beer to be brewed in the area where it is sold, so the three large groups which dominate brewing in Canada – Molson, Labatt and Carling – have breweries scattered across the provinces, often producing beers under a myriad of local labels. Originally the beer they produced was typical of the top-fermenting ales that reflected the English origins of the founding brewers, but they soon switched to bottom-fermenting lagers, and Labatt's pioneered the introduction of "ice beer" in 1993 which has proved so popular.

Since the early 1980s there has been a small-scale brewery revolution, particularly in British Columbia, Ontario and Quebec. By 1995, some 40 micro-breweries had been set up, bringing a new wave of beers to the bar. But many of these small breweries have had to struggle against stifling regulations.

Above: Molson is the oldest brewer on the North American continent. The company merged with Carling in 1989 to form a giant international company.

THE BEERS

Alpine Lager

This refreshing lager (5%) is produced locally by the independent Moosehead brewery for the Maritime provinces.

Anniversary Amber Ale

A red-amber, Bavarian-style, all-malt brew (5.5%) was created to celebrate 10 years of production at the Granville Island micro-brewery.

Arkell Best Bitter

Wellington County produces this light, bitter ale (4%) with a malt aroma in the brewing town of Guelph in the state of Ontario.

Big Rock Pale Ale

This quality pale ale (5%) is brewed at the Big Rock brewery in Calgary, which was founded by Ed McNally in 1985. Big Rock has created its own stampede, with demand rising for its tasty, all-malt, unpasteurized ales brewed by Bernd Pieper, who was formerly a head brewer with Löwenbräu in Zurich.

Black Amber

An extra-strong, amber ale (7%) from the small Big Rock brewery.

Blanche de Chambly

A cloudy, spicy, bottle-conditioned wheat beer (5%) from the Unibroue micro-brewery. This tart, refreshing brew won the Silver Medal in the 1995 World Beer Championship.

Brador

A rich, fruity, top-fermenting specialist ale (6.5%) from Molson.

Brasal Bock

An amber-brown, sweet-roasted, hoppy bock (7.8%), which is matured in oak barrels for three months.

Brasal Légère

The lightest lager brewed by the Brasal micro-brewery of LaSalle. The companion brew Brasal Hops Bräu (4.5%) is also quite light.

Brasal Special Amber

A malty, strong, German-style lager (6.1%).

Brick Bock

A strong, unpasteurized German-style bock (6.5%) from the Brick micro-brewery.

Brick Premium Lager

This excellent, hoppy, golden lager (5%) is one of the award-winning brews from the Brick micro-brewery of Waterloo, Ontario.

Brick Red Baron

An unpasteurized ale (5%) produced by the Brick micro-brewery.

Brock's Extra Stout

Brock extra stout porter (5.8%) is one of the specialist beers brewed by the innovative Niagara micro-brewery.

Canadian Lager

An unexciting, but not unpleasant, standard lager (5%) produced by Moosehead.

Carling Black Label

A light-tasting, pale-gold, standard lager (5%) from Molson, which has proved to be a best-selling export to the UK.

Colonial Stout

This stout porter (4.8%) comes from the Upper Canada micro-brewery.

County Ale

This excellent, amber, malty, traditional ale (5%) with a hoppy aftertaste is a slightly stronger ale produced by the Wellington County micro-brewery.

Frontenac

This light ale (5%) comes from the popular small brewery, McAuslan, which is based in Ontario.

Granville Island Dark Bock

This delicious, amber bock (6.5%) brewed by Granville Island Brewing Company in Vancouver, British Columbia, is one of the finest beers in Canada. It has a rich, malt nose, a hearty, roasted-malt and hop flavour, good balance and an exceptionally long and well-balanced finish.

Grasshopper Wheat

This all-malt, unpasteurized wheat beer (5%) is produced by Big Rock of Calgary.

Griffon Brown Ale

A mahogany-brown, complex, full-bodied, slightly sweet, hoppy ale (4.5%) produced by Brasserie McAuslan.

Griffon Extra Pale Ale

This bright-gold, pale ale (5%) has a hoppy, fruity-malt flavour. It comes from the Brasserie McAuslan.

Gritstone Premium Ale

This strong ale (5.5%) is produced by the Niagara Falls Brewing Company.

Imperial Stout

This dark stout (5.5%) from Wellington County has a faint chocolate-malt nose, a light but complex malty flavour and a hoppy finish.

Island Lager

A full-bodied, hoppy, deep-gold lager (5%), from Granville Island Brewing.

John Labatt's Classic

This gold, highly carbonated lager (5%) from Labatt has a mild, hoppy aroma and a dull, malt and hop flavour.

La Fin du Monde

Unibroue produces this deep-yellow, fruity, spicy, extra-strong, triple-fermented ale (9%). It is conditioned in the bottle.

La Gaillarde

This unusual bottle-conditioned beer (5%) from Unibroue uses herbs and spices in place of hops.

Labatt Ice Beer

This pioneering ice beer, with a golden, malt and hop flavour and full body, weighs in at 5.6%.

Labatt's Blue

This grainy, deep-amber, slightly dry lager (5%) is Labatt's flagship brand.

Labatt's 50 Ale

This refreshing, bright-gold ale (5%) has a medium body, a light hop nose with fruity hints and a crisp, fresh flavour with a slightly sour malt finish.

Lord Granville Pale Ale

This all-malt, copper-red, fruity pale ale (5%) from the Granville Island brewery is brewed in accordance with the German beer purity law, using only barley malt, hops, water and yeast in the brew.

McAuslan Pale Ale

This zesty pale ale (5%) from Brasserie McAuslan has a smooth, well-balanced hop and malt flavour.

McNally's Extra Pure Malt Irish Style Ale

This deep-amber, extra-strong, unpasteurized, all-malt beer (7%) from Big Rock brewery has a powerful, roasted-malt nose, a rich malt flavour, and a hop and malt aftertaste with hints of caramel.

Magpie Rye

This is an unpasteurized, tart-flavoured rye beer (5%), which comes from the Big Rock brewery in Calgary.

Maple Wheat Beer

A strong, syrupy wheat beer (8.5%) from the Niagara Falls Brewing Company.

Maudite

A warming, mellow, bottle-conditioned red ale (8%), from the Unibroue micro-brewery.

Mitchell's ESB

A copper-coloured, English-style ale (5.5%) from the Spinnakers brewpub.

Molson Canadian Lager

The most famous of Molson's products (5%) is pale gold with a dry malt nose and hints of hops. Its flavour is smooth and well-balanced with malt and hops and a long, dry finish.

Molson Export Ale

This light, brownish-gold ale (5%) is a little fuller than the lager, with a crisp, hoppy taste, good body and a long malt and hop aftertaste.

Molson Special Dry

A slightly stronger lager (5.5%) from Molson.

Moosehead Lager

This is the popular, mild, pale-malt lager (5%) that gave its name to the brewery.

Moosehead Pale Ale

This pale-gold ale (5%) has a yeasty, malt-hop nose, a well-hopped, slightly sweet malt flavour, and a dry malt-hop finish. It is brewed at the Moosehead brewery.

Mount Tolmie

This dark ale (4.2%) is brewed by the Spinnakers brewpub, using four malt types and Mount Hood hops.

Ogden Porter

This strong porter (6.2%) comes from the Spinnakers brewpub in Victoria, British Columbia.

Okanagan Spring Brown Ale

A deep-brown, top-fermented ale (5.6%), brewed with two-row barley malt and Hallertauer hops by the Okanagan Spring brewery, British Columbia.

Okanagan Spring Pilsner

A light, golden, hoppy Pilsner (4.5%) from the Okanagan Spring brewery, British Columbia.

Pacific Real Draft

This light, pleasant lager (5%) is the best-known brew from the Pacific Western brewery.

Publican's Special Bitter

The Upper Canada micro-brewery produces this special top-fermented, amber-brown, English-style bitter (4.8%).

Raftman

This gold, smoky, bottle-conditioned beer (5.5%) is brewed using peat-smoked whiskey malt by the Unibroue micro-brewery.

Rebellion Malt Liquor

This deep-gold, malt liquor (6%) has a sweet, full, honey taste with a malty hop finish. It is a very pleasant, well-rounded beer from the Upper Canada Brewing Company.

Red Baron

This pale-gold lager (5%), brewed by the Brick Brewing Company, has a light hop and malt aroma, a mild malt flavour and a hoppy finish.

Red Cap Ale

The Brick Brewing Company produces this classic beer (5%) using the original Carling recipe.

Red Dog

A golden, German-style ale (5.5%) with a faint malt and hop nose and a dry, malty flavour.

St-Ambroise Framboise

A Belgian-style, light, pink-red, raspberry fruit beer (5%), from the Brasserie McAuslan.

St-Ambroise Oatmeal Stout

A black, chocolatey, malt and roasted barley, traditional, dry stout (5.5%), brewed using oatmeal in the mash by McAuslan Brasserie, St Ambroise, Quebec.

St-Ambroise Pale Ale

A reddish-gold, robust, malty ale with a clean taste – a characteristic of the Cascade hops used in the brew by Brasserie McAuslan.

Signature Amber Lager

This amber, all-malt lager is brewed under the Signature label by Molson.

Signature Cream Ale

A characterful, all-malt ale. It is one of Molson's prestige Signature brews.

Sleeman Cream Ale

As with all Sleeman brews, this tawny-gold, malty cream ale (5%) is sold in a distinctive embossed bottle.

Sleeman Original Dark

This dark-amber ale (5.5%) has a malty aroma and is lightly hopped. It comes from the Sleeman brewery.

Spinnaker Ale

An amber, English-style ale (4.2%) from Canada's first brewpub, Spinnaker.

Spinnaker Hefe-Weizen

This spicy, cloudy beer is a speciality brew from the Spinnaker brewpub.

Trapper Lager

A deep-gold lager with a grapey nose and a thin, sweet taste from the Niagara Falls Brewing Company.

True Bock

This is a red-amber German-style bock beer (6.5%) with a complex, warm, soft malty flavour and a pleasant hop nose. It is the most interesting beer from the Upper Canada micro-brewery in Toronto. The brewery also produces a light wheat beer (4.3%) with a tart, fruity aroma, a standard lager (5%) and an English-style IPA (4.8%).

Warthog Ale

The Big Rock Brewery in Calgary produces this all-malt, unpasteurized ale (4.5%).

Waterloo Dark

An unpasteurized dark draft ale (5.5%) from the Brick Brewing Company.

Wellington Imperial Stout

A rich, brown-black, top-fermented stout (5.5%) brewed using speciality malts by the Wellington County Brewery.

Legal restrictions

The legal restrictions on the Canadian brewing industry stem from the Prohibition of the 1920s and rigid state laws. Micro-breweries have had to struggle against these barriers. In spite of this, Canada has always been at the forefront of brewing developments.

THE BREWERS

Big Rock

Founded by Ed McNally in 1985, the Big Rock brewery is dedicated to the batch-brewing of premium beers following the German beer purity law. It uses a cold multi-microfiltration system rather than pasteurization. Among its best-known brews are Buzzard Breath Ale, a light to medium-bodied ale, McNally's Extra Pure Irish-style Ale, Warthog Ale, which is copper-coloured and nutty, Magpie Rye Ale and Grasshopper Wheat Ale.

Brasal Brasserie Allemande

This is Quebec's largest micro-brewery. It was founded in the city of LaSalle, Montreal in 1989, by the Jagerman family to brew German-style lagers according to the German beer purity law.

Brick

The Brick Brewing Company was established in 1984 in Waterloo, Ontario. Brick laid the foundations for the new brewery movement in eastern Canada. Its unpasteurized beers, many of them award-winners, are mainly European-style lagers developed by founder Jim Brickman.

Carling

One of Canada's leading international brewing names, Carling was founded in Ontario in 1840 by Sir Thomas Carling. Later in the 19th century Carling merged with the rival brewery O'Keefe, founded by Eugene O'Keefe in 1862, forming Carling O'Keefe. The company was taken over by the Australian giant, Foster's, in 1987, but that company overreached itself and Carling was merged with Molson in 1989. They then formed the largest brewing group in Canada, with vast overseas interests. The flagship brew, Carling Black Label, is one of the best-selling lagers in the UK. Because of the state laws in Canada that stipulate that beer must be brewed within the state boundaries, the company runs a large number of breweries, which produce local beers under various labels.

Granville Island Brewing

Businessman Mitch Taylor set up Canada's first micro-brewery in Vancouver's waterfront crafts area in 1984. It brews Bavarian-style all-malt lagers, notably Island Lager.

Labatt

One of Canada's two brewing giants, Labatt was taken over by the Belgian brewing company Interbrew in 1995. It also owns Latrobe (Rolling Rock) in the US.

The brewery was founded in London, Ontario, in 1847 by John Labatt. Despite the brewery being burned down twice in the 19th century, the company persevered, surviving Prohibition to take over many rival regional brewers after the Second World War.

Today it runs seven breweries across Canada, and at one time it marketed almost 50 brands. Its main lager is Labatt's Blue (5%). Local beer brands include Kokanee and Kootenay in the West and Schooner and Keith's IPA in the East, besides Blue Star in Newfoundland.

Labatt pioneered ice beer (introduced in 1993). During the brewing process the beer is chilled to 4°C (39.2°F) to form ice crystals, which are then removed leaving a stronger (5.6%) but rather bland brew behind.

McAuslan

After two years preparation this small brewery in Montreal began brewing in 1989. The famous British brewer Alan Pugsley helped to formulate the recipe for its first brew – St-Ambroise Pale Ale. The brewery has since gone from strength to strength, and in the seven years since launching, it has introduced four new beers, St-Ambroise Oatmeal Stout, Griffon Extra Pale Ale, Griffon Brown Ale and Frontenac, a golden, lightly hopped extra pale ale.

Molson

The oldest brewer in North America dates back to 1786 when English immigrant John Molson set up the Molson brewery in Montreal. Now based in Toronto, it is the rival giant to Labatt, with nine breweries and about 50 brands. Molson merged with Carling O'Keefe in 1989 to make it the brewmaster Conrad Oland was killed in an explosion in 1917 when two ships collided in Halifax harbour – the company moved to St John's, New Brunswick. In 1931 George Oland renamed his main beer Moosehead and this proved to be such a successful innovation that the company name was changed to Moosehead in 1947.

The beer is enormously popular in the US. It also brews local Alpine Lager (5%) for the Maritime Provinces, and a dry Moosehead Pale Ale.

Niagara Falls

This innovative micro-brewery on the Canadian side of the Niagara falls produced the first North American ice beer, the smoothly malty Niagara Eisbock (8%) in 1989. It was inspired by the local Eiswein.

Niagara was set up by the Criveller brothers, Mario and Bruno, after their Ethiopian brewery in Addis Ababa was nationalized. Since then the brewery has added an Apple Ale and a Kriek (both 6.5%) made with cherries.

the largest Canadian brewer, with 53% of the market. Best known for its Molson Canadian Lager (5%) and Molson Special Dry (5.5%), it introduced a new range of all-malt beers in 1993, which are marketed under the Signature brand name. These brews have found a ready acceptance in the home market.

Moosehead

Moosehead, Canada's oldest and largest independent brewery, was founded by Susannah Oland in Halifax, Nova Scotia, in 1867. The company used old family recipes from Britain and then won the contract to supply beer to the Canadian forces. It became known as the Army and Navy brewery.

After a troubled history –

Okanagan Spring Brewery

A small, specialist brewery established in Vernon, British Columbia. Their most prestigious brew is the Old English Porter, full-bodied and rummy (8.5%), but the company also produces a golden, malty Premium Lager, a Pale Ale and an Old Munich Wheat Beer that has a dry cider aroma and roasted-malt flavour.

Sleeman

The fourth-largest brewer in Canada (behind Molson, Labatt and Moosehead), Sleeman was first founded in Guelph, Ontario, in 1834, but closed in 1939. In 1985, John Sleeman decided to resurrect the family brewing business, opening a new plant in Guelph in 1988. Its beers are sold in distinctive embossed bottles.

Spinnakers

Canada's first brewpub had to overcome a succession of legal hurdles before opening in Victoria, British Columbia, in 1984. Permission to brew and sell beer on the same premises required a change to federal law and a local referendum. Spinnakers had to make the bar into a restaurant and build another storey to house the bar. Paul Hadfield brews mainly English-style ales and some lambic-style brews.

Unibroue

Quebec's largest micro-brewery was founded in 1991 in Chambly, Montreal, by Belgian beer enthusiast André Dion. It produces a range of characterful beers, such as Eau Bénite, that are even exported to France.

Upper Canada

Frank Heaps founded this Ontario micro-brewery in 1985 in a Toronto warehouse. It is now one of the largest new breweries in North America, and exports its beers to Europe. It uses water from the Caledon Hills 48 km (30 miles) away, trucking it in daily to ensure the purity of its beers.

Wellington County

The small Wellington County plant was set up in the Ontario brewing town of Guelph in 1985 to brew English-style ales, including some of the first cask-conditioned beers in North America to come from a commercial brewery, besides an Imperial Stout (5.5%) and Iron Duke strong ale (6.5%).

UNITED STATES OF AMERICA

The United States is the largest brewer in the world and its big-name lagers are famous the world over. Recently it has become the land of the born-again brewer, as micro-breweries spring up to meet the growing demand for variety.

ONCE THE US heaved with Europe's best beers – from English ales and Irish stouts to Czech Pilsners. Many of the leading brewers were German immigrants and brought with them that country's rich range of styles. Then came Prohibition. The Volstead Act of 1919 destroyed a thriving and colourful brewing industry by outlawing the manufacture and sale of alcohol. By the time Prohibition was repealed 14 years later in 1933, most of the original companies had vanished. The way was open for a few combines to dominate the trade – with a much-reduced range of beers.

When most Americans asked for a beer in the 1970s, they expected to receive a chilled pale lager, low in hops and light in flavour. Nothing much else was produced. This bland lager was increasingly sold in cans through supermarkets and stores. With little to distinguish between beers in taste, the emphasis was on marketing. The brand image became bigger than the beer, and the big brands gradually squeezed out those with less marketing muscle.

America is the home of light beer, a low-calorie lager launched by Miller in 1975. By 1995, three of the top four best-selling beers were light beers.

At the end of the 1970s, new small-scale breweries began to appear. Some, like New Amsterdam, used the spare capacity at established breweries to brew their beer. This contract brewing system helped struggling regional breweries to survive, while launching colourful new beers. By the 1990s new brewery business was booming. Some micro-breweries produced draft and bottled beers for local bars and stores, while others set up brewpubs to serve their beers direct to the customers. There are now about 1,000 new ventures with 92 micro-breweries and 138 brewpubs opening in 1995 alone. This speciality market is relatively small, but it is growing all the time.

Above: Anchor Steam Beer, brewed in San Francisco, was one of the pioneering brews of America's modern beer renaissance.

THE BEERS

Abita Amber

This light-amber, sweetish, malty European-style beer (3.8%) is brewed by Abita Brewing Co. Inc., Louisiana's first micro-brewery. Abita also brews a Golden Lager, a brilliant-amber, hoppy Fall Fest, an amber Bock Beer and Purple Haze Raspberry Wheat Ale.

Acme Pale Ale

This famous Californian brand was revived in 1996 by North Coast, the award-winning Californian brewery in Fort Bragg, which began as a brewpub in 1988. Other beers include Scrimshaw Pilsner (4.5%) and Blue Star Wheat (4.8%). It also brews a rich, intense Old Rasputin Russian Imperial Stout.

Adirondack Amber

This amber-coloured, Bavarian-style lager (5%), with a classic Pilsner flavour, is part of the Saranac range from FX Matt.

Alimony Ale

This famous nut-brown, orange-tinged ale ("the bitterest beer in America") is brewed by beer enthusiast Bill Owens. Alimony's bitter finish is complemented by a sweet-malt entry. Owens originally brewed the beer in honour of an employee who was going through a divorce. Bill Owens opened America's third brewpub, Buffalo Bill's, in Hayward, California, in 1983.

Amber

This unpasteurized, golden, smooth, malty lager (4.5%) is brewed by the Thomas Kemper Brewing Company.

American Originals

Anheuser-Busch sells its speciality beers, based on turn-of-the-century recipes, under the American Originals name. Beers include Muenchener Amber and Black and Tan Porter.

Anchor Steam Beer

A bright, copper-coloured cross between an ale and a lager (5%) with a well-rounded, malty taste and a crisp finish. Fritz Maytag's brewery revived this gold-rush-era beer, produced using a shallow-fermenter brewing method, perfected by forty-niners when no refrigeration was available.

Apricot Ale

This mild ale (3.5%) has a subtle apricot taste from start to finish. It is made with real apricots by Hart Brewing.

Auburn Ale

This ale is brewed by the family-run Leinenkugel lager brewery in Chippewa Falls, Wisconsin.

Augsburger

This is the brand name for speciality German-style beers from the US's fourth largest brewer, Stroh. Augsburger beers were originally developed by the Wisconsin brewer, Huber.

Bachelor Bitter

This copper-coloured, cold-conditioned, English-style ale (5%) with hints of grapefruit and evergreen is brewed by Deschute's brewery in Bend, Oregon. This Pacific Northwest brewery began life in 1988 as a brewpub but has expanded rapidly to meet demand.

Baderbräu

These German-style lagers from Chicago's Pavichevich brewery (set up in 1989 in Elmhurst, Illinois) comply with the German Reinheitsgebot beer purity law. The beers included a hoppy, bronze-coloured Pilsner (4.8%) and a light-brown, malty bock (5.4%).

Ballantine's Ale

Once one of the best-selling ales in America, Ballantine's was originally brewed in Albany, New York, in the 1830s before moving to Newark, New Jersey. In the 20th century, the beers have been brewed by a variety of companies, but are now produced by Pabst in Milwaukee. The best-known Ballantine beer is the copper-coloured hoppy IPA, but there is also a lighter Ballantine Ale.

Ballard Bitter

This strong, caramel-coloured bitter (5.9%), brewed by Redhook, is aggressively hopped, but offers some maltiness and a dry finish.

Banquet Beer
This pale-gold lager put Coors on the map when it was launched in the 1960s.

Bert Grant's
A range of "real ales" from the Yakima Brewing and Malting Co. brewpub in Yakima, WA. The brews include an English-style IPA (4.2%), a fruity, malty Scottish Ale (4.7%), a chocolatey Imperial Stout (6%), a hoppy Hefe Weizen (4.2%), a rich Perfect Porter (4%) and the flowery Amber Ale (5.5%).

Big Butt Doppelbock
A German-style doppelbock from Leinenkugel, Wisconsin.

Big Shoulders Porter
This chocolate-brown porter has a slightly roasted taste with a good hops balance. It is produced by the family-run Chicago brewery, the only commercial brewery left in the "windy city".

Bigfoot Barley Wine
This powerful, bottle-conditioned, russet barley wine (10.6%), brewed by Sierra Nevada, has a fruity, bittersweet taste.

Black and Tan
A dark-brown mix of a specially made stout and Saranac Adirondack Lager. The Black and Tan has a chocolate-malt nose, a medium body and roasted barley flavour with hints of fruity hops.

Black and Tan Porter
This dark-amber-coloured speciality beer by Anheuser-Busch has a toasted-malt aroma, a smooth, dry malt flavour and a dry malt finish.

Black Butte Porter
A dark-reddish-brown, cold-conditioned, unfiltered porter (5.5%), with a tan head and a rich, roasted-malt taste with a touch of chocolate, was a surprise success for Deschute's in Bend, Oregon.

Black Chocolate Stout
This potent stout (8.3%), produced annually by the Brooklyn brewery, is a classic imperial stout with a rich, creamy texture and a deep-malt, burnt-coffee taste.

Black Hawk Stout
This light-bodied stout, brewed by Mendocino – California's first micro-brewery – is fruitier than either Irish or English stout, with a flavour of chocolate, caramel and coffee.

Blackened Voodoo
This dark, ruby-brown beer (5%) with a light, malt aroma and slightly sour tang, brewed by Dixie, caused some outrage and was banned in Texas when launched in 1992, with allegations that it was the devil's brew.

Blackhook Porter
This dark-chestnut porter (4.9%) has a robust malt and coffee nose and a bitter, roasty finish with hints of coffee. It is brewed by the Redhook Ale brewery in Woodinville, WA.

Blue Fin Stout
This ebony stout (5%) has a roasted malt nose with hints of molasses. It has a medium body and a bitter coffee finish. It is brewed by Shipyard in Portland, Maine.

Blue Heron Pale Ale (Bridgeport)
This attractive, copper-coloured, malty American pale ale (5.8%) with a white head has a sweet malt and complex, bitter flavour and a dry finish. It is available in cask-conditioned form in the brewery bar of Oregon's oldest micro-brewery, Bridgeport.

Blue Heron Pale Ale (Mendocino)
This excellent, hazy-gold, English-style pale ale (5.9%) from Mendocino Brewing has a dry, hoppy character and a touch of fruit and sweet maltiness.

Blue Moon
In 1995, the brewing giant Coors launched this range of speciality beers with a Belgian White, Nut Brown and Honey Blonde Ale. They were developed in its Sandlot micro-brewery in Denver, Colorado. The beers are brewed under licence by F.X. Matt of Utica, New York.

Blue Star Wheat Beer
A good version of American wheat beer (4.8%) brewed by North Coast. It is a pale, clean, dry brew with a soft, refreshing flavour.

Bohemian Dunkel
This rich, well-rounded, unpasteurized, dark lager (5.6%) is brewed by Kemper, using chocolate-malt and Styrian hops.

Boulder Amber Ale
A robust, bright-amber ale (4.5%) with a yeasty, malty nose and a well-balanced malt and hop taste. It is brewed by Rockies Brewing in Boulder, Colorado.

Brooklyn Lager
Dubbed the pre-Prohibition beer, the dry-hopped Brooklyn Lager (4.5%) was launched in 1987 in New York. Originally all the beer was contract-brewed upstate by F.X. Matt of Utica, but in 1996 the company opened its own brewery in Brooklyn, reviving the area's brewing traditions. Once Brooklyn was one of the country's top beer towns with breweries like Piels, Shaefer and Rheingold. It also brews a

strong Brooklyn Brown Ale (5.5%), a dry Brooklyn IPA (7.4%) and an annual Black Chocolate Stout (8.3%).

Budweiser

The world's leading beer brand from Anheuser-Busch of St Louis was first launched in 1876 and named after the famous brewing town in the Czech Republic. Budweiser is the epitome of a light American lager, using rice in the mash to give a crisp, clean taste that belies its alcohol content of 4.7%. Despite using eight hop varieties, it is very lightly hopped. Anheuser-Busch also takes pride in maturing the "King of Beers" in tanks containing beechwood chips to smooth out the flavour. In 1995, about one in four beers sold in America was a Budweiser.

Cascade Golden Ale

Another unfiltered, cold-conditioned, English-style ale (4.1%) from Deschute's.

Celebration Ale

This is one of the best of the American IPAs. It is a copper-coloured ale (5.1%), brewed by Sierra Nevada Brewing. It has a pungent,

floral nose with hints of caramel malt and a roasted malt and earthy hops flavour and a long, full-bodied finish. This is a real gem.

Celis White

This is a Belgian-style wheat beer (5%), flavoured with coriander and orange peel, from the Celis brewery in Austin, Texas.

Cerveza Rosanna Red Chili Ale

This odd, slow-burning speciality beer, flavoured with red chillies, is occasionally produced by the Pike Place brewery of Seattle. It goes well with Mexican food.

Chesterfield Ale

A golden, bottom-fermented ale with a flowery hop aroma, from Yuengling, America's oldest brewery.

Christian Moerlein

A malty lager brewed by Hudepohl-Schoenling of Cincinatti, named after an early brewer in the city. A Reinheitsgebot brew with plenty of body and a full, smooth finish.

Cold Spring Export Lager

This mild, crisp, gold lager, brewed by Cold Spring Brewing Company in Cold Spring, Minnesota, has a crisp, malty flavour and a dry, hoppy finish.

Coors

A range of lagers from this American giant. There is a full-bodied Original, a refreshing clean-flavoured Extra Gold, a Light, and a variety of Winterfest beers.

Crazy Ed's Cave Creek Chili Beer

This golden, hot-pepper specialty beer has a nose, taste and finish dominated by jalapeño peppers. It is brewed by Evansville Brewing Company in Evansville, Indiana, for the Black Mountain brewery of Cave Creek, Arizona.

Cream City Pale Ale

This top-fermented amber ale (4.2%) has a complex, hoppy nose with woody and citrus hints, a spicy hop taste and a long, dry hop finish. Brewed by the Lakefront micro-brewery.

Dortmunder Gold

This is a malty, dry, full-bodied, strong, export-style lager (5.4%) in the Dortmunder style. It is brewed by Great Lakes.

Dundee's Honey Brown Lager

A tasty brown lager from Genesee in New York.

East Side Dark

A deep-chestnut bock (6.5%) with a brown head, from Lakefront Brewery in Milwaukee, Wisconsin. This medium-bodied beer is sweet, with a deeply roasted malt flavour and a velvety smooth finish.

Eliot Ness

This amber-red, Vienna-style lager (5.4%) with a roasted-malt, buttery, fruity taste, is named after the man who jailed the notorious 1920s Chicago bootlegger Al Capone, and is brewed by Great Lakes.

Elk Mountain Amber Ale

Made with 100% barley malt, whole cone hops and English sale yeast, this amber ale (4.1%) has a malt and hops nose, a hoppy flavour with touches of sweet malt, and a dry hop and malt aftertaste. Brewed by Anheuser-Busch.

Espresso Stout

In keeping with its name, this deep-brown stout with a dark-brown, creamy head boasts a long coffee-like aftertaste. It has a good thick body, a rich chocolate and charcoal nose and a powerful roasted-malt flavour. It is made by Hart Brewing Company in Kalama, Washington, the makers of the Pyramid line of brews.

Esquire Extra Dry

A deep-gold, rich, malt-flavoured lager from the small regional Jones Brewing in Smithton, Pennsylvania.

Esquire Premium Pale Ale

This straw-coloured pale ale from Jones Brewing in Smithton, Pennsylvania, is hoppy from nose to finish.

Eye of the Hawk

A well-balanced, strong, amber ale (7.6%), brewed by Mendocino. It has a fruity nose, followed by a malty taste with assertive hopping.

Fall Fest

This sweetish, malty, European-style beer (4.9%) is brewed by Abita in Louisiana.

Full Sail Nut Brown Ale

This English-style brown ale (5.4%) has an auburn colour, a nutty nose and a rich, roasted-malt flavour with hints of fruit and smoke. It is brewed by Full Sail in Hood River, Oregon.

Frontier

A cloudy, dark-amber American pale ale (4.2%) with a spicy, hoppy nose and a big, complex, highly carbonated flavour with a dry finish. An award-winning beer from Alaskan Brewing in Juneau, Alaska.

Genny Bock

An occasional deep-amber, malty bock, brewed by Genesee in Rochester, New York.

George Killian's Red Ale

This pale, copper-red ale from Coors (3.9%) has a light body, a toasted-malt nose and a fresh hop and malt flavour.

Gerst Amber

This malty beer is brewed by Evansville, a small former Heileman brewery in Indiana, which was bought out by its employees.

Grant's Scottish Ale

This reddish-amber American ESB (5%) with an off-white head, a hoppy, fruity aroma, a roasted-malt entry and an earthy hop finish, is brewed by Bert Grant of Grant's Yakima Brewing in Yakima, WA.

Great Northern Porter

A dark, reddish-brown porter (5.4%), brewed by Summit Brewing in Minneapolis, MN, with a rich, dark aroma and a big, fruity, roasted-malt and chocolate flavour, and hints of liquorice.

Growlin Gator Lager

A yellow-gold, light, refreshing lager (3.7%), brewed with pale malt and Yakima and Saaz hops by the August Schell Brewing Company.

Hampshire Special Ale

A strong, intensely malty winter ale (7%) with an earthy nose and a bitter-sweet finish, from Geary's Brewing in Portland, Maine.

Heartland Weiss

This hazy-gold, refreshing white wheat beer with a spicy, malt flavour is produced by the Chicago brewery.

Hefeweizen

This pale-yellow, hazy, unfiltered, unpasteurized, wheat beer (5%) is brewed by Thomas Kemper. It has a crisp, refreshing flavour.

Heimertingen Maibock

This powerfully pale German-style spring beer (7.5%) is brewed by Summit.

Helenbock 1992 Oktoberfest

This amber-coloured, German-style beer (4.2%) is made with Hallertau and Saaz hops and Munich malts. It has good body with a light head, a hearty hop aroma, a powerful malty flavour with a hop bite and a dry finish. It is contract-brewed by August Schell Brewing in New Ulm, MN, for Friends B.C. in Helen, Georgia.

AMERICAN BEERS OVERSEAS

The major American brewers have been relatively slow in going international, mainly due to the attraction of the massive domestic market on their doorstep. This insular attitude is in sharp contrast to the soft drinks industry in which American brands like Coca-Cola dominate the world. The world's largest brewer, Anheuser-Busch of St Louis, only established Anheuser-Busch International in 1981. Its top beer, Budweiser, is now brewed in eight overseas countries and sold in 70 others. Second-placed Miller of Milwaukee only seriously developed overseas interests in the early 1990s, spurred by the realization that, while the beer market has peaked in the United States, it is still growing abroad. The company is now making a major push to double its foreign business by the year 2000.

Hell Doppel Bock

This rich and warming Bavarian-style beer (7.2%) comes from Heckler, a Californian venture set up in Tahoe City in 1993 by Keith Hilken after he had trained at a number of German breweries. Heckler produces only Bavarian-style lagers with German ingredients, brewed according to the Reinheitsgebot beer purity law. Hell Doppel Bock, like all Heckler beers, is currently contract-brewed by the Schell Brewery in New Ulm, Minnesota.

Hell Lager

This Bavarian-style lager (4.9%) comes from Heckler of Tahoe City. Made with German ingredients, it complies with the Reinheitsgebot beer purity law.

Helles Gold

This German-style lager (4.5%) is one of a range of German-style beers brewed by Pennsylvania, a pioneer of craft brewing on the East Coast. Set up in 1988 by Thomas Pastorius in the former Eberhardt and Ober brewery in the Deutschtown area of Pittsburgh, the brewery uses imported German plant.

Henry Weinhard's Private Reserve

This medium-gold beer (3.75%) is brewed by the G. Heileman Brewing Company, using Cascade hops. It has a medium body, an inviting hop nose and a well-balanced malt and hop flavour with a light hop finish. Each bottling is numerically identified on the neck of the bottle.

Hickory Switch Smoked Amber Ale

This ale (4.4%) is brewed using cold-smoked malt by Otter Creek in Middlebury, Vermont. It has a beautiful chestnut colour, a delicate smoky aroma and smoked-malt taste.

Honey Double Mai Bock

A golden, refreshing, strong German-style bock (7%) with a tall white head and a blend of sweet malt and tangy hops. It is traditionally brewed to be served in May, hence the name, but Stoudt's Brewing makes it available year-round.

Honeyweizen

Brewed with local honey in Washington State, this unpasteurized beer (5%) is produced by Kemper.

Hudy

This range of beers is produced by the Hudepohl-Schoenling brewery, formed in 1986 by the merger of Cincinnati's last two breweries in a city once famous for its brewers.

Iron City Lager

This lager from the Pittsburgh Brewing Company in Pennsylvania attracts strong local loyalty, despite the fact that it is a very bland American-style lager, in the same vein as Budweiser.

Jax Lager

This golden lager is produced by the Pearl brewery, the Texas rival to Lone Star, based in San Antonio.

Jax Pilsner

This light, refreshing yellow-gold Pilsner is a good thirst-quenching hot-weather drink. It has a pleasant malt nose, a mild but slightly sweet malt and hop flavour and a lot of carbonation. It is brewed by Pearl in San Antonio, Texas – now part of the S & P Company Brewing Group.

Jazz Amber Light

This amber-coloured, light beer (3.2%) is brewed in New Orleans by Dixie.

Jubelale

A mahogany, strong ale (6%) with a tan head, a fruity malt aroma and a roasted-malt, fruit and hops flavour. It is brewed by Deschute's, using an unfiltered, cold-conditioned technique.

Kilsch Lager

A striking German-style Pilsner (6.5%) with a cloudy-gold-coloured body, and a white head. It has a hoppy aroma and a sweet, malt entry followed by a long crisp finish. It is brewed by Lakefront brewery,

Latrobe

See Rolling Rock.

Legacy Lager

A bottom-fermented, German-style Pilsner (4.8%) with a deep-gold body, a tall white head, and a malty taste with a hint of butterscotch. It is brewed by Chicago Brewing, the only commercial brewery apart from Miller that is left in the "Windy City".

Legacy Red Ale

A bright, copper-coloured Irish-style red ale (4.9%) from the Chicago Brewing Company. It has a roasted-malt nose, a full-bodied malty entry and a tangy bitter finish.

Leinenkugel

This light, flowery premium beer is popular in Wisconsin where it is brewed by the family-run Leinenkugel Brewery in Chippewa Falls.

Liberty Ale

A strong, hazy bronze American IPA (6%) with a big malty hop nose, a powerful malt flavour with spicy hops, and a grapefruity finish. This is the first American beer to be dry-hopped in modern times. It is one of the best IPAs available.

Little Kings Cream Ale

This cream ale (5.5%) is brewed by Hudenpohl-Schoenling of Cincinnati.

Lone Star

This gold, crisp, light malt lager (3.5%) from the famous Texas brewery (part of Heileman) is regarded as the state's national beer.

Mactarnahan's Scottish Ale

This bright-copper-coloured, malty American pale ale (4.8%) has a fruity flavour with hints of caramel. Brewed by Portland Brewing.

Meister Bräu

A low-budget beer brewed by Miller. It used to sell itself by saying it tasted like Bud, but cost less.

Michelob

Made with a high percentage of two-row barley malt and imported hops, this gold lager has a balanced hop and dry malt flavour, and a medium long finish with a slight hop character. It is named after a town in Czechoslovakia.

Milwaukee's Best

Another cut-rate beer brewed by Miller. Just like Meister Bräu but with different packaging.

Mirror Pond Pale Ale

A deep-gold, unfiltered, cold-conditioned American-style pale ale (5.3%) with a creamy head and a flowery flavour with earthy hints, from Deschute's.

Moondog Ale

A pale-copper-coloured English-bitter-style ale (5%) with a dry, well-hopped flavour. Brewed by the Great Lakes Brewing Company in Cleveland, Ohio.

Moose Brown Ale

Brewed by Shipyard in Portland, Maine, and available on tap at the Great Lost Bear in Portland, this brown ale has a faint hop and malt nose, and a strong malt flavour balanced with a dry hop aftertaste.

Muenchener Amber

This ale, based on a turn-of-the-century recipe, is one of Anheuser-Busch's speciality American Originals beers.

Mystic Seaport Pale

This English-style pale ale (4.8%) from the Shipyard brewery in Portland, Maine, is bright-amber with a beige head. It has a perfumey, earthy nose, a fruity entry and a dry finish.

Northwoods Lager

This Germanic lager is brewed by the family-run Leinenkugel lager brewery in Wisconsin.

Obsidian Stout

This dark-brown, ruby-tinted, potent stout (6.9%) is brewed by Deschute's using an unfiltered, cold-conditioning method. It has a fresh, full-bodied malty flavour with a dry, roasty finish.

Oktoberfest

This strong, Bavarian-style lager (6%) comes from Heckler of Tahoe City. It is brewed with German ingredients and complies with the beer purity law.

Old Bawdy Barley Wine

A golden, oak-aged barley wine (9.9%) brewed by Pike Place brewery using peated distillers malt, which gives a smoky edge to the taste.

Old Crustacean

A cloudy, copper-coloured, strong, hoppy beer (10.2%) with a creamy head. It has a rich malt and apricot nose, a sweet caramel and roasted-malt entry, followed by fruit and scorched malt. It is one of the most complex and interesting beers available and is brewed by the Rogue micro-brewery, founded in Newport, Oregon, in 1988.

Old Foghorn

A deep-copper barley-wine-style ale (8.7%) with a creamy tan head, a hoppy, malty nose and a taste of fruit, hops and roasted malt. It is Anchor's strongest beer.

Old Knucklehead

A dark-copper ale with a sweet, roasted-malt nose, a malty, bitter-sweet taste and a long warm finish. This ale is produced by the Oregon micro-brewery Bridgeport, and is served in cask-conditioned form in the brewery bar.

Old Milwaukee

A range of lagers from the Stroh Brewery, Detroit. It includes a standard pale-gold Old Milwaukee Beer with a good malt flavour (3.6%), a pale, yellow-gold, clean-tasting Premium Light Beer, the highly carbonated, golden Genuine Draft and a deep-gold, strong Ice Beer.

Old No. 38 Stout

This award-winning stout (5.6%), named after a steam engine, is brewed by North Coast. It is very dark black, with a ruby hue and a dense brown head. The nose is of roasted malt and barley, and it has a rich barley flavour with a bitter, burnt, malt flavour.

Old Rasputin Russian Imperial Stout

A dark, reddish-brown, rich, intense stout (7.8%) with a hoppy roasted malt nose, a roasty flavour and a bitter finish. It is brewed by North Coast.

Old Thumper

This is an American version of the English ale (5.7%), brewed in Portland, Maine, by Shipyard.

Oregon Honey Beer

A pale-gold honey beer (4%) with a gentle, earthy aroma of hops and a malty flavour, from the Portland brewery.

Pearl Lager

This golden lager is produced by the Pearl brewery, the Texas rival to Lone Star, based in San Antonio.

Pennsylvania Dark

This German-style, deep-ruby-brown lager (5%) has a delicious roasted taste with hoppy notes.

Pennsylvania Oktoberfest

A German-style lager (6%) brewed by Pennsylvania.

Pennsylvania Pilsner

This clear-gold, sweet, malty, lightly-hopped German-style lager (5%) is one of a range of German-style beers brewed by Pennsylvania in the Deutschtown area of Pittsburgh, using imported German plant.

Perfect Porter

This rich, dark Scottish-style porter (4%) is brewed by Bert Grant of Yakima.

Pete's Wicked Winter Brew

A delicious, red-amber ale (4.2%) with hints of nutmeg and raspberry in its flavour. It is one of the wide range of speciality brews from Pete's Brewing Company.

Pike Pale Ale

The bold Pale Ale (4.5%) is the best-known brew from the Seattle Pike brewery founded by famous "Marchand du Vin" beer importer Charles Finkel in 1989. Pike also brews a 5X Stout, an IPA and a lusty, oak-aged Old Bawdy Barley Wine. In 1996, Pike opened a new brewery with a pub attached.

Pike XXX

A dense, black stout (6.2%) with a creamy dark-brown head and a malt and coffee nose. The flavour starts off sweet and is then followed by a strong coffee flavour and a bitter, burnt, hoppy finish. This excellent stout has a rich, creamy body and texture.

Pintail

This ale is produced by the Oregon micro-brewery in Bridgeport, and is available in cask-conditioned form in the brewery bar.

Point Special

This better-than-average American lager is brewed at the Wisconsin Point brewery founded in 1857 at Stevens Point.

Portland Ale

This malty ale (5%) was the first beer to be produced by the Portland brewery when it opened in Oregon in 1986. The brewery has two pubs in Portland.

Pottsville Porter

This bottom-fermented, dark porter is produced by America's oldest brewery, Yuengling.

Premium Verum

This malty lager is the most notable beer brewed by the Kentucky brewery, Oldenburg. The Fort Mitchell brewery is famed for its occasional weekend beer camps, when visitors taste the brews, tour the brewery and visit the neighbouring American Museum of Brewing History.

Pullman Pale Ale

This pale ale (5.9%) comes from the Californian Riverside brewery set up in Riverside in 1993.

Pumpkin Ale

This beer is made using huge, home-grown pumpkins and is spiced with cinnamon, nutmeg and cloves. It is another delicious and interesting beer from Bill Owens.

Raincross Cream Ale

This mellow pale ale (5.9%) is produced by the Californian Riverside brewery, which was set up in Riverside in 1993.

Rainier Ale

The fruity Rainier Ale was a much sought-after beer in the years before the micro-brewery revolution hit the north-west.

The ale was known as "The Green Death" owing to the colour of its label and high alcohol strength. It is produced by the Rainier brewery.

Red Bull

A strong, golden, malt-liquor brand (7.1%) produced by Stroh in Detroit for the Canadian market.

Red Hook ESB
This deep-amber, strong extra-special bitter (5.4%) comes from the ground-breaking Red Hook brewery founded in 1981 by Paul Shipman and Gordon Bowker in the Ballard area of Seattle.

Red Hook Rye
This golden, unfiltered beer (5%) with a dry grainy flavour is brewed by Red Hook. Red Hook has embarked on a series of expansions and is rapidly becoming a national brewer.

Red Sky Ale
This amber-coloured, complex, strong ale (5.6%) is produced by St Stan's brewery, whose other beers tend to be German-style alts.

Red Tail Ale
This hazy, copper-coloured, strong English-style ale (6.5%) is brewed by Mendocino.

Riverwest Stein Beer
A striking, bright-copper Märzenbier (6.5%) with a delicate beige head, a buttery caramel nose and a caramel flavour with hints of scorched smoke.

Roggen Rye
This golden, unfiltered, unpasteurized rye beer (5%) is brewed by Thomas Kemper, using flaked grain and pale barley malt.

Rogue-n-Berry
Marionberries are used to flavour this beer from the Rogue micro-brewery.

Rolling Rock
This lager brand revived the fortunes of the Latrobe brewery of Pennsylvania, founded in 1893. The light lager stands out from the crowd due to the fired-on label on its green bottles.

Ruedrich's Red Seal Ale
This rich, amber-coloured, award-winning beer, brewed by North Coast Brewing Company, is the epitome of a good American ale. It is a pleasant combination of hoppy dryness and malty flavours with fruity notes.

Samuel Adams Boston Lager
This bright-amber Pilsner has a fresh, hoppy nose, a sweet-malt entry, a caramel flavour and a dry, malty finish. It is brewed by Boston Beer Company,

Samuel Adams Boston Stock Ale
This bright-amber ale (5%) has a complex, earthy nose and a hoppy, off-dry palate. It is brewed by Boston Beer Company.

Schaefer Beer
A light-gold lager, produced by the Schaefer Brewing company in Detroit and promoted as the US's oldest lager beer.

Schlitz
A range of beers from the Stroh brewing company. Schlitz beer is the standard pale-gold lager; there is also a Light Beer, a Malt Liquor, a Draught and an Ice Beer.

Schmaltz's Alt
This strong, dark alt (6%) is brewed by the family-owned Schell brewery in New Ulm, Minnesota.

Scrimshaw Pilsner
Brewed by North Coast, this well-balanced lager (4.4%) has a sweet, malty entry and a crisp finish.

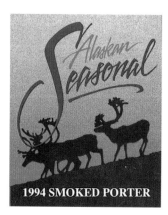

Seasonal Smoked Porter
The distinctive, intense taste of Alaskan's award-winning annual porter (6.4%) comes from using malt kilned over alder wood in the local fish smokehouse.

Shakespeare's Stout
An ebony-coloured export stout (6.1%) with a creamy, dark-brown head. Shakespeare has a complex hoppy, chocolatey, smoky, malt nose and a bittersweet, fruity flavour with a dry, burnt, bitter finish.

Shea's Irish Amber
This traditional East-Coast ale is brewed by Genesee in Rochester, New York.

Shiner Bock
This dark, amber bock (4.4%) is brewed by a small local brewery in Shiner, Texas, called Spoetzl, founded in 1909.

Shipyard Export
This export beer (5.1%) comes from Portland's Shipyard brewery.

Signature
See Stroh's.

Snow Goose
This complex old ale (6.4%) is brewed by the Wild Goose micro-brewery in Maryland. It has a beautiful dark-copper, orangey colour, a pungent, hoppy nose and a caramelized malt flavour, followed by a long, bitter, malty finish.

Stegmaier
Stegmaier lager and porter are the best-known brews from the Lion brewery in Wilkes-Barre, Pennsylvania.

Stoney's Lager
This light lager is produced by the small regional Jones Brewing in Smithton, Pennsylvania.

Stoudt's Festbier

A copper-coloured Märzenbier (5.1%) from the Stoudt brewery in Adamstown, Pennsylvania, which complies with the German Reinheitsgebot beer purity law. Festbier has a beautiful head, a roasted malt nose and a caramel finish.

Stroh's

This lager is one of the ranges of beers from the Stroh brewing company. It includes a copper-amber bock, a Light Beer (3.1%), a standard American Beer and Signature lager.

Tabernash

This small Denver micro-brewery produces a range of four beers. The golden Weiss is a top-fermenting German-style wheat beer with a spicy, fruity flavour. It is bottle-conditioned. Golden is a light-gold, hoppy Pilsner.

Munich is a deep-brown, rich, malty, Bavarian-style dunkel, brewed using six different malts in the mash. Amber claims to be a traditional ale brewed according to 19th-century methods to produce a deep-amber ale with a light, crisp lager finish.

Triple Bock

This heavyweight beer (17.5%) is brewed at the Bronco Winery in Ceres, California, using a champagne yeast, primed with maple syrup and matured for three months in former Tennessee whisky casks. It is the most powerful of the contract beers from the Boston Beer Company.

Turbo Dog

This is Abita's deep, ruby-amber, strong, darkish, dry-hopped beer (4.9%) with a roasted-malt flavour and long, dry aftertaste.

Twelve Horse Ale

This bright-gold, refreshing lager (3.8%) with a dry hops finish, is brewed by Genesee in Rochester, New York.

Victoria Avenue Amber Ale

A dark, scarlet-amber ale (5.8%) with a tan-coloured head, from Riverside. It has a malty nose with hints of fruit, a sweet malt and caramel palate and a slightly bitter, malty finish.

Wassail Winter Ale

Brewed by Full Sail, this strong winter warmer (6.5%) is a hazy, dark-amber ale with a fruity nose and a complex malt flavour with a bitter, tangy finish.

Weizen Berry

This rosy-gold, unfiltered, unpasteurized fruit and wheat beer (5%) has a raspberry nose and a malty raspberry flavour. It is brewed by the Thomas Kemper Brewing company in Poulsbo, Washington.

Wheat Berry Brew

This malty beer (4.5%) is made from local Oregon marionberries. It is brewed by Portland.

7th Street Stout

This potent, ruby-black, rich stout (6%) is brewed by Riverside Brewing in Riverside, California. It has a rich, malty aroma and a burnt, bitter, malt, full-bodied flavour.

Above: Customers outside the Second Class Saloon in Alaska, 1899, which was owned by Wyatt Earp during the Gold Rush.

THE BREWERS

Abita
Set up in 1986 at Abita Springs near New Orleans, Louisiana's first new brewery produces sweetish, malty European-style beers.

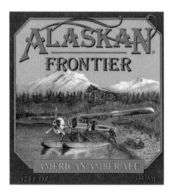

Alaskan
This highly regarded brewery was established in the Alaskan capital of Juneau in 1986. Its rich beers have won many awards.

Anchor
See panel right.

Anderson Valley
The Californian brewery at the Buckhorn Saloon in Boonville has been famous for its richly flavoured beers since 1987.

Anheuser-Busch
The undisputed giant of the American brewing industry has 12 breweries and 44% of the US beer market. In 1995 it sold 87.5 million barrels, nearly double that of its nearest rival, Miller. Its leading brand Budweiser is the biggest-selling beer in the world, brewed in eight overseas countries and exported to more than 70.

Anheuser-Busch is a family company. The story started in 1860 when German immigrant Eberhard Anheuser (1805-80) bought a failed brewery in St Louis, Missouri. His energetic son-in-law Adolphus Busch (1839–1913) turned it into a national success. Busch used the new rail system to introduce the first fleet of refrigerated wagons, he pioneered the use of pasteurization and in 1876 launched the first national beer brand, Budweiser. Twenty years later he added a premium brew, Michelob. Sales reached a million barrels by 1901.

During Prohibition the company brewed the non-alcoholic Bevo. After the Second World War, sales soared, with eight regional breweries built to meet demand.

The original brewery in St Louis is now a tourist attraction and houses the company's Clydesdale horses.

Besides Budweiser and Michelob, the company brews about 30 beers. In response to the micro-brewery movement Anheuser-Busch has introduced its own speciality beers.

Boston Beer Company
The Boston Beer Company has its beers produced to order by other breweries in Pennsylvania, New York and Oregon. Formed in 1985, ten years later the company was the ninth-largest US brewer, with sales of a million barrels per year. The brews are named after Samuel Adams, one of the organizers of the Boston Tea Party of 1773. Jim Koch revived his ancestors' brewing recipes with his Boston Lager and now produces a wide range of beers. The Boston Beer Company also has its own small brewery.

Catamount
A small brewery started in White River Junction, Vermont, in 1985 by Steve Mason, who had trained in England. He named his new enterprise after the cougar or mountain cat – catamount.

Celis
See panel opposite.

ANCHOR

Anchor is the guiding light of the new brewery revolution in North America. When Fritz Maytag, the heir to a washing-machine empire, bought a bankrupt brewery in San Francisco in 1965, his main aim was to preserve a piece of Californian history. The Anchor brewery, founded in 1896, used a unique American method of brewing perfected in the California Gold Rush days when no refrigeration was available. Very shallow fermenters cooled the brew, producing a cross between a lager and an ale. Maytag maintained this tradition and his Anchor Steam Beer (5%) gained a national reputation. It helped inspire the new brewery movement by showing that quality beers of character had a market in America. Maytag has since added a range of other brews, including Liberty Ale (6.1%), Anchor Porter (6.3%) and Old Foghorn (8.7%).

In 1989, Maytag extended his exploration into beers from the past by making a brew using an ancient Sumerian recipe.

CELIS

The Celis story is one of the most remarkable in the world of beer. Pierre Celis started not one but two pioneering breweries – each on a different continent.

Born in Belgium, Celis grew up next to a brewery. When the local "white" wheat-beer style disappeared, he decided to revive it, setting up the De Kluis (the Cloister) brewery in Hoegaarden in 1966. Its refreshing, spicy Hoegaarden beer proved so popular that, after expanding the brewery a number of times, he sold up to Belgium's largest brewer Interbrew in 1989. He had revived a beer style that was widely copied in his home country.

Hoegaarden had also been successful as an export to the United States. Celis decided to cross the Atlantic, and in 1992, he opened the Celis Brewery in Austin, Texas, to brew his Belgian-style wheat beer now called Celis White. It too proved a huge success and was soon copied by others.

History also repeated itself in another way. In 1995, Celis sold a controlling interest to American brewing giant Miller. In 1996 the company doubled capacity. The Celis brewery also brews other Belgian-style beers, including Celis Raspberry (5%), a richer Grand Cru (8.7%), a Pilsner Celis Golden (5%) and a Pale Bock (5%).

Coors

Coors boasts the biggest single brewery in the world, filling the town of Golden, near Denver, Colorado. The plant is capable of brewing 20 million barrels a year. The US's third-largest brewing company has just one other brewery at Memphis, Tennessee.

A family firm founded by Adolph Coors in 1873, Coors was an unremarkable regional brewery until its Banquet Beer developed a cult following in the 1960s, spurred on by its fresh Rocky Mountain water image. Now Coors Light is its flagship brand. A slightly more malty Extra Gold is brewed under licence by Scottish Courage in England. Coors is noted for its refusal to pasteurize its beers, only chilling and micro-filtering them. Its most distinctive beer is its annual Winterfest. Coors also pioneered the first red ale, George Killian's, which was introduced back in 1978. The brewery launched a range of speciality beers under the Blue Moon name in 1995.

Dixie

This legendary New Orleans brewery was founded in 1907. It still ages its "slow-brewed" beers in cypress wood vessels. Its main beers are the malty Dixie (4.5%) and Jazz Amber Light. It also brews the notorious dark beer, Blackened Voodoo.

Dock Street

An innovative restaurant brewery in Philadelphia, which produces a wide range of beers such as a ginger wheat and a juniper rye. Its bottled beers – notably Dock Street Amber (5.3%), Dock Street Bohemian Pilsner (5.3%) and Dock Street Illuminator (7.5%) – are contract-brewed by F.X. Matt of Utica, New York, for the Dock Street restaurant in Philadelphia.

Frankenmuth

The Michigan town of Frankenmuth was founded in 1845 by Bavarian immigrants from Franconia, in Germany, the world's most brewery-packed region. Inevitably, the town built its own brewery, dating back to 1862. In 1987, the Frankenmuth brewery was rebuilt. Its German-style beers include Frankenmuth Dark (5.2%), Pilsner (5.2%), Old Detroit Amber (5.9%) and Bock (6.4%).

Full Sail

Founded in 1987 at the windsurfing centre of Hood River, Oregon, this brewery's fruity ales have grown in popularity on the West Coast. Bottled beers include Golden (4.4%), Amber (5.9%) and Nut Brown, as well as a range of seasonal beers.

Geary's

New England's first micro-brewery opened in Portland, Maine, in 1986. Its founder David Geary had worked in various Scottish and English breweries and the influence is obvious in the beers.

The flagship beer is Geary's Pale Ale (4.5%), but the brewery also produces a dark Geary's London Porter (4.2%), Geary's American Ale (4.8%) and a warming winter Hampshire Special.

Genesee

The largest independent regional brewery in the US was founded in Rochester, New York, in 1878. It still follows the north-eastern tradition of ale brewing, notably with the soft, sweetish Twelve Horse Ale, Cream Ale and Shea's Irish Amber. It also produces an occasional Genny Bock and other speciality beers such as Dundee's Honey Brown Lager.

Great Lakes

This extensive range of widely acclaimed beers has poured from Cleveland's first micro-brewery, which was set up in an old saloon in Ohio in 1988. The range of beers includes Moon Dog Ale, Dortmunder Gold, a Vienna-style lager Eliot Ness, a Porter (5.9%) and a Great Lakes' IPA (6.9%).

Harpoon

The Mass Bay brewery has been brewing Harpoon ales in Boston since 1987, notably a Harpoon Ale, Light, Pilsner, IPA and Stout. Its bottled beers are contract brewed by F.X. Matt of Utica, New York.

Heileman

The fifth-largest brewing company in the US is based in La Crosse, Wisconsin, where it is known for its Heileman Old Style and Special Export lagers. This brewpub in Davis, California, has been operating close to the university brewing school since 1990. It is known for its extensive range of German-style lagers, including a Hübsch Hefe-Weizen (5%), Märzen (5.5%) and Doppelbock (7.5%).

Matt

F.X. Matt has been brewing in Utica in upstate New York since 1888, originally as the West End brewery. Now it mainly contract-brews speciality beers for other companies. The first was New Amsterdam in 1982. In 1985, the firm also introduced its own successful Saranac range of beers including Adirondack Amber, Pale Ale, Golden (5.2%) and Black and Tan.

Mendocino

Mendocino is one of the standard-bearers of the new brewery revolution in the United States. In 1983 it was California's first brewpub, opened in an old saloon. The brewery in Mendocino County now brews a wide range of excellent English-style ales.

Miller

The second-largest brewer in the United States, Miller has more than a fifth of the beer market and runs the five main brewing plants. Founded in 1855 when German immigrant Frederick Miller bought a small brewery in Milwaukee, the company was taken over by tobacco giant Philip Morris in 1970. Miller Lite, which was launched in 1975, created a huge new market for low-calorie beers. In little more than ten years, production soared from around five million barrels to more than 40 million per year.

Its other high-profile brand is bottled Genuine Draft, launched in 1986 using a special cold-filtered process, which means that the beer does not need to be pasteurized. The oldest brand Miller High Life, is now part of Miller's popularly priced

range, which also includes Miller Meister Bräu and Milwaukee's Best. In addition, Miller brews a non-alcoholic beer called Sharp's and a Magnum Malt Liquor.

The Miller company has responded to competition from the fast-growing speciality beer market in a number of ways. In 1990 it introduced a range of all-barley beers under the Miller Reserve brand name, including an Amber Ale. It also markets various brands under the company's original name, Plank Road Brewery. In addition, Miller has also directly taken over smaller breweries. In 1988, for example, it bought the old Leinenkugel brewery of Wisconsin, which still sells its lager under the Leinenkugel name. In 1995 Miller bought a majority interest in the successful Celis Brewery of Texas and Shipyard of Maine.

New Amsterdam

The original contract brewer, New Amsterdam was founded in New York in 1982 by Matthew Reich. He contracted established brewer F.X. Matt of Utica to brew his New Amsterdam beers, selling them as if from a micro. New Amsterdam's best-known beers are its Ale and Amber.

New Glarus

This Wisconsin village brewery was set up in 1993 by a former Budweiser brewer who trained in Germany. In 1996 it revived a famous old Californian brand – Acme Pale Ale. It specializes in European lagers, notably Edel-Pils, Wisconsin Bock and Weiss.

Pabst

The US's sixth largest brewery, Pabst, is best-known for Pabst Blue Ribbon lager, "the working man's beer". Founded in Milwaukee in 1844 as Best Brewing, Frederick Pabst married into the Best family, rapidly expanded sales and in 1889 the company's name was changed to Pabst. After being recognized as America's Best Lager at the World Exposition in 1893, Pabst began fixing blue ribbons to its bottles, giving their flagship beer its name.

Below: A gleaming copper in the modern Pyramid micro-brewery.

Pete's

Home-brew enthusiast Pete Slosberg has been marketing his Pete's Wicked Ale with wicked success since 1986. Contract brewed in St Paul, Minnesota, nine other speciality beers have since joined the original chestnut ale (5.1%) including Pete's Bohemian Pilsner and Pete's Amber (both 4.9%) and summer and winter brews.

This table shows the largest brewers, with their market share and number of barrels sold in 1995. Although the top three brewers account for 77% of the market, their grip is slipping – the previous year they controlled 81%. The new speciality brewers are creating a more diverse market, with one of them, the Boston Beer Company (Samuel Adams) becoming the ninth-largest US brewer.

BREWER	MARKET SHARE	NO. OF BARRELS
1 Anheuser-Busch	44.1%	87.5 million
2 Miller	22.7%	45.0 million
3 Coors	10.2%	20.3 million
4 Stroh's	5.4%	10.8 million
5 Heileman	4.0%	7.9 million
6 Pabst	3.2%	6.3 million
7 Genesee	0.9%	1.8 million
8 Latrobe	0.6%	1.2 million
9 Boston	0.5%	1.0 million
10 Pittsburgh	0.5%	0.9 million

Plank Road Brewery

This was the original name of the Miller brewing giant. It now markets various beers under this brand name, including Icehouse and Red Dog.

Pyramid

One of the success stories of the craft brewery movement, the Pyramid brewery was set up as Hart Brewing in 1984 in the small logging town of Kalama in Washington State, brewing Pyramid Pale Ale. Since then, Pyramid has grown into the third-largest

new venture in the United States. Pyramid ales include Pyramid Pale Ale, Pyramid Wheaten Ale, Pyramid Best Brown and Pyramid Rye (all 5.1%). It also brews a range of seasonal brews including Porter (5.4%) and Snow Cap (6.9%).

St Stan's

Inspired by visits to Germany, Garith Helm built a brewery in Modesto, California. St Stan's is best-known for its original unpasteurized Amber Alt.

Schell

This rare midwest regional brewery was founded in 1858 by German immigrant August Schell in New Ulm, Minnesota, and it is still family-owned. It produces pre-Prohibition-quality lagers. The family's elaborate 1858 mansion and beer garden are now a site of national historic importance. Its lagers include an all-malt Schell Pilsner (5.3%), a Schell Weizen (4.4%) using 60% wheat and an Oktoberfest (5.3%).

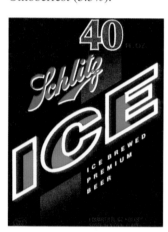

Schlitz

Once one of the best-known breweries – and brands – in the US, "The Beer that made Milwaukee Famous" is no longer brewed in the city since the brewery was taken over by Stroh's in 1982.

Sierra Nevada

One of the leaders of the craft brewery revolution, Sierra Nevada has grown to be the largest in the west. It was founded by keen home-brewers Ken Grossman and Paul Camusi in Chico, California, in 1981. Its flagship beer is the highly acclaimed Sierra Nevada Pale Ale (5.5%). It also brews a Sierra Nevada Porter (5.9%) and Sierra Nevada Stout (6%).

Sprecher

The former Pabst brewer Randall Sprecher revived the German brewing arts that Milwaukee had largely forgotten when he set up his own brewery in the town in 1985. His robust beers include an all-malt Sprecher Special Amber, Sprecher Black Bavarian (6%) and an unfiltered Sprecher Hefe-Weiss. He also brews an occasional Sprecher Irish Stout (6%).

Stoudt's

The first American micro-brewery to be designed and developed by a woman, Carol Stoudt's German-style beers have won about 20 medals at the Great American Beer Festival since she set up her brewery in Adamstown, Pennsylvania, in 1987. Her beers, brewed to the Reinheitsgebot beer purity law, include Stoudt's Gold Dortmunder (5%). In addition, she brews two Belgian Abbey ales, plus English-style ales and stout.

Straub

This small, long-established, family-owned brewery in rural Pennsylvania at St Mary's produces a light Straub Beer.

Stroh's

The US's fourth-largest brewing company was originally founded in 1850 in Detroit. Bernhard Stroh emigrated to America from Germany in 1849 where his family had started brewing in the late 1700s at Kirn. The next year he started a small brewhouse in Detroit, and five generations of the Stroh family have run the brewery ever since. During Prohibition, the company continued to operate producing "near" beers and alternative products made from brewing ingredients, including a popular malt extract that was a favourite of local home-brewers. Recently the company has expanded with a series of acquisitions, culminating in the takeover of the Heileman Brewing Company of Wisconsin in 1996. A number of the Stroh beers are advertised as being "fire-brewed", meaning that direct heat on the coppers is used to boil the wort, a process that was started by Julius Stroh in the early 1900s. The best-known brands are Stroh's Lager and Signature. The company also produces maltier German-style beers under the Augsburger name and has recently developed a number of low-alcohol beers, especially Stroh's Non-Alcoholic beer.

Summit

This midwest brewery was opened by Mark Stutrud in 1986 in St Paul, Minnesota, and has steadily grown in size and reputation. Best known for its Extra Pale Ale and IPA, it also brews seasonal German-style beers including a Hefe Weizen and a Düsseldorfer Alt (4.9%).

Tabernash

This micro-brewery in Denver, Colorado, concentrates on brewing German-style beers, such as its malt-accented dark Munich lager and an unfiltered Bavarian-style wheat beer, Tabernash Weiss.

Thomas Kemper

Thomas Kemper was founded in Washington State in 1985 specifically to brew German-style lagers, soon establishing itself near the coastal town of Poulsbo. In 1992 it merged with another north-west brewer, Pyramid Ales. It produces a range of unpasteurized beers. Seasonals include a Belgian White (4.4%) and Maibock (6.5%). See also Pyramid.

Twenty Tank

The Twenty Tank brewpub opened in a former sheet metal shop in 1990 in the heart of San Francisco's SOMA club district. The brew-kettle and mash vessels are in plain view for customers in the bar and restaurant. It offers a wide variety of house-brewed ales.

Widmer

North America's first modern Hefeweizen, a cloudy draught beer, surprised drinkers when it was launched by the Widmer brothers, Kurt and Rob, in Portland, Oregon, in 1986. The Widmer brewery uses a top-fermenting German alt yeast, and its original beer was a rich-copper-coloured alt. There is an unfiltered Hefeweizen available, and the brothers also brew an Amber, Blackbier and a fruity Widberry.

Wild Goose

One of the first micro-breweries in the mid-Atlantic states was founded in Cambridge, Maryland, in 1989. It brews a range of English-style ales, including Wild Goose Amber (5%) and IPA (5.3%).

Yakima

The Yakima Brewing Company was set up in 1982 in the heart of the hop-growing area in Washington State by Bert Grant, an engaging ale pioneer who opened the first modern brewpub in the US. Grant was an experienced brewing chemist. In 1982 he branched out on his own to brew better-quality beers, starting with the Yakima brewpub. He built a larger commercial brewery in 1991. Many of the beers produced by Yakima reflect his Scottish ancestry.

Yuengling

The oldest brewery still operating in the United States was founded in 1829 in Pottsville, Pennsylvania, where deep cellars were dug into the hillside to keep the beer cool during maturation. Still family-run, it is best known for its bottom-fermented Pottsville Porter and Chesterfield Ale, which are now enjoying renewed sales with the revival of interest in specialist beers. Yuengling also brews a Premium and Traditional Lager and a blended lager-porter called Black and Tan.

Zip City

This sophisticated New York brewpub and restaurant was established in the former headquarters of the National Temperance Society in Manhattan. It brews mainly unfiltered German-style lagers, including a Märzen and a Dunkel, to accompany its gourmet food.

Below: At the beginning of Prohibition in the US government agents closed down hundred of saloons.

LATIN AMERICA

Now best known for light, thin lager drunk straight from the bottle with a wedge of lime, Central and South American beer has a much richer tradition than is widely appreciated.

THE MAYANS were brewing beer from fermented corn stalks long before Spanish conquistadors made their mark. Meanwhile, in northern Mexico, the Aztecs enjoyed a fermented drink made with sprouted maize. Even after the conquest, peasants in isolated areas remained loyal to pulque, a drink brewed with the juice of the agave plant. It keeps for just a day or two (the name means "decomposed") and can still be found today, along with other indigenous drinks. An Inca legend claims that specially chosen maidens would chew cooked maize to a pulp to prepare it for brewing – their beauty and the purity of saliva were considered an aid to fermentation.

The Spanish conquistadors set up small breweries – cervecería – across the continent from the 16th century onwards. Beer came a poor second to distilled spirits, such as mescal or tequila, however, until Bavarian, Swiss and Austrian brewers introduced lager to Mexico in the 19th century, and ice-making machines arrived on the continent.

During Prohibition, which devastated the North American brewing industry from 1919 to 1933, the sleepy Mexican town of Tijuana became an outpost of alcohol tourism for thirsty Americans. As a result, at one point there were 75 bars on its 200m (600ft) main street.

Mexico remains the leading beer producer in Latin America. Its two biggest breweries, Cervecería Modelo and Cervecería Moctezuma, dominate the home market. Brazil, which was colonized by the Portuguese rather than the Spanish, and has a brewing tradition that looks to Germany, is the second-largest producer. Brazil also produces a traditional black (negra) beer. Lagers are the popular drink of choice in Latin America, with most brewers offering a Pilsner. Light, cheap and cheerful lagers made using rice, corn or other adjuncts in the mash are widely available, although other, more eclectic and traditional brews can also be found.

Above: Dos Equis, "Two Crosses", is a rich, dark, high-quality lager brewed in Mexico which has proved popular in many export markets.

THE BEERS

Africana

This rich, dark lager (5.5%) is a cross between a Munich-style dunkel and a Vienna Red, brewed with hops, rice and maize. It has an aroma of roast malt, a smooth chocolate taste and a hoppy aftertaste. It is brewed by Argentina's Bieckhart brewery in Buenos Aires.

Ancla

Columbia's Ancla brewery offers a range of all-malt beers. These include Cerveza Ancla which is made with German and Canadian hops and matured for four weeks, Ancla Premium (4.8%) and the amber-coloured Ancla Roja (4.1%). Ancla also offers the all-malt Naval Super Premium (4.8%) and an all-malt, alcohol-free beer.

Antarctica Pilsen

This Brazilian beer, the eighth most popular beer in the region, is gold-coloured and highly carbonated, with a strong hop aftertaste.

Bavaria Gold Beer

Golden-coloured and unremarkable, this fruity, slightly malty lager-style beer (3.5–5%) is brewed by Cervecería Costa Rica S.A.

Belikin Beer

The malty, golden, dryish lager (3.5–5%), from the Belize Brewing Company in Ladyville, is a pleasant, fizzy beer, best served cold.

Belikin Stout

A strong, dark-brown, faintly hoppy, rich stout (6–7.5%) with a sweet, malty aroma from the Belize Brewing Company.

Biekhart Cerveza Pilsen

A malty Pilsner-style lager (4.8%), made using pale malt from Argentinian barley, rice, maize and American Cascade hops. It is brewed by the Argentinian Biekhart brewery.

Biekhart Especial

This golden premium lager (5%) is more aromatic and fully flavoured than its sister brand, Cerveza Pilsen, from the Biekhart brewery.

Bohemia

This superior, strong lager (5.4%) from Cuauhtémoc in Mexico is made with Saaz hops, to give it a malty, full-bodied taste with a hint of vanilla. In 1995, Bohemia was the most popular beer in Mexico.

Brahma Chopp Export

From Brazil's Companhia Cervejaría, this yellow-gold, malty, slightly sour beer was the fourth-best-selling beer in South America in 1996.

Brahma Pilsner

This quality, hoppy Pilsner (5%) from Brazil's Companhia Cervejaría, based in Rio de Janeiro, has a rich malty, bittersweet taste with a hint of vanilla.

Corona Extra

Corona Extra (4.6%) is a lager made with about 40% rice and a relatively low proportion of hops. Cheap to make and refreshing when served very cold, this beer was designed for the taste-buds of the Mexican working man, and is served in a distinctive clear bottle. It was taken up eagerly by American tourists, who took to drinking it with lime, much to the amusement of the Mexicans, although the lime and lager fashion is now taking off in Mexico as well. Corona is the best-known brew from the Modelo brewery of Mexico City, one of the country's two major brewing companies. It is now widely exported and is a familiar designer beer which can be found in the bars of many of the European capital cities.

Cuzco

This very pale, yellow-gold, fizzy, malty, Pilsner-style lager (5%) is brewed using 100% barley by the Compañía del Sur del Perú S.A. It takes its name from the ancient Inca city in the high Andes of Peru.

Mexico's malty legacy

One of the few legacies of the Austrian Emperor Maximilian's short and inglorious reign over Mexico between 1864 and 1867 is a strongly Germanic influence on that country's brewing industry. The malty, dark-amber beers of Vienna may be hard to find in Austria today, but the old style is still very popular in the former colony.

Naval Superpremium
A Brazilian all-malt beer (4.8%) from Ancla.

Negra León
Brown rather than black, León is made by the Yucatán brewery (owned by Modelo) in Mexico. It is chocolatey in taste and quite similar to its sister brew, Negra Modelo.

Peru Gold
A dry, tart and refreshing lager (5%), Peru Gold has a rich corn-and-vanilla aroma. It is brewed by Peru's Cervesur. The bottle label features a memorable Peruvian Indian face mask.

Polar Lager
Venezuela's leading brand is a light, thin lager (5%) that takes the style of Sol and Corona to an extreme. Despite this, it is the second-best-selling beer in South America, where the Polar Brewing Company sells over 12 million hectolitres (264 million gallons) of it each year.

Porter
A rich, top-fermenting, dark beer (8%) from the Companhia Cevejaría of Brazil. Some say it takes its name from Portugal, the country that colonized Brazil, rather than from the beer style.

Dos Equis
Dos Equis ("Two Crosses") is a rich, dark-red, high-quality, Vienna-style lager (4.8%) with a fruity, chocolatey taste. Brewed in Mexico by Moctezuma, it has also proved popular in export markets.

Kaiser Bock
Introduced by Cervejarías Kaiser in 1994 as a cold-weather drink, this amber-coloured, pasteurized beer was the first bock to be produced in Brazil.

Kaiser Gold
This premium pasteurized Pilsner was initially launched as Kaiser Copa 94, to mark Brazil's entry in soccer's World Cup. Due to their success, it was renamed Kaiser Gold in 1995.

Negra Modelo
Despite its name, Negra Modelo (Black Model) (5.3%) is more of a deep amber-brown colour. It is a cross between a spicy Vienna red and a softer Munich dunkel, with a chocolate aroma, a hint of fruit and spices, and a hop finish. This classic, first-rate Mexican beer enjoys a justified reputation among beer connoisseurs both at home and abroad.

Sol
In the 1980s, the Moctezuma brewery's Sol succeeded Corona Extra as the fashionable Mexican beer to drink. Sol (4.6%) is a thin, light lager with a high proportion of adjuncts. Like its arch-rival, it is sold in a distinctive, embossed bottle.

Superior
This pale lager (4.5%) from Moctezuma has more hop character than its stablemate Sol.

Tecate
Launched in the 1950s by Cuauhtémoc of Mexico, this pale, light ("clara") lager (4.5%) is low in flavour, but good for satisfying thirst in a hot climate. It was originally served with salt and fresh lemons – a custom that probably inspired the recent craze for drinking Mexican lagers with a slice of lime.

Xingu
This Brazilian black beer (5%) is a modern version of the historic Amazonian drink. It is brewed commercially by Cervejaría Cacador, using hops rather than lupins to add flavour and act as a preservative. Sweet and malty, Xingu, named after a tributary of the Amazon River, is the fourth-best-selling beer in South America.

BLACK BREW

Black beer was first produced in the parts of the Upper Amazon Basin in the 15th century, using roasted barley and dark-pigmented grains to give its distinctive colour, and lupins for flavour (the lupin is a distant relative of the hop). A modern version, Xingu, is brewed commercially by Cervejaría Cacador in Brazil.

THE BREWERS

Ancla

Cervecería Ancla S.A. in Columbia produces a range of quality beers made with 100% pure malt, which come in amber glass bottles as well as in cans. The company has positioned itself at the top end of the domestic market and uses the marketing slogan "Por cultura es colombiana". A modernized plant opened in 1996, with a capacity of 1.2 million hectolitres (26 million gallons) per year.

Bieckhart

Cervecería Bieckhart has a range of German-influenced beers, even though its home is in the capital city of the former Spanish colony Argentina, Buenos Aires. It brews a golden lager and the rich, dark lager Africana.

Cardenal

Venezuela's second beer company after Polar is home to a typical Latin American light, thin lager called Andes, as well as a range of interesting Germanic beers,

among them the golden, malty beer, Tipo Munich (in the Munich style) and an authentic-tasting Nacional "Cerveza Tipo Pilsen" (in the Pilsen style).

Cervecería La Constancia

The San Salvador brewery in El Salvador offers a range of bottom-fermented lager beers: Pilsener of El Salvador Export Beer, Suprema Special Beer, Regla Extra, Noche Buena Special Dark Lager and Cabro Extra.

Cervesur (Compañia Cervecera del Sur del Perú S.A.)

Based in southern Peru, Cervesur has been brewing since 1898, when it was founded in Arequipa under the name Sociedad Industrial Ernesto Günther & Francisco Rehder. It adopted its present title in 1926. It brews using Andes water, barley from its malting plant in Cuzco as well as imported barley, malt and hops. Unusually for Latin America, it concentrates on 100% barley beers and does not use adjuncts. Brews include both

Pilsners and dark beers. Export brews are Cusqueña Pilsner and Cuzco Beer, Cusqueña Dark and Cuzco Dark (both 5.6%), as well as Peru Gold. In 1996, it was the first brewery in Latin America to be awarded a quality certificate by TUV Bayern. Cervesur first began exporting beer to Chile in 1978. By 1995, it controlled 17.5% of the beer market in Lima and accounted for 69% of Peru's beer exports.

Companhia Cervejaría

This Brazilian group brews a quality malty Brahma Pilsner, Brahma Chopp, as well as a top-fermenting, extra-strong porter (8%). The company produces more than 31 hectolitres (660 gallons) of beer annually.

Cuauhtémoc

Now merged with Moctezuma, this brewery offers a pale ("clara") lager called Chihuahua (named for the Mexican state) similar to Corona or Sol, as well as Tecate, another "clara" lager, the best-selling beer in Mexico, and the fuller-bodied, malty Bohemia, brewed with Saaz hops.

Kaiser

Kaiser, Brazil's third-largest brewery, was set up in 1983. The first plant was opened in Divinópolis in Minas Gerais State. Today, it has six plants across the country. The brewery is run by specialist technicians, trained by master brewers in Belgium. Beers, available both bottled and on draught, include Kaiser Cerveja and Premium Pilsner. It was the first Brazilian company to develop a bock, in 1994. In

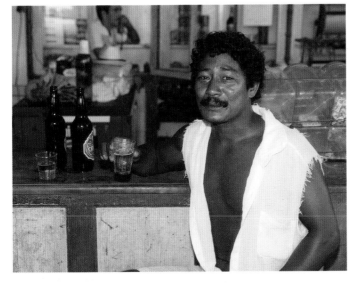

Above: Bars in Mexico tend to be an all-male preserve – a place for a quiet drink after a hard day's work.

Beer and chilli

Light, cheap lagers like Sol and Corona are reputed to go well with spicy Mexican food, but Mexico's dark and amber lagers are a better match for hot, robust flavours.

1995, it changed its name to KAC (Kaiser Consumer Relations). The company's marketing strategy has fixed it firmly in the minds of Brazilian beer drinkers in just ten years, partly due to the company's distinctive spokesman, "Shorty".

Moctezuma

Since merging with Cuauhtémoc, the Cervecería Moctezuma of Monterey has since overtaken Modelo and has become Mexico's largest brewery. The merged group, which controls seven breweries in the country, is owned by a large holding company called Valores. Moctezuma was founded in 1894 in Orizaba, Veracruz.

Modelo

The Cervecería Modelo of Mexico City is one of Mexico's two brewing giants. Modelo produces its beers at the single largest brewing plant in the country. Beers include the cheap, refreshing Corona Extra and tasty, Vienna-style dark lagers, Dos Equis and Negra Modelo.

Polar Brewing Company

This Venezuelan company is best known for the extremely light and thin Polar lager which is the country's leading lager brand.

THE CARIBBEAN

Rum, fermented from locally grown cane sugar, is the region's favourite tipple but, perhaps surprisingly for an area with a warm climate that grows little grain, there is also a strong beer culture, and drinkers show a marked preference for dark stouts and strong lagers.

INHABITANTS OF THE CARIBBEAN islands have been producing beer for centuries, using maize to brew a kind of porridge, which was then left to ferment. The recipe and name may vary from island to island (*chicha, izquiate* and *sendecho,* to name a few), but the technique remains the same.

The arrival of European brews and brewers in the 19th century had a great impact on the drinking and brewing habits of the region. Today in the Caribbean, lager is a popular drink and international giants, such as Heineken, brew many conventional Pilsner-style beers. They are often served ice-cold as a thirst-quencher for the beach, as an alternative to rum and coke, or sipped in relaxed island bars, as an accompaniment to seafood. There are also many strong, relatively sweet, full-flavoured lagers available. Jamaica's most popular exported beer, Red Stripe, which is now a familiar sight in the US and the UK, is a classic example of this Caribbean-style golden brew. Another European beer style that has been wholeheartedly taken into the bosom of the Islands is rich, strong, dark stout. Many in these exotic climes believe dark beers to possess aphrodisiac or virility-enhancing qualities. Guinness Stout, the classic of this type, has been brewed here for over 150 years and is now produced under licence at the Central Village Brewery in Spanish Town, Jamaica. Other breweries in Trinidad, Granada and St Vincent produce similar dark brews. These "exotic stouts", as they are often known, are usually brewed with a higher alcohol content than stouts produced in England or Ireland.

At the other end of the scale, but continuing the theme of rich, dark brews, another popular product from many breweries in the Caribbean is a dark drink made from malt extract. It is more of a soft drink than an alcohol-free beer.

Above: Carib is a relatively dry lager from Trinidad that bucks the trend for sweet, strong lagers and dark, heavy stouts throughout the Caribbean.

THE BEER

Banks Lager Beer
A pale-gold, sweet, malty lager (4.5%) from the Banks brewery in Bridgetown Barbados.

Bohemia Cerveza
A hazy, pale, amber-gold standard lager (5%) brewed in Ciudad Trujillo, Dominican Republic, by the Cervecería Bohemia.

Caribe
A dry, light-flavoured, pale-yellow lager (4.5%) from the Caribe Development Company, Port of Spain, Trinidad.

Corona
A pale, golden-yellow lager (4.5%) from the Cervecería Corona in Puerto Rico.

Dragon Stout
A deep-brown, sweetish, rich, malty stout (7.5%). It is brewed in Kingston, Jamaica, by Desnoes & Geddes. This potent brew is believed by some to aid virility.

Ebony Super Strength
A deep-brown ale (8%) with a high alcohol content that gives it an almost port-like quality, from the Banks brewery in Barbados.

Kalik Gold
A golden, rich, malty lager which is high in alcohol, from the Commonwealth Brewery in the Bahamas.

Red Stripe
A pale-gold, lightly hopped, strong lager (4.7%) with a full flavour, from the family-run Desnoes & Geddes in Kingston, Jamaica. It is now brewed under licence in the UK, where it is a particular favourite with the West Indian population.

Royal Extra Stout
A deep-brown, classic stout with a malty flavour. Brewed by the Caribe Development Company in Port of Spain, Trinidad.

THE BREWERS

Banks (Barbados) Breweries Ltd
This major player in the Caribbean market is also a familiar name on the South American mainland, where it has a brewery in Guyana.

Desnoes & Geddes Ltd
A family-owned firm set up in 1918 in Kingston, Jamaica, by Eugene Desnoes and Thomas Geddes. Heineken now has a small shareholding.

Granada Breweries Limited
This bright idea by the Caribbean Development Company was first registered as a company in 1960, but it wasn't until the 1970s that it really began to thrive.

St Vincent Brewery Ltd
Set up in 1985 on the island of St Vincent, this small brewery produces its own-brand, Hairoun Lager, as well as brewing Guinness and EKU Bavaria under licence.

Salty liquor
In 1994 Granada Breweries unveiled the solution to its problem of water shortages during the dry season. It had drilled its own borehole to tap underground water and installed a desalination plant.

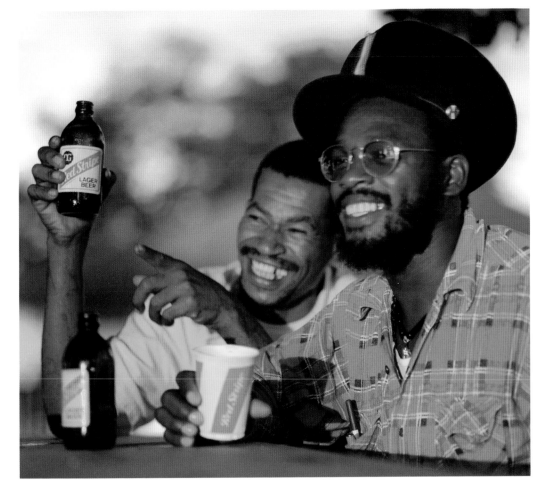

Left: Enjoying a beer and chewing the fat is part of the relaxed Caribbean way of life. Red Stripe is the region's leading lager.

INDEX